Women
in the
Organization

ATE DUE

Women
in the
Organization

HAROLD H. FRANK

University of Pennsylvania Press
1977

To:

Sally Garry Frank, Barbara Kellerman Frank,
Mildred Kreeger Frank, Ellen S. Frank, Sofia Frank Berger,
Toby Berger Holtz, Sylvia Garry Kofsky, Jeanne
Van Kuyk de Monch, and Jany Muench Frank,

working women all.

Contents

Preface

At a time when the enrollment of women in professional schools and their participation as workers outside the home is increasing dramatically, this book serves several purposes. It will be useful as a supplementary text in management courses or as the principal text in more advanced seminars. Designers of women's studies programs will find within it appropriate material for discussion sessions. Companies who wish to acquaint managerial personnel with issues relating to female employees should find in this book highly relevant cases and readings suitable for discussion and analysis.

The body of the text consists of two parts. Part I is a collection of case studies dealing with women in managerial and professional positions. Each is an account of actual events; only names and some locations are fictionalized. These cases were not chosen to illustrate specific principles or theories of management, or to show effective or ineffective handling of organizational problems. They were selected for inclusion because of their potential for challenging the reader's analytical skills, increasing the understanding of basic issues, and inviting lively and productive discussion.

The cases present management problems as they relate to social, cultural, and psychological factors. The women described in this book achieve success, make mistakes, are well-treated, or are ill-treated. In short, they are direct and active participants in the social and technical configurations through which work is accomplished.

Four of the cases describe situations in health care institutions because the representation of women in positions of influence in this field has undergone especially rapid growth in recent years. Although medicine has in many respects its own traditions, the managerial and organizational problems are not essentially different from those in other fields.

Conventional management texts unfortunately deal almost exclusively with male subjects. Female students have, as a consequence, too few role models and often feel left out and neglected when only these texts are used. Discussion of the cases in this book will, it is hoped, promote interaction between male and female students and force them to confront and deal seriously with their own and each other's prejudices.

Part II is a collection of readings drawn from a variety of sources. They have been selected for their readability and relevance to the issues which confront working women. Each one is relevant to several and in some instances all the cases. (See Appendix.)

This book, then, is intended as a tool for facilitating the exchange of ideas on women in business and the professions. There is a need for a casebook of this sort, and I hope that it will further more extensive and intensive study of its subject.

Acknowledgments

Nearly fifteen years ago, as an undergraduate in an experimental program at what was then the School of Business Administration at the University of California, Los Angeles, I was first introduced to the case method for studying behavior in organizations. The experience set the stage for a doctoral program in Behavioral Science at the same institution, now called the Graduate School of Management. I learned much there about analyzing cases from James V. Clark and Warren H. Schmidt, and from Peter B. Vaill, now Dean of the School of Government and Business Administration at George Washington University, who supervised the doctoral dissertation I wrote. It was based on a case study of a secretarial training program developed primarily for black women from the Watts area of Los Angeles.

Issues of sexism, like those of racism and of superior-subordinate relations in general, become deeply rooted in the psyche. Whatever understanding I have of these things was influenced significantly by my experience as an analysand at the Los Angeles Psychoanalytic Institute and by my study of psychoanalytic theory and social behavior during the same period in my doctoral program.

The idea for this book first took shape at Harvard University where I spent my sabbatical leave with Robert Freed Bales of the Department of Psychology and Social Relations. He helped me hone my observational skills and provided encouragement and advice at various stages of the research. Eric Trist of the Department of Social Systems Science at the University of Pennsylvania, my mentor and friend, formulated the notion of the sociotechnical system—the framework within which data for the cases was collected. Henry W. Riecken and Aaron H. Katcher, of the School of Medicine at the University of Pennsylvania, also gave freely of their time and advice.

xi

Donald C. Carroll, Dean of the Wharton School, and Edward B. Shils, as Chairman of the Management Department, provided assistance with funding and gave their support to the establishment of B.A. 506L, Women in Management, an advanced research project which produced several of the cases reported in this book. I am indebted to other colleagues at the Wharton School, including Jules J. Schwartz for "Women's Medical College of Pennsylvania" and "First Shelter Corporation," and to Ross A. Webber for "Northside Child Health Care Center." The case "Sue Garson" was prepared by Sherrie S. Epstein for use in the Graduate Program in Management, Simmons College.

Numerous people participated in the collection of data for the cases. For reasons of their own, some have requested that their names not be used in association with particular cases, while others have requested that pseudonyms be used. All are grouped together in the list that follows. Linda Pierce Johnson, Helen Sandberg, Mary Pat Johnson, Diane L. Simon, Judith S. Katzenellenbogen, Pam Wallis, Joanne Stern, Douglas Singer, Bonita Rothman, and Nina Robinson.

I would also like to thank the many publishers and authors who granted permission to quote copyrighted material. Some did so without charge, making it possible to donate a portion of the proceeds from the sale of the book to the National Organization for Women Education and Legal Defense Fund.

My greatest debt is to Janet Novack, an editor on the staff of the Daily Pennsylvanian, and to Katherine Hooks, a former news reporter and writer currently enrolled in the Master of Business Administration (MBA) Program at Wharton. Both participated in major redrafting of many of the cases and edited them all, not only for clarity but for sex bias as well. My thanks also to my wife Jany Ingrid Frank, a former doctoral candidate in Classics at UCLA, a housewife, mother, a recent recipient of an MBA in Accounting from Wharton, and a full-time employee of a large corporation. Her experiences in meeting the competing demands women face as parents, spouses, students, and employees provided me with invaluable insight.

Finally, I want to acknowledge the help of Miss Cynthia L. Kee and Mrs. Joanne R. Cohen for their help in the preparation of this manuscript.

Although I welcome the opportunity to acknowledge the many and varied contributions of others to this book, as its author I am fully responsible for its contents and accept all its faults.

Harold H. Frank

Philadelphia, Pennsylvania
May, 1976

Introduction

SOME NOTES ON CASE ANALYSIS

In a management curriculum, case studies are often a welcome respite from strictly theoretical materials. They help to bridge the gap between lectures and texts on the one hand and actual practice and fieldwork on the other, and provide an immediate opportunity for students to apply newly acquired knowledge.

The essence of case analysis, the pedagogic use of stories, is quite appropriately best captured by a tale Aesopian in nature:

Once upon a time not so long ago, an ambitious young man came to the laboratories of an old biologist of international reknown and requested that the scientist accept him as a pupil. The biologist politely responded that he would take the matter under consideration, and asked his would-be student to remain in the laboratory while he attended to some personal business. "During my absence," he added, "I would like you to observe the goldfish in my fishbowl."

Thinking it best to humor the eccentricities of an old but brilliant scientist, the student complied. Upon his return an hour later, the biologist inquired of the young man, "What have you noticed about the goldfish?" The student replied, "Well, sir, during your absence the goldfish swam back and forth in his bowl emitting bubbles." The old man nodded his head knowingly and then announced his intention to leave for a luncheon engagement, adding, "While I'm gone, why don't you remain with the goldfish?" Anxious to curry the scientist's favor, the young man complied once more.

The biologist returned to his laboratory after a leisurely two-hour lunch and greeted his potential disciple with the query, "And what else have you observed about our goldfish?" "Well, sir," was the reply, "the goldfish has scales, fins, and a tail." "I see," said the old man as he again headed for the door, "I have an afternoon seminar to attend and must be going now, but I am sure the goldfish will keep you well occupied." The student, struggling to suppress his annoyance, gave a weak, sycophantic smile.

Upon his return three hours later, the scientist posed the question the young man had been anticipating with dread, "Is there anything else you have noticed about this goldfish?" Feeling more than a little foolish, he answered, "Well, the goldfish is gold, sir." "He is at that," smiled the biologist, and added, "I'm off for the day now. Why don't you spend the night observing our goldfish?" But for the old man's impeccable reputation, the student might have left right then, attributing this odd scenario to the progression of arteriosclerosis.

In the morning, the biologist, looking well-rested and certainly in possession of all his wits, returned to find the young man haggard but lucid, staring intently at the goldfish in the bowl. When asked to report any new observations, he replied, "Well, sir, the left side of the goldfish appears to be the same as the right side." "Congratulations, my boy!" exclaimed the biologist, "You have just discovered the principle of bisymmetry, which describes the structure of all living things." And he welcomed the young man to the study of biology.

This is the process of inductive logic, the fundamental intellectual approach employed in case analysis. Often the most valuable insights stem from simple observations that, because of our preoccupation with the sophisticated and the complex, may take the longest to discern.

But people are not as reliable or predictable as goldfish. While the student of management, like the student of biology, may discover basic principles through observation and inductive reasoning, management principles are notorious because of the number and variety of their exceptions. Therefore, the case analyst must cultivate not only his ability for inductive reasoning, but also openmindedness and flexibility of thought. Particularly those students who have actual field experience in management must resist the temptation to draw precise analogies between the subject in a case and other individuals they may have dealt with. Comparing and contrasting individuals is a useful technique, but the indiscriminate use of analogy can too often lead to pat solutions.

Another important element of successful case analysis is a good measure of self-knowledge. Especially when dealing with histories of career women, a topic that is likely to arouse considerable controversy and debate, the student must be aware of her/his own values, prejudices, and preconceived notions. Few managerial decisions are value-free; it is unrealistic and perhaps undesirable to insist that they should be. Nevertheless, the analyst must acknowledge the social, cultural, and psychological assumptions s/he is operating on and question their applicability.

PREPARATION OF A CASE

While individual study techniques vary, there is a general approach to case preparation which I recommend.

First, the analyst should immerse her/himself in the facts of a case with an eye toward capturing the atmosphere and personalities involved. Next s/he should identify the specific problems faced by each individual in the case and attempt to discover the causes for the difficulties. Some information presented in a case may prove to be superfluous; discerning relevant data is one of the elements of the analytic process. At times the student may find it necessary to use conjecture in establishing the roots of a management problem. At other times the causes may be too obscure. Case study has no ready formula.

It is advisable to generate as many alternative workable solutions as possible. The thorough and creative case analyst will formulate solutions which transcend her/his prejudices and often the bounds of conventional management practice. The student must then choose among these alternatives and designate a recommended course of action. S/he should be prepared to justify her/his selection on logical and practical grounds and finally give her/his personal reasons for the choice, for in the end a person's own value system should be taken into account.

A WORD OF ADVICE

Students often come to class discussions armed with a "definitive" solution replete with facts and figures and supporting information garnered from outside readings. Thorough preparation is commendable and necessary, but one should also bring to class a willingness to listen, debate, and give thoughtful consideration to differing opinions.

I
CASES

1
Barbara Parker

PART I

ABSTRACT

Barbara Parker, a young woman with an M.A. in Urban Arts Management, joins the staff of the Museum of Science as Director of Special Projects and begins to assume a wide range of duties, including many belonging to the Museum Director. When the Museum Director resigns, Ms. Parker, who has been with the organization for less than two years, is appointed acting director. As the Museum begins the long process of selecting a permanent Director, Ms. Parker must deal with severe budget and personnel problems without receiving any added compensation for her expanded responsibilities. She begins to perceive an element of sex discrimination in her problems.

Organizational Structure

The Museum of Science Foundation, headquartered in New York, is a strongly research-oriented institution. The Foundation relies primarily on federal and private research grants, although a small percentage of the budget is derived from memberships and donations to the Museum itself. Both financially and intellectually, the Museum is often regarded as the stepchild of the Foundation.

Officially, the governing body of the Museum of Science Foundation is the forty-member Board of Directors, but considerable power is exercised by the Chairman of the Board, Dr. Davis, a well-known, well-funded scientist. Dr. Davis, who is engaged in several research projects, lectures a great deal, and participates frequently in scholarly conferences, is in his office at the Foundation an average of one day a week. Among his staff members Dr. Davis is not noted for his managerial abilities.

3

The Museum of Science Foundation's Managing Director is Dr. Hobbs, who spends three days a week at the Foundation offices overseeing both the Research and Museum branches of the Foundation. (See Exhibit 1.)

In February of 1975, Museum Director Dr. Sam Dill announced his resignation, creating a vacancy that, given the past performance of the Foundation, could have easily taken a year to fill. A Development Director had only recently been hired after that post remained vacant for a full year. As one staff member relates:

In 1974 our whole public relations effort for the Foundation was disrupted because we didn't have a new development division chief. And the research group and the science branch people really needed a better publicity effort for what they were doing at the time. I'll tell you, we suffered. But the directors were weighed down by their search committees that met once a month. They were really out of touch with what was going on around here.

Acting Museum Director

Six weeks after Dr. Dill's resignation, twenty-six-year-old Barbara Parker was appointed Acting Museum Director. She was a striking contrast to Dr. Dill: she was young, she did not have her doctorate, and she had been with the Museum for less than two years. To Ms. Parker the temporary appointment was at first welcome, for it was a promotion from Special Programs Director and an official recognition of the range of responsibilities she had already assumed. (See Exhibit 2.)

When Ms. Parker graduated from U.C.L.A. at age twenty-one with a B.A. in Anthropology, she went to work as a department supervisor in a small midwestern hospital. Hoping to find employment related to her academic concentration, Ms. Parker traveled to the East Coast where she found research opportunities for B.A.'s just as limited. She finally accepted a position as a Foundation Research Assistant in the Development Office of Flower Fifth Avenue Hospital in New York. She recalls:

While I was at the hospital, I decided to go back to school part-time. I felt the M.P.A. would make me more employable as a manager. To find work in anthropology I would have to earn a Ph.D., and that would cost a lot and take at least four years.

Ms. Parker matriculated at New York University and within two years had earned a masters degree in Public Administration, specializing in Urban Arts Management. As part of her second year studies, Ms. Parker served an internship at the Museum of Science Foundation by working in the Special Programs Division. Upon receiving her M.A., she was appointed Director of Special Programs at the Museum.

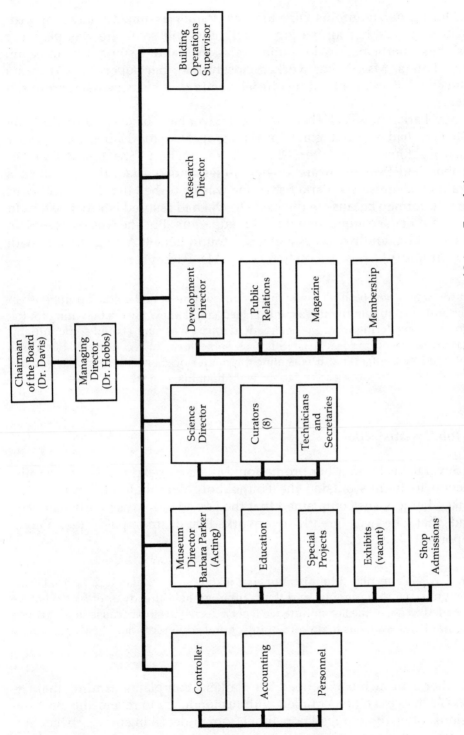

Exhibit 1: Table of Organization for the Museum of Science Foundation

5

During her tenure as Director, Ms. Parker assumed many responsibilities outside her formal job description, and soon she was planning exhibits, participating in public relations, and issuing the museum newsletters. Ms. Parker worked closely with her supervisor, Museum Director Dill, often attending official meetings as his personal representative.

Ms. Parker now feels that she might never have been appointed Acting Director had she not gone to Managing Director Hobbs for a salary increase four weeks after Dr. Dill's resignation. She found that Dr. Hobbs had been unaware of her duties and the fact that she held a graduate degree. Ms. Parker says she was disturbed that Dr. Hobbs was so uninformed because in the past Dr. Dill had assured her that he would mention her accomplishments to his superiors. But she was pleased with the meeting, and two weeks later she found herself Acting Director with the promise of a raise "soon to follow." Ms. Parker recalls:

At the time I was both pleased with the appointment and a little apprehensive. Certainly the appointment was unexpected, and I knew I was a bit young for the job. But considering what I was already doing, I was sure I could settle into it. I was overworked, and at least this was some form of recognition. But I was bothered by the fact that it was almost a matter of chance that I got it, and appalled at how uninformed Dr. Hobbs was about his own staff.

Job Dissatisfaction

Several weeks after her promotion, Ms. Parker expressed her dissatisfaction to friends outside the Foundation. Although she professed to "like" her job, she complained that the Foundation was poorly managed and that she was greatly overworked and underpaid. Ms. Parker reported:

Dr. Davis is a terrible administrator. For instance, we'll plan a project, allocate the funds, get things going, and then, although he's already approved what we intended to do, at the last minute we'll get a decree to stop because he's changed his mind and wants us to do something entirely different—and he wants it done immediately.

Other staff members echoed Ms. Parker's complaints, adding that Dr. Davis's inaccessibility, coupled with his tendency to reverse his own decisions, often discouraged personnel from undertaking new projects. According to Barbara Parker:

It was no use trying to get a commitment from Dr. Hobbs, because he was afraid to go out on a limb and support anything that wasn't sure of getting Dr. Davis's okay. Dr. Hobbs was just as intimidated by Dr. Davis as everyone else was. He was unwilling to confront Dr. Davis in defense of his own subordinates. I think this whole mess is the reason Sam Dill left, though he would never come out and say it.

Despite her recognition of general managerial malaise within the Museum of Science Foundation, Barbara Parker felt personally exploited. Even when Sam Dill had been with the Foundation, Ms. Parker told friends, she had assumed a heavier work load than she thought equitable. However, she had never complained directly because "when I first came here, I decided to make myself indispensible. It was important to me to have the chance to prove my competence."

The work load which Ms. Parker had felt compelled to assume had now grown to the point that she resented it, and she felt the quality of her performance was jeopardized. She said:

The Exhibits Director post has been vacant for two years. Guess who gets to fill in there? And in addition to my usual overload of work, we also have the Bicentennial exhibition to plan. I've been making use of our volunteers in many capacities, but I need more regular staff to do a professional job. We don't have the money to hire any additional staff, and I'm beginning to wonder if my own raise will ever come through.

As the situation worsened, Ms. Parker told friends that if her raise was not forthcoming, she would consider filing a complaint of sex discrimination with the Equal Employment Opportunity Commission (EEOC). Although she said she was sure her age, lack of a doctorate, and the fact that her graduate work was in a nonscientific field would prevent her from being considered for the permanent appointment, Ms. Parker observed:

I'm certainly doing just as much work as the other Directors, and I'm just not making anything close to their salaries. It's true I don't have the same credentials, but if I'm talented enough to function on this level, then I deserve to be paid for it.

Ms. Parker, who was still awaiting the promised first raise, had been brought in with a starting salary of $10,200. The other directors earned from $17,500 up.

PART II

ABSTRACT

Ms. Parker becomes increasingly rebellious over the volume of her workload, which she believes to include many functions inappropriate to her position. She is caught in the tensions between administrative and scientific personnel, and perceiving sex discrimination as an important factor in her problems, she files a complaint with the EEOC (Equal Employment Opportunity Commission).

Special Assignment

Soon after Ms. Parker discussed her problems at the Museum of Science Foundation, an incident occurred which she considered representative of her mistreatment. Dr. Davis was planning to host a conference of researchers specializing in his narrow field, an event which would generate considerable personal prestige for him. With the permission of the Board of Directors, Dr. Davis planned to use the facilities of the Museum for both the seminars and a formal reception for the participants.

Although the Museum's regular exhibits were geared toward laymen and scientific personnel in other fields, Dr. Davis wanted a special, highly technical exhibit constructed for the conference which would concentrate on current research methods and highlight the work of his own laboratories. Dr. Davis called Ms. Parker to his office and explained:

> *Davis:* Please understand that this exhibit is important to the total success of the conference and the reputation of the Foundation. As the only Director of Special Projects we have, and since we have no one in Exhibits at present, I'd appreciate it if you'd direct this project personally. My experience has been that no matter what the quality of the work presented, if the logistics of a conference are not handled properly, the meetings are not well received. In view of that, I'd consider it a personal favor if you yourself would handle the arrangements for conference rooms, slide projection, the reception, coffee breaks, and what have you. I've certainly got a great deal of confidence in your ability.
>
> *Parker:* I'm not sure I'm really up on the latest developments in your field of investigation.
>
> *Davis:* I'll send you copies of our latest published papers and related works to read. And, of course, we'll work together in planning this. Don't think I'm leaving you without direction. You know I appreciate this. You're so much more adept at creating posters and the like than the people in my laboratories.

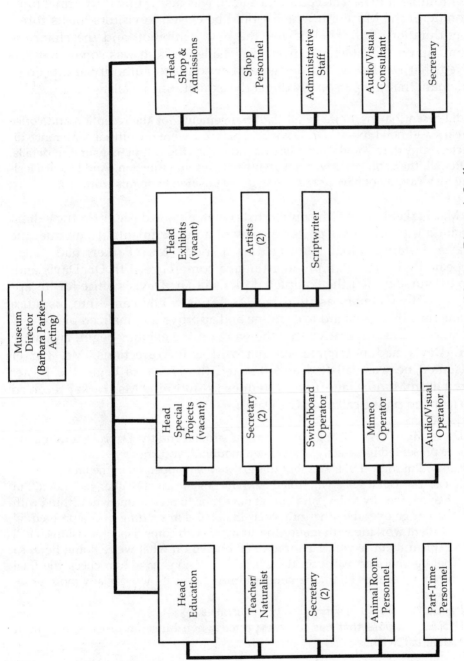

Exhibit 2. Table of Organization—Musuem Director's Staff

9

Ms. Parker found the work relating to the conference interfered with her routine duties. The conference itself was disrupting the normal functioning of the Museum, which would be closed to visitors for its three-day duration. Still, she viewed the new exhibition and the chance to bone up on the latest advances as a challenge, and was somewhat flattered that Dr. Davis had delegated her so much authority and been so adamant that she personally direct the exhibit. She recalls:

I did resent having to make all the arrangements for the reception and coffee breaks and hotel rooms. Dr. Davis and his crew were the official conference directors and they should have been handling all those time-consuming details. After all, the conference was not an official museum function. And I have a feeling they would not have asked a man in my position to do this work.

Ms. Parker and the Museum artists created scale designs for the exhibit including proofs for a poster display of an experimental technique, the Davis Determination. During this period, Ms. Parker had failed repeatedly in her attempts to arrange a conference with Dr. Davis and, on a Thursday, left the completed plans in Dr. Davis's office for his approval. His secretary assured her Dr. Davis would come into his office some time that weekend to examine and approve the finalized plans.

Since it was imperative that the work on the exhibits begin, and since Dr. Davis had not contacted her with any corrections, Ms. Parker assumed he was satisfied and directed the artists to begin the poster exhibit on Monday afternoon. Wednesday morning Ms. Parker received an agitated phone call from Dr. Davis:

Davis: Miss Parker, I've gone over these proofs, and the Davis Determination is presented incorrectly. It has been modified, you know.
Parker: I'm sorry, Dr. Davis, but this is the way it appeared in the literature.
Davis: Yes, but it's been modified, and the posters must be changed. Look, I'm leaving the city today, and I don't have time to review this whole thing with you or go over the other proposals in detail. I'm sending over a premedical student working with me for the summer with some lists of revisions. He'll explain them to you. He's very well briefed on what we're doing here, so before you start work on the corrected version, have him check the final proofs. Perhaps I'll phone you tomorrow to see if there are any more problems.
Parker: Yes, well, I'm sorry about the mistakes.
Davis: I suppose that has to be expected when Museum officials are out of their bailiwick.

The following day Ms. Parker wrote a letter of inquiry to the EEOC.

2
Nina Ritchie

PART I

ABSTRACT

Nina Ritchie, an English major with some professional writing experience, enters the publishing world after her college graduation. She finds, however, that the entry-level positions on major magazines are unsatisfying and takes a more challenging job with a new publication. Workplace friction and her own writing problems combine to make Ms. Ritchie unhappy on the job.

Personal History

Ms. Ritchie was raised in an upper-middle-class family in the New York suburbs. Her father was a successful corporate lawyer, and her mother was a museum curator who had earned her M.A. in art history while Nina was in grade school. Ms. Ritchie recalls:

My mother was lively, level-headed, and intelligent, but certainly not an intellectual. My father, on the other hand, was a brilliant attorney and legal scholar.

The Ritchie household was strongly career-oriented, with a premium placed on excellence and financial success. Nina Ritchie remembers:

My parents were loving, but I always felt an undercurrent of pressure to succeed. Mom and Dad kept telling me to plan for a career. My father really didn't believe women were as capable as men, but he thought I could be successful and urged me not to underrate myself.

11

Beginning Her Career

At Cornell University, Ms. Ritchie developed her creative writing talents, receiving a prestigious $500 literary award for a short story and serving a summer internship at *Esquire* magazine. Upon graduation, unlike many of her peers, Nina did not have to agonize over a career choice. She recalls:

I had already received positive recognition for my writing, and I certainly enjoyed the "in the know" atmosphere I felt at *Esquire*. It just seemed obvious that I should go into magazine work.

Ms. Ritchie's first employment experience after college was at *Harper's* magazine as a $100-a-week proofreader. Despite the low salary, there was considerable competition for the position, a circumstance for which she was prepared. She notes:

There are hordes of girls who want to go into publishing, and I wanted to get a foot in the door, which generally meant as an editorial assistant, really just a glorified secretary with a college degree. So at Cornell I took a night course in shorthand, and now I'm quite good at it.

Ms. Ritchie's major job responsibility was to proofread articles for grammatical and spelling errors, a process which she and two other proofreaders repeated three times for each article. Nina recalls the lack of personal involvement:

There was no feeling of individual responsibility. I really disliked the work, and I wanted to quit, but I thought I should stick it out for at least a year. I didn't want to get a reputation as a "job hopper," and I hoped something better might turn up, you know, like an opportunity to do some research or writing for the magazine.

City Magazine

After only five months on the job, Nina read in *Editor and Publisher* of a new magazine being established in New York by the publisher of a successful Hartford, Connecticut, weekly. Attracted by the prospect of helping to shape a new magazine, Ms. Ritchie, who had never read *Hartford*, sent a note to Michael Hall, the executive editor of both publications, stating, "If *City* is going to be like *Hartford*, that's where I'd like to be. I think we may be right for each other." Ms. Ritchie followed the note with several phone calls to Hall. Impressed by her persistence and enthusiasm, Hall interviewed Ms. Ritchie and soon thereafter hired her.

Nina's duties at *City* were diverse. She wrote a monthly column high-lighting interesting places to eat, shop, or visit around the city, contributed story ideas, wrote headlines, edited manuscripts, and proofread finished articles, the latter duty taking much of her time. She also wrote a number of feature pieces; however, during her year and a half with *City*, only three of these were published. Ms. Ritchie recalls:

I had to write the column to stay in my boss's good graces, but it was always a chore. I was frantically nervous each time and put off actually writing until the last minute, although I never missed a deadline. I kept telling myself I would get better with practice. I did enjoy reading and editing for content, but straight copy editing bored me as it had at *Harper's*.

Transfer To Hartford

In June 1972, Ms. Ritchie married a second-year Yale law school student and ex-college athlete whom she had known and dated since her high school days, and moved with him to Hartford, Connecticut. She kept her maiden name, but was forced to go to court to assure its legality. She explains:

I just knew I couldn't give up my name. I would look at marriage announcements which read, "Mrs. John Smith, the former Miss Ann Jones," and I would wonder, where had Ann Jones gone? I had to go to court and present a notarized statement from my husband, Steve, giving me "permission" to keep my maiden name. The IRS gave us trouble and the banks were impossible. It was still a relatively unusual situation for them.

Despite her insistence on retaining her maiden name, Nina says she was not reluctant to change her residence and her job in order to live with her husband. She notes:

I like to move, and will always be willing to move with Stephen.

Asked if her husband would feel the same way if the circumstances were reversed, Nina replied:

I don't know, we've never discussed it. It would probably depend on which job was easier for us to give up.

After approaching Editor Hall several months earlier about transferring to the staff of *Hartford*, Ms. Ritchie was hired by *Hartford* as an editorial assistant to Managing Editor Cynthia Elliot. Commenting on Nina's request, Hall said:

Nina is witty, personable, and creative, but she lacked the discipline to take on more responsibility. I had a talk with Cynthia Elliot at *Hartford,* and we agreed to try her out up there for six months as an editorial assistant. My hope was that under Cynthia's guidance, Nina would develop into a disciplined writer and take on the associate editorship position, which is fairly demanding. We knew that position would be vacant then.

Staff Friction

Managing Editor Elliot, a thirty-four-year-old mother of two, was the only woman prominent in the *Hartford* hierarchy. A Phi Beta Kappa graduate of Michigan State, she began with the publication as a secretary when she was twenty-two, left three years later to bear children, and returned when she was twenty-nine as a member of the editorial staff. One long-time *Hartford* employee, a middle-aged female secretary, observed:

Cynthia was very shy when she first started here, very unsure of herself. She had freelanced while she was away, and had several published articles to her credit. I was impressed with how self-confident she had become.

Ms. Elliot told the casewriter:

When Nina first started at *Hartford,* my husband, an artist, was unemployed, and I was the family breadwinner. I make a decent salary now as Managing Editor, but I've had to fight for respect. Some of the people remember me from the time I worked here as a secretary.

When Nina Ritchie assumed her new duties, her association with Cynthia Elliot began on an antagonistic note, the latter taking pains to inform Ms. Ritchie of her place in the magazine structure. Ms. Ritchie recalls:

My first day of work, Cynthia was very hostile. She said to me, "These are your duties. Water the plants, type the reporters' letters, answer the phones while the rest of the staff is at editorial meetings, order supplies, retype manuscripts, clip relevant news articles and maintain files." She also said quite pointedly that it was my job to make the afternoon coffee, and should I "ever have to report a story," she would get me a temporary press card. I resented her attitude, but I was overwhelmed by it. And her description of the job certainly didn't fit my notion of an editorial assistant.

After discussing the situation with her husband, Nina decided to "straighten Cynthia out"—she deliberately made very weak coffee. At the time, none of the staffers commented, but Mike Jones, the sports editor, recalls:

We all knew what she was doing with the coffee. I was irritated. Lots of people do time with the coffeemaker when they're starting out. What made her special? It was very unsportsmanlike, and it didn't help her make friends quickly on the staff, that's for sure.

Within a month, Nina was asserting herself in less covert ways. She went over Ms. Elliot's head to Michael Hall to obtain a permanent press card and to gain access to the editorial meetings. Ms. Ritchie, reflecting on these incidents, states:

Others probably thought I had come on too strongly with Cynthia, but I didn't feel I was being aggressive. I belonged at those meetings, and I had a right to a permanent press card. I knew Hall would back me up.

Changing Job Design

Nina's relations with Cynthia Elliot "were pretty strained" for several weeks after these incidents, as sports editor Jones describes it:

Nina had bucked Cynthia—the rest of us thought it was a game with them, Nina being spunky enough to contest Cynthia's power, and Cynthia making life difficult for Nina by giving her lots of clerical work.

With time, however, relations between the two improved, and Nina began receiving more desirable assignments. Six months after she came to *Hartford,* Nina took over the job of Associate Editor from Bill Holt, who left to start a weekly paper in Maine. Her job responsibilities included a monthly column on offbeat places and happenings, with the option of writing feature stories on a fairly regular basis as well. Though her duties were still largely editorial, she enjoyed a greater degree of autonomy.

Less than a month after her promotion, Ms. Ritchie clearly defined the limits of what she would and would not do to retain her job. Her predecessor had worked weekends, even when there were no pressing deadlines, but Nina had decided she was not being paid enough to warrant unnecessary overtime work. The previous Sunday, Cynthia had telephoned Nina at home and asked her to come to the office to proof some copy. That week she worked overtime on three days, and when Cynthia again asked her to work on Sunday, Nina flatly refused. Nina recalls:

No one else was expected to work overtime on Sunday. I told Cynthia I would be in promptly Monday morning to do the work, since in my opinion it wasn't urgent, and reminded her I was not one to shirk my duty. She wasn't happy, but she hasn't had the nerve to call me on the weekend since then.

Ms. Ritchie's writing commitments, meanwhile, had increased, and she was distressed over her inability to produce work in volume and with ease. From time to time she consulted with Editor Hall by telephone, or during his weekly visits, and often incorporated his suggestions in her writing, but even this approach did not give her the extra confidence and zest for writing she had hoped to develop. She recalls her feelings at the time:

There was little I actually liked about my job. I wasn't getting anywhere with the writing, and I had always abhorred copy editing. In fact, the only part of my job I did like was revising manuscripts, sketching out articles for others, and generally organizing office details. I had found the only contact I really enjoyed with the other writers was to joke around or to discuss news that came in over the wire machines. Frankly, most of the people at *Hartford* were dull. None of them were as incisive, or as interesting, as Stephen, my husband.

PART II

ABSTRACT

Nina Ritchie undertakes a major feature article for Hartford *on a sensitive local issue. In the course of the project, she clashes with her* Hartford *superiors and faces a crucial turning point in her career.*

Challenging Assignment

Within three months of her promotion to Associate Editor, Ms. Ritchie had completed several articles for the magazine's light features section. She had not, however, undertaken any major feature assignments, preferring instead to edit and coordinate projects originated by other staff writers. By this time, however, the magazine had stepped up its commitment to offering its readership an "inside" look at current problems in the city, and accordingly was encouraging an in-depth feature article on at least one major issue per month. Writers contributing to this series were relieved of other assignments, and their articles were given top priority. Several writers, as a consequence of their features, had been offered the chance to specialize in the topics which their series had covered, thus shifting the image from that of a generalized light publication to a more sophisticated, issue-oriented periodical.

Editor Hall encouraged Nina Ritchie to develop such a feature series of her own and suggested she start by picking up on a lead he'd gotten in

New York concerning a Jewish Defense League chapter being organized in Hartford. He gave her the name of a local J.D.L. leader who had written a political tract detailing why the organization had taken vigilante action against the street gangs which were roaming Jewish neighborhoods. Hall was impressed by the political potential of the author's views, given current attitudes towards crime, and wanted someone at *Hartford* to collaborate with him for a feature.

Difficulties in Teamwork

Nina followed up the lead and arranged for lunch with Mitch Berger, the J.D.L. writer. She recalls their conversation:

Berger was an intense, radical person. He felt any violence was justified in response to violence against Jews. I didn't relish working with him, but the story certainly seemed right for a *Hartford* feature. We arranged for me to spend several days familiarizing myself with the political and religious background for the story. Then I planned to work with him and others involved on both sides of the violence in order to develop an analytical piece which would objectively present the J.D.L.

On the second day of the assignment, after she had spent several hours in Berger's office listening to him argue the "national significance of our neighborhood crisis," Nina challenged the legitimacy of vigilante groups. She reported the following conversation:

Berger: Hey, what's the matter with you? Don't you realize that if Jews had resisted Hitler when his Brownshirts started pushing us around he never would have gotten away with what he did to us? It could happen the same way here—sure it could, if we don't fight. What sort of Jew are you?
Ritchie: I don't think that my religious involvement—or lack of it—is an issue . . .
Berger: But you *are* a Jew, aren't you? You're part of this.
Ritchie: Listen, I was brought up to respect the rule of law—I think we should be Americans first, before we're Jews.
Berger: Wrong! It's God before country, Mrs. Ritchie. The Jews in Germany were loyal to Germany, and look where it got them!

For several days after this confrontation, Nina Ritchie continued to work on the assignment, but found it increasingly difficult to translate Berger's rhetoric into reasoned, balanced background information. Finally, in a discussion of the article with Cynthia, she brought it up:

Ritchie: I really don't feel this story I'm working on merits the time I'm spending on it. I picked up a lead on the Jewish Defense League and started working with their chief publicist, Mitch Berger, just like Michael (Hall) wanted. But this guy Berger is a political fool, and the other side's leaders are no better. I can't see working the story through. I'm going to try to interest one of the reporters in it as a short news item and work on something else.

Elliot: Can't you get along with Berger just long enough to get your story?

Ritchie: Listen Cynthia, I could if I thought it would give the magazine one of its better features, but I just don't believe this is a major piece now. Sure, Berger bothers me. He's arrogant, and too intent on shoving his views down people's throats. If I'm going to take time away from my other work for a feature, I want it to be a significant story.

Elliot: Nina, I think, and Michael thinks, this feature should be done, and we thought you could handle it. I'll help you with it if you'll bring in what you've got so far, and bring along Berger's original article too. We've already allocated space for a feature from you in the next issue. If you were going to back out of this thing, you should have done it sooner.

Nina was upset by Cynthia's unsympathetic response, but she nodded silently and left the room when Cynthia answered a ringing telephone. She now recalls:

I wasn't sure whether my problems were due to conflicts within me about being Jewish, or to a lack of talent, or to an inability to discipline myself. I had long-term goals for money, status, and job satisfaction, but I also wanted to be happy getting wherever I was going professionally. My trouble at the magazine—just before I quit—was in feeling that Cynthia and Hall had dumped an unnecessary, low priority feature on me as a "test." I don't like being manipulated. I wanted to take on features, but at my own pace, and on pieces I believed in. I'd had it with *Hartford* and its office politics.

PART III

ABSTRACT

Nina Ritchie reenters the academic world to obtain a master's degree in business management and embarks on an intense study routine for two years. She discovers the extent of her abilities in new areas and eventually takes a position which draws on both her managerial and creative talents.

Applying to Business School

Nina Ritchie ruled out an immediate return to journalism because, she explains, "I was unwilling to put in more time in a lowly position, and I had no assurances that I would be good enough to get anywhere." Each spring since graduating from Cornell, she had applied and been accepted to graduate programs in both creative writing and communication, but had deferred matriculation because "school was an escape valve I didn't want to use unless my job became really unbearable."

After five months of "just being a housewife," as she puts it, Nina decided to apply to business school. She recalls:

I knew how to write, but not how to make money or organize my time productively. A business school seemed just what I was looking for at the time.

Ms. Ritchie's husband had been offered a clerkship with a federal judge in Philadelphia, so Nina filed an application to the MBA program at the Wharton School of the University of Pennsylvania, and, she relates:

Even though my ATGSB (Advanced Test for Graduate Study in Business) scores were low, they admitted me. Suddenly, I found I was entering a man's world. I was tired of being one of millions of girls in lousy publishing positions. The thought of competing with men changed my perspective . . . I felt imposing. Business school had always retained a certain mystique for me. . . . I was still unsure, however, how I would fit into the business world.

Preparing for a New Career

Although Nina Ritchie's experiences at Wharton were by and large positive, she suffered from periodic spells of depression and feelings of inadequacy. She maintained an intense study routine in the marketing curriculum, concentrating on course work which she found most challenging, mathematics and statistics. Midway through her first semester, Ms. Ritchie underwent an "MBA identity crisis," and seriously questioned how she could integrate her creative abilities with the demands of the business world. She briefly considered dropping out of the program to write, and decided to visit the placement director to discuss her doubts. She remembers:

He was very reassuring, but also condescending. He said, "Don't worry, we'll find you a job where the only numbers you'll have to deal with will be the annual budget, and you can bring that home to your husband." In one sense I was infuriated by his attitude, but that was the kind of job I wanted, and I needed his cooperation, so I said nothing.

Nina gradually gained more confidence in her abilities, and considered entering advertising, which she believed would provide a wider range of experience and more opportunities for advancement than product management, the other marketing specialty.

In the spring of 1975, Ms. Ritchie prepared her résumé for one of the toughest job markets in recent years. She received a number of job offers and accepted what she considered to be the most attractive one, as an advertising manager of a television station. A few weeks before she was to begin in her new position, Ms. Ritchie commented:

I hope this is what I want. This job certainly is a long way from feature writing. I haven't abandoned the arts, and I still love some aspects of the publishing world, particularly the atmosphere of excitement. Perhaps after a few years of this [work], I'll end up in the business or management end of publishing.

3
Marlene Rubin

PART I

ABSTRACT

Marlene Rubin received a masters degree in Art Education, a traditionally female concentration, at the age of twenty-two. Determined to secure a "creative" position which allowed her a maximum degree of independence and individuality, Ms. Rubin was prepared to work in temporary, low-paying jobs until such a desirable position could be found. Instead, the combination of a temporary placement and her own talent and drive catapulted her into one of the most intensely competitive sectors of the corporate world.

Entering Business

While searching for a position capable of fulfilling her high expectations, Ms. Rubin took a temporary job through a Kelly girl-type employment agency as an executive secretary with the large Belmont Company. At the urging of her high school career counselor, and as a means to lucrative summer employment, she had acquired typing and shorthand skills years before.

Ms. Rubin served as a secretary to Mr. Shore, a division manager of Organization Planning and Development. Impressed by the range of Marlene's abilities, Mr. Shore attempted to locate a position within the firm which would satisfy her long-term personal career goals.

Job Development

On the strength of Mr. Shore's recommendation, Ms. Rubin was offered a short-term position at Belmont as a project coordinator in the Creative Marketing Center and given a raise commensurate with her new

21

position. In this capacity she wrote a speech for the division manager, Robert Clark, entitled, "How Our Company is Moving towards More Economically Sound Sales Contracts." Ms. Rubin's lack of training in the field made it necessary for her to conduct extensive research, during the course of which she interviewed all of the division managers in the Marketing group, establishing contacts which a new employee would not normally have.

After an interview with an associate in the Folding Carton and Label Division, Marlene realized she had been given some inaccurate data, and she arranged a meeting with the division manager, Mr. Jules, to verify the correct figures. When they finally met, Marlene remarked in a slightly sarcastic yet not unfriendly tone:

Mr. Jules, I'm Marlene Rubin and I have been trying to reach you for three days. Did you know that your division is holding up my entire report?

Mr. Jules, noting that Ms. Rubin was young, attractive, and stylishly dressed, responded:

Well, if I knew you were Marlene Rubin, I would have spoken to you much sooner.

They proceeded to correct the errors and ended their meeting with a conversation regarding Ms. Rubin's future at the Belmont Company. Ms. Rubin recited her litany of job expectations and discussed her intention to eventually pursue an MBA through an evening school program. Mr. Jules remarked:

Marlene, you're one of the most ambitious girls I've ever come across.

Later, when Ms. Rubin discussed with friends outside the Belmont Company her relationships with her superiors, she would make light of the incident:

So, when I finally met the unreachable man, I said, "Hi! My name's Marlene and you're holding me up, so get out of my way." He would never take that from any of the males my age or in my position, but somehow I'm not a threat when I say something like that. They assume that I'm not after their jobs but just have a great sense of humor, and who am I to disabuse them of that little fantasy? It's funny, but they'll start talking to me and they'll end up revealing top management conflicts that are supposed to be hush-hush. I put them at ease.

Robert Clark was impressed by both the style and substance of the speech Ms. Rubin wrote for him, and he found the background material she had prepared of such value that he based a company-wide seminar on it. He asked Ms. Rubin to write another speech, this time on "1975 Strategic Planning," and gave her a sizable raise with her new assignment.

Solo Woman Experience

The speech, as well as supporting data, were to be delivered to a meeting of the Board of Directors with Ms. Rubin, along with several other executives, playing an active role in the presentation. The participants held several evening planning and practice sessions, during which Ms. Rubin was a "solo woman," the only female present among ten males. Because her assignments had previously been independent projects, this was the first time Ms. Rubin was confronted with such a situation. Both Ms. Rubin and several participants in these sessions reported later that male executives, in the company of their peers, were less familiar and jocular with Ms. Rubin than they had been on an individual basis. While they related to her in a group in a more formal, professional manner, Ms. Rubin felt the executives also began to challenge her status to a greater degree. She told a female friend:

At the beginning of the sessions I was doubted because I didn't have a sufficient business background and because I was young. I got the impression they were thinking, "What does a twenty-two-year-old woman know about sales contracts?" It was an unspoken challenge and I knew I had to excel. So I tried to prove myself able by asking pointed questions . . . but being an extremely young woman is a difficult problem to overcome. Somehow I lacked credibility and, I guess, competence, in their eyes. It convinced me that a woman in my position must have concrete proof of her competence, something she can hang on her wall like a hunting trophy. An MBA is a "must."

Relations with Office Personnel

Although Ms. Rubin usually worked alone or in association with upper level management, she found herself most in conflict with employees of both sexes at or below her level in the company hierarchy. Ms. Rubin described one ongoing antagonism:

I shared an office with a male who had less responsibility and earned less than I did. When he found out what I earned he was outraged. There was a strong undercurrent of resentment between us, especially since I always spoke with top people. He used to make snide remarks intimating I was in some way a "spy" or infiltrator working for top management.

Ms. Rubin's relations with other women in the corporation were generally unsatisfactory, although this did not impair her job performance. Ms. Rubin told a male friend:

There are no other women now in Marketing Services, though I suspect what with pressure from the EEOC (Equal Employment Opportunity Commission) they just might bring one in. I'm not sure how I feel about that. If they want to do their part for women, they can promote me. A few women around the office who are my age or older act like they resent me, probably because I achieved my superior position so quickly. I think they might also resent the fact that I insist on maintaining my femininity—you know I'm no women's libber. But some of the women seem to feel they have to be "tough" to earn respect in business. I don't buy that. I'm very conscious of being a woman and use it to the utmost advantage without compromising myself or my values—around the office I'm appreciated for being a woman who accepts the fact that she's a woman.

Ms. Rubin's male friend joked:

Well, doesn't that create complications?

She answered seriously:

Occasionally it does. Any time I'm in the presence of a male, others see it as an opportunity to make some sexist comment like, "Excuse me, I'll leave you two alone." It's hard to have a male friendship in the office for this reason. But if I'm with one of the more important executives they don't dare make a comment to my face, at least not while he's around.

A female sales representative of a major office equipment concern, who during her frequent visits to the Belmont Company struck up a casual friendship with Ms. Rubin, recalls:

We went out to lunch together a few times but Marlene rarely ate with the women in her office. She was very young and very ambitious, but most of the other women in the office were stuck in traditional or dead-end jobs. The way Marlene was treated made it difficult for her to become one of the girls, and she certainly couldn't be one of the boys. It was hard for her because the office was sexually segregated as far as lunch dates and all that.

Ms. Rubin undertook several additional writing projects and was commended each time for the thoroughness of her research and the originality of her ideas. Mr. Clark awarded Ms. Rubin another substantial raise, her third in ten months.

Further Advancement

In the division budget for the next fiscal year, Ms. Rubin was officially approved as a permanent employee. The position had become a highly lucrative one, and Ms. Rubin told friends she was convinced that a career in business was the most appropriate use of her talents.

After a year with the Belmont Company, Ms. Rubin was presented with a new and challenging assignment. As head of Creative Marketing Services, Clark asked her to design a campaign promoting use of certain of the company's products by Belmont employees. The objectives of the campaign were ambitious: to boost employee morale and foster pride in company products. Ms. Rubin worked closely with Mr. Clark for three months developing campaign strategy. At the end of this period the basics of the promotion were approved by upper management, and it was necessary to mobilize a task force of personnel from several areas to finalize and distribute the promotional material.

Ms. Rubin had prematurely assumed she would direct this task force, since the project had been hers from its inception. However, management required for this position an executive who not only had contacts in many of the divisions but experience in dealing with employee groups as well. While Mr. Summers, a project specialist from the Employee Relations Division who had directed other internal company campaigns, was given the assignment, Ms. Rubin was named Creative Director of the project. Mr. Summers assumed final control over the text and presentation of promotional materials. Ms. Rubin complained to friends:

I know I won't be able to work with this Summers man. He's arrogant and he's only a few years older than I am, so we'll never get along. I'm the one with the ideas; I've got the creative ability; and then they appoint him to destroy them with his implementation plans and even let him modify the creative aspects. It's humiliating. It seems they didn't consider me for the post very seriously, most likely because I'm a woman. In the past Clark has always given me raises and praised my work, but when they proposed someone else to handle the campaign, he didn't even fight for me.

Determined to find out "where she stood" with Mr. Clark, Ms. Rubin approached him for a raise. She knew company policy was fairly rigid on this issue and, due to rapid promotions, she had already received an unusual number of raises within her first year with Belmont. Explained Ms. Rubin:

I assumed that if Clark wanted me working for him enough he could bend the rules. And anyway, I started out as a secretary on a level which a man would never have accepted, and I didn't think the first raises should count.

PART II

ABSTRACT

Ms. Rubin is offered a position with a creative division of a major fast food chain. In line with company policy, Ms. Rubin is required to first gain experience in one of the company's high volume outlets. She finds herself in an unknown, hostile environment with no upper-level executives looking out for her interests.

Career Redirection

Mr. Robert Clark, Creative Marketing Services Division manager, informed Ms. Rubin that her request for a raise had been refused, on the basis that it violated company policy limiting the number of salary increments any employee could receive within his or her first two years of affiliation with the company. Further, Clark reminded Ms. Rubin that she lacked an MBA degree, which most management personnel at her level held.

The following week, Ms. Rubin sent Clark a terse letter of resignation. However, this time she was not prepared to work another temporary stint as a secretary while searching for an "ideal" job.

Two months earlier a "talent scout" from a major, national fast food chain, "Buddy's," had discretely approached Ms. Rubin with a job offer. Because of a recent discrimination judgment rendered against "Buddy's" in federal court, Ms. Rubin was aware that "Buddy's" was under a legal obligation to seek out and hire more female executives. Wishing to keep her options open at the time, she had entered into unofficial discussions with "Buddy's."

Ms. Rubin left the Belmont Company for a tentative offer of an executive position with Buddy's Employee Training and Policy Division. Buddy's employed almost exclusively high school and college students as "crew members" in their outlets, and averaged a 300 percent yearly turnover in crew personnel. The hazards of short-term teenage employees handling expensive, though easily operated, kitchen equipment worth $50,000 per outlet were a major concern to the company. Employee education was highly standardized throughout the Buddy's Company, and novel approaches were often introduced in hopes of maintaining employee interest.

Theoretically, before an employee could handle a Buddy's milkshake machine or fry station, he or she was required to view films on its operation, memorize instructions, and pass a simple written test. New campaigns were initiated monthly to revive interest in work and increase employee productivity and allegiance to the company. With her master's in Art Education, her experience with the Belmont employee purchasing promotion, and her demonstrated writing ability, Ms. Rubin was offered an attractive position in the Creative Promotions Section of the Employees Training and Policy Division. She would be an "idea woman" dreaming up ways to interest adolescents in performing tedious, low-paying jobs with a fair degree of accuracy and speed.

Training Experience

The management of the Buddy's Company had a reputation for being extremely competitive both internally and externally. However, Buddy's also assigned considerable weight to company fealty, and top management preferred to see "their people" come up through the ranks rather than moving laterally from another corporation. For that reason, Ms. Rubin's offer in the Creative Promotions section was made conditional upon her passage through an arduous initiation rite. She was first required to spend six months in training and store work, so that, as the company explained, "You'll know our product, the way we operate, and get an idea of what our problems with crew members are." She revealed:

I was impressed that, even at this end, the type of creative propaganda I was to produce was treated with great importance. I made the mistake of telling one man in my training class that I had been promised an executive position. He made no attempt to hide his resentment. After that I was careful not to tell any of the other students, all of whom were male, but I'm sure it got around. I think they believed I hadn't gotten the job on my merits, because when there was a classroom discussion on how to avoid discriminatory practices, one man made a joke about affirmative action, and they all glared at me.

Ms. Rubin was then assigned as an assistant manager of a high-volume outlet in an inner city area. Although she knew it would be difficult, she was quite unprepared for what she experienced. She recalled:

I had heard horror tales, but living them is something different. The twelve-hour days, the six-day weeks, I was expecting them, but it was physically exhausting. You're not supposed to sit down for a minute. When you're supervising a shift, you're supposed to be constantly checking up on the crew, helping them during rush hours if necessary. A few managers, male and female, in other stores I knew used stimulants to keep going, but I wouldn't.

Ms. Rubin, an athletic and vigorous woman, was able to handle most of the physical rigors of working in a fast food outlet, but found some of the human problems more vexing.

On the Job Difficulties

The male crew members, some of them just three or four years younger than I, used to take great pleasure in standing over me in a threatening pose when I spoke to them, although usually they'd follow my orders. Most of these kids are just working at the store long enough to make a few dollars for a stereo or a car, or to put in the bank, and they don't much like the work. And unless you can really intimidate them, which for me was out of the question, it was better to be popular with them. But it was hard for me to let the male crew members play their games, and I blew up some of the time. When I kept quiet, they were happy and did their jobs, though I doubt they really respected me. The kids used to "cut down" the training material, which by and large was viewed as an insult to their intelligence, and they had little time for the company-wide contests. I thought, "My God, am I going to spend my life writing inane jingles and designing color-coded charts, so these kids can use them as scrap paper?" Among themselves, they'd talk primarily about poor working conditions and intolerant managers—those were their chief concerns.

Ms. Rubin developed what she describes as a "working relationship" with crew members, but for the first time in her career, found she had difficulty communicating with her superiors. The Buddy's Company, despite its emphasis on "team work," fostered a competitive attitude among its young managers. According to company policy, any store-hired employee who was not deemed worthy of promotion within two and one-half years was dismissed.

Ms. Rubin, who was in a sense just "passing through," encountered considerable antagonism from the other assistant and store managers, who were less sure of their futures. Store personnel were generally not supportive of one another. She recalls:

All the managers hated each other. The only sense of camaraderie that existed occurred when a district manager came to town. After he'd cut a few throats, the survivors would go out with him and get stinking drunk. I did not ever consider going along, nor was I invited; it was a "men only" affair. One of the managers was, I believe, an alcoholic. When he was drinking alone, and I was on night shift, he would often come to the store after the crew had gone home and while I was doing paper work, and he would harass me.

Ms. Rubin became increasingly disillusioned, and friends expressed concern that she was abnormally tense. One incident in particular, according to a male friend, "sent her nearly to the brink." Ms. Rubin was persuaded to relate the incident:

I was scheduled for the afternoon shift, and because of an illness in the managerial staff I had to cover the morning shift also. I had been on my feet for twelve straight hours and still had paper work to do. When the two men assigned to the busy evening shift arrived, they told me to take off and they would finish my inventories, time cards, and cash register count, which is against company policy. I accepted their offer.

Early the next morning, Ms. Rubin received an agitated phone call from the store manager, which she recounted for the casewriter:

Manager: The money from your shift is $200 short. The guys on the night shift brought it to my attention. Why didn't you notify me immediately?
Rubin: I didn't know. I left before it was counted.
Manager: You what? You just committed two cardinal sins, Marlene . . . breaking company policy and gross stupidity.
Rubin: What should I do?
Manager: The only thing you can do is make good on the money out of your salary. It won't look good on your record.
Rubin: But I didn't take that money. They counted my shift—they must have it.
Manager: Can you prove it? What is it, your word against theirs? Anyway, the shift is your responsibility! Don't add another black mark to your record by making wild, unsupported allegations.

Ms. Rubin did not speak with the two men again. Her efficiency, which had not been high to begin with, suffered greatly and her supervisor gave her an unsatisfactory rating. Crew members complained that her disorganization made extra work for them. During one shift she supervised, a fist fight with racial overtones broke out between two male crew members, and she called the police rather than ask the manager in a Buddy's, just four blocks away, for assistance.

Ms. Rubin now believes:

In retrospect, I handled myself poorly. I came in very sure of myself and where I was going, and I didn't recognize just how much hostility there was. Perhaps part of it was my personality, part the cutthroat attitude, and a good part sexist. I was not very efficient, and I let a lot of the extra work fall on the men. After all, I was hired to be creative, not fix milkshake machines. A lot of people, and even more, ethics, fell victim to the competition. Before, in an office, the favor of my superiors had always been enough, and I didn't have to deal with my peers or subordinates. But in this case, my 'guardians' were way off in a central office in another city, and I was in over my head. I realize now that the money stolen was not the important thing. What those men were hoping was that it would throw me off my keel, and it did. I heard later that a regional supervisor once had an entire shipment of hamburger meat "lost" for him by his coworkers and he survived. A lot of these incidents remind me of locker room pranks. I had never had to handle this sort of thing before.

Because she received unsatisfactory ratings for her work in the outlet, the original job offer with the Creative Promotion Section was withdrawn. A supervisor with whom she had been friendly later told Ms. Rubin:

It wasn't just that short money incident that ruined your chances. Word travels fast. Everyone knew what had really happened. In general, though, you weren't very good as a manager. You were unwise to take the job to begin with. Most of our trainees have already had years of experience in a high-volume, high-pressure store. You were a bit too precocious for your own good. And management didn't really care but was anxious to get the court and the EEOC off its back. They hire people, but they sure don't make it easy for them to last.

A Career Decision

After losing her job with Buddy's, Ms. Rubin received a flood of advice from concerned family and friends. Her parents, who had always stressed a career, now pressured her to get married "for security" and suggested she might enjoy taking a vacation as a housewife. Several friends suggested she search for a job in advertising or go to graduate school. Ms. Rubin expressed confusion about her future:

I'm rather unsure of myself at the moment. But I believe that I never would have gotten as far as I did if I didn't have a fair degree of talent and the ability to apply myself. I'm drawn to the business world, but I may want at least a breather from it. One of the questions I'm confronting right now is whether it's possible for me, with the proper training, to cope with some of the same problems I faced and not become too tough and cynical. I've always been very careful to guard my femininity, perhaps been too self-conscious. But now I suppose I'm rethinking my definition of femininity. If I return to the business world, I might like to specialize in personnel problems, something I never was interested in before. But I'm not sure that I'd be terribly good in this field.

At present Marlene Rubin is debating between pursuing an MBA or a doctorate in English. She has been accepted into both programs.

4
First Shelter Corporation*

ABSTRACT

Ann Brooks accepts reassignment from a position as a financial analyst to one in the Investor Services Department. Despite good performance, conflicts between her and her supervisor lead to Ms. Brooks' firing and her supervisor's resignation.

The lawyer waited for Silas James to answer his phone call. "Mr. James, I'd like to talk to you about a former employee of yours. I think you might want to hire her back. I'm not calling in my capacity as counsel to the Company, but I know her work and I think a mistake has been made in firing her."

After a brief discussion the two men hung up, and Mr. James thought back over the past few years. He had formed First Shelter Corporation in January 1970 as a small company with himself as president, four executives—all recent graduates of the Tuck School—and a few secretaries. By September, three additional administrative positions had opened up and were filled by secretaries, whose jobs were then taken by new recruits.

Prior to its incorporation the company had been the tax shelter department of a prominent retail brokerage house. When tax laws were changed to allow significant benefits in syndicating tax shelters centered around low income housing, Mr. James, as the head of the tax shelter department, sought to innovate in the area. The management of the brokerage house, however, did not want to bear the risk. An agreement was

*This is a shortened version of a case prepared by Anita Bright under the supervision of Jules J. Schwartz. It is used here by permission of Professor Schwartz.

31

worked out whereby the tax shelter department was incorporated, with 15 percent of the voting common stock retained by the brokerage house.

First Shelter was registered as a broker-dealer with the National Association of Securities Dealers and in each of the states in which it did business. The first year was slow since the marketing of the tax shelter syndications was carried on independently of the parent brokerage house. Only six syndications were sold during the first six months; however, during the last part of the year another twenty deals were sold, for a total of $11 million in sales the first year. The next year, sales more than doubled.

The nature of the business was quite hectic. The sooner a project was syndicated and sold, the more tax deductions would accrue to the investors. The ultimate deadline was the end of construction, since the investors had to enjoy first-user status with any building, or substantial tax deductions would be lost. On the other hand, the syndication could not be completed until the costs of construction were firm. This meant that the commitments for permanent construction loans and construction project estimates had to be obtained before negotiation of the syndication could begin. As a result, deadlines were short, both for syndicating and for marketing.

All of the activities occurring after the time of closing of each syndicate were performed initially by First Shelter's Marketing Department. The tasks had been handled previously by a marketing executive who had been hired at the founding of the company. This was her first job. After the management decided that such activities did not constitute a marketing function, it was decided to set up an Investor Services Department.

The Investor Services position was first offered to Mr. James' secretary, who had been very efficient at her job. When she accepted the job offer, she was told that the marketing executive would help her get on her feet. After several weeks the secretary began to complain that she spent all day typing letters dictated by the executive and did not have time to cope with the volume of letters that had to go to investors. Soon after that she was demoted back to a secretarial position and later left the company.

The job was then offered to another secretary with about eight years experience. She took the job with the understanding that she would run the department. After two months, however, she also complained that she was still typing letters dictated by the marketing executive and doing various record-keeping tasks for her. She too quit the company.

The job was next offered to Ann Brooks, who for nine months had been working at First Shelter running financial simulations in the computer room for three of the firm's officers, and subsequently for one vice president exclusively. She agreed to take the offer on the conditions that she would be autonomous, and that she would have a secretary. It seemed to her that part of the problem the two previous people had was that they were expected to do two jobs: one administrative and one secretarial. Her conditions were agreed to, and she began work by writing letters under the marketing executive's tutelage but over her own signature, and redesigning the existing systems that were meant to trigger the various cyclical activities the department was to become involved in. The marketing executive had no further relationship with the Investor Services Department after that.

The job involved a large volume of letters sent out to investors. The information in the letters came from the developers of the real estate projects. A great deal of skill was involved in getting this information from the developers since First Shelter had only temporary financial leverage with them. The typical initial reaction Ms. Brooks received over the phone was, "It takes too long to work up an estimate," or "I'll look into that." Either way the information was slow in coming. However, after a couple of months she built up a rapport with the developers and found ways to extract the information from them.

Through trial and error she initiated several new systems. As soon as any area was routinized, she let her secretary handle the administration and went on to work on some other problem. After the collection of installment payments was systematized, another secretary was promoted to take care of this area, also reporting to Brooks.

Six months later, the Executive Committee decided that a person with real estate and accounting backgrounds would be useful, both to catch potential problems in the projects First Shelter had sold, and to steer shaky projects back to a stable course. They hired an accountant, Tony Laird, who had been an auditor at one of the developers. First Shelter was aware of his background. He was a CPA and had several interests in small real estate dealings of his own. He had worked for a large public accounting firm for five years and had been fired from his job there as a supervisor. Brooks was to report to him.

When Laird first joined the firm, one of the vice presidents, who was relatively familiar with Brooks' progress in heading the department, told him what she had been doing and that the situation seemed to be under control. Laird asked whom he was to report to and did not get a clear answer. He later said that he came away with the impression that he had been hired to straighten out a mess.

The first day that Laird started to work he wrote a letter, gave it to Brooks' secretary, and ordered her to type it. The secretary said she was much too busy and couldn't possibly type anything. She later complained to Ms. Brooks about Laird's brusque manner. Laird then took the letter to another woman who did her own typing but did not consider herself a secretary. She also refused to type it. Later in the day Brooks spoke to him: "If you have any trouble getting things typed, give them to me and I'll see to it that they get done." She later confided to one of the vice presidents that she thought it was crucial for Laird's work to get typed, and that if he couldn't deal effectively with the secretaries she would have to handle the situation.

Brooks had no problem getting her own work typed. In fact, some of the secretaries in other departments of the company were in the habit of offering their assistance when they had no other work. As Brooks' secretary became more proficient, she learned to apportion the delegation of heavy work loads to other secretaries. At times, during peak periods, there were seven people in the office typing Brooks' messages on magnetic card typewriters that recorded text so that the same letter could be sent to many people with a minimum of secretarial time. This freed Brooks' secretary to do higher level jobs. Brooks had given her one raise after she had been with the company only six weeks and another after four months. She asked the Personnel Department to give her still another raise four months later but was told that the company could not afford it. The next month Brooks went on vacation for three weeks, and upon her return she again asked Personnel for the raise for her secretary. She was told that a raise had just been settled; Laird had given it to the secretary while Brooks was on vacation.

Soon after, Laird hired his own secretary and there were no more incidents of refusal to type his work, although one afternoon while his secretary was not at her desk he asked Ms. Brooks if she knew how to work the typewriter and, if so, if she could type an envelope for him. She answered that she knew enough to show him how to use it. He said he would wait for his secretary to return.

Two weeks later a letter had to be written to some of the investors. The letter was a fairly sensitive matter in that it involved asking for an additional and unexpected payment. Ms. Brooks wrote the letter and showed it to Laird before sending it out to show him the type of problem that arose in the investor relations area. Laird made changes in the letter even though it was to go out over Ann Brooks' signature. In the past she had balked at other people changing her letters, but she let Laird work over eight drafts of this particular letter because he was new on the job. The ninth draft she took to him and said, "Here's the final draft. I thought you'd like to see it before it goes out." When Laird started putting further changes in the letter, she protested that this was the *final* copy. Laird countered that the letter would go through several more drafts before it was ready to go. Brooks said she would put these changes in and send it out. She then gave the letter to her secretary and asked her to send it out to the twelve investors.

Laird stopped in her office two days later and asked where the letter was. She said it had been sent to the investors. He glared at her and walked out of the office. That afternoon he returned after the secretaries had left for the day and said, "I want to talk to you about the letter. It was an act of insubordination." Ms. Brooks replied, "I don't think so. This company has no visible hierarchy. The way I look at my job is that there is a large amount of work to do. It has to get done on time and it has to get done right. There is such a volume of work we cannot afford to make mistakes; on the other hand, we cannot afford to spend too much time on any one thing. I think that ten drafts of a letter are enough to weed out any mistakes. My action in sending out the letter was not done for personal reasons, but for business reasons." The company subsequently received all of the funds the letter was intended to collect except for one recalcitrant's share.

Laird had been with First Shelter perhaps two months, when Ann Brooks received a letter from a wealthy matron. She wrote that she wanted to sell her unit of tax shelter and asked what the sale price would be. Since the company had a policy of discouraging sales of units, Ms. Brooks asked Laird for advice on how to answer the letter. He said not to answer it and referred to the woman in less than gentlemanly terms. He had had a fight with her on the phone earlier and complained that she was hard to deal with.

Brooks began working on an answer by herself. The next day one of the marketing men saw the investor's letter on her desk and asked Laird what he intended to do about it. Laird's answer was, "Nothing." The marketing man exploded and started shouting things about keeping the investors happy. Laird shouted back in self defense, his usual poor grammar at a low ebb. Ann Brooks, who was present, got their attention by saying, "Both of you calm down. I've written the draft of a response." She handed it to the marketing man who relaxed and then offered some constructive criticisms that were later incorporated in the letter.

Late in the year Ms. Brooks went into Laird's office to say that she had plenty of free time on her hands and was willing to take on any new long term projects he could think of. Laird got up from his desk and closed the door to his office:

Laird: A decision has been made to terminate you.

Brooks: Why?

Laird: You know perfectly well why. You've been expecting it. Last night I handed in my own resignation. I am taking another job at the end of this month.

Laird had been with First Shelter for some nine months. Brooks had been looking for another job because she often disagreed with the way he ran things. The fact that First Shelter's president would walk into the office they both shared for a time and would ask her, not Laird, how the department was going and what problems there were, was an indication to her that she was respected. However, she felt that Laird saw her as a threat.

Laird gave her the impression that the Executive Committee had decided to fire her, and when asked, told her that the president knew of the decision. All of this was untrue. The next day, no one in the company knew she had been fired, except her secretary whom she had called immediately after leaving work the previous evening. Mr. James was visibly upset when he found out. Brooks' secretary was in tears all day. Morale among the secretaries was generally lowered, and at least one of the senior executives was stunned that the top two people in the Investor Services Department were leaving the company within a month of each other. Furthermore, it was January, and tax returns were due out to the seven hundred investors within two months.

5
Donna Fogel

PART I

ABSTRACT

Donna Fogel is, at the age of thirty, in the midst of a career change. After graduating from college, Ms. Fogel worked briefly in a publishing firm but then turned towards the field of education, furthering her own in the process. Now, already working on her dissertation, Ms. Fogel again begins to re-think her life goals. From another perspective, however, her current activities may be seen as an attempt to establish new direction in her personal life and to achieve a greater measure of self-determination.

Personal Background

Ms. Fogel was the second child in a lower-middle-class family and grew up in a community where approximately 10 percent of the high school seniors went on to college. While Ms. Fogel always did well in school—in fact, was usually at the top of her class—her family expected, at most, that she would become a public school teacher. She recalls:

My father often extolled the virtues of a school teacher's life. He would have been just as happy to see me become a secretary. His aspirations for me came, I think, as much from his traditional notions of what is proper and *possible* for a woman to do, as from his intense memories of the Depression and his desire for financial security. He seldom spoke to me of marriage, or of finding a man to support myself, under any circumstances. This meant, of course, not taking any risks as far as education or a career was concerned. Even the spring after my first year in business school, when I was having trouble finding a summer job, he said to me that, if necessary, I could always type or do clerical work. My mother, too, often reminds me that if this new venture into the business world doesn't work out, I can always go back to teaching.

First Work Experience

Ms. Fogel fought these expectations, but in an unorganized and unplanned way. She received a scholarship to a small eastern women's college, and though she was later admitted to a more prestigious school—one of the seven sisters—Ms. Fogel attended the small college fearing that she would not do as well and would not be accepted socially at the other school. While Donna Fogel graduated *cum laude,* she found herself, like many liberal arts graduates, unskilled and unmarketable. She took one of the first jobs offered her, as secretary and assistant to the production manager in a publishing company. Although her responsibilities included editing and research, her job was, she recalls, tedious and without direction. She notes:

Only now, eight years later, does it dawn on me that I really had no expectations for myself, in terms of a career or otherwise. I had, through the duration of my college years, some vague notions of a career in literature or publishing, but not the least idea of what kinds of jobs were available, what kinds of skills might be required, and, in general, the parameters of a professional career and life.

When my boss left the firm, it never occurred to me that I might have acquired sufficient skills and experience to do his job and that I might have presented myself to management as a possible candidate. When a friend suggested this to me at the time, I dismissed it out of hand, thought it an absurd suggestion, and, probably was pretty frightened by the whole idea.

Further Education and New Involvements

After a year with the publishing concern, Ms. Fogel quit her job to return to school for a master's degree in teaching, hoping that would prove more interesting and satisfying. After receiving her master's, Donna entered teaching, but found she disliked it. She remembers:

The amazing thing to me now is that I went into teaching without a clear desire or reason to do so. What I do remember clearly, however, is the overwhelming sense of waiting, of passively and constantly waiting for something to happen which would give definition to my life and somehow release the hidden powers which I didn't have the strength or ability to release myself. I was literally unconscious of the possibility of making a clear choice and giving direction to my life.

After teaching for a year and a half, Donna met a man whom she describes as "outwardly confident and strong," a man she felt would give her life some of the meaning she believed it lacked. She recalls wanting to link her life to his—in fact, she found a new job in another city in order to live with him. She remembers:

At the same time I wanted Roy to direct my life. It took a long time before I realized that this was a responsibility he definitely did not want to take on, and that much of what eventually went wrong in our relationship was attributable to my unconscious attempts to make him accept that kind of burden. I had no compunctions about leaving my teaching job and no concern about finding another job in a new city. My only priority and concern was to be with Roy, for that was, indeed, my life.

Donna's new job was with a university-sponsored project. For the next three and a half years, she recalls, it all seemed "convenient and very cozy" to her—she and Roy lived together, on and off, and she in turn developed what she considered to be a critical relationship with her employer, Lorraine Allen.

Ms. Fogel came to view Ms. Allen as an egocentric, domineering, and in some ways maternalistic woman. This naturally fostered constant, though unspoken, conflict and resentment, which remained unspoken partly because Ms. Fogel felt her job was only of secondary importance, as her relationship with Roy seemed to have some hope of being permanent. Yet she found herself involved in a complex and ambivalent relationship with Lorraine; she feels Lorraine became her mother, sister, mentor, and alter ego. Ms. Fogel relates:

A dozen times a day, I wanted to argue with Lorraine, to disagree with her singular and narrow view of our work and the people we were dealing with. I wanted to improve the quality of our research and the efficiency with which we ran the project. However, I was afraid of her and of her rather caustic tongue, and so I kept quiet.

During the course of her work with the project, Ms. Fogel also entered a doctoral program in education at the same university. It seemed the reasonable thing to do, she explains, adding that her philosophy was, "another degree can't hurt." Getting a Ph.D., however, turned out to be a chore. She was uninterested and undisciplined in fulfilling the requirements of the program—just a week before the preliminary exams, Ms. Fogel was still trying to fill out papers transferring credits to achieve qualifying status. Nevertheless, she continued in the program, viewing it as her only link to some kind of independent professional status because her concurrent job did not give her confidence in her own abilities. Ms. Fogel believes her lack of confidence was in part caused by her feeling that everything she did was dominated and overshadowed by Lorraine's hand. At one point, while juggling the school requirements and a report due on a project at work, Ms. Fogel encountered unavoidable delays, which caused the report to be handed to Lorraine too late to meet a deadline. Donna Fogel recalls:

I gave her the draft to read, and she was angry because it wasn't finished. She hadn't kept track of that project, and she obviously hadn't even read the report. But she was angry at the delay and said, "You're getting paid to do this, aren't you?" It was like a knife. When I explained the delays, she said, "Oh, well, fine, then we'll be all right. *You* can explain what happened (to the clients) and it'll be okay." But she never said she was sorry.

Despite the tension, Ms. Fogel at other times felt "very close" to Lorraine and wanted "to feel myself her equal." She admired Lorraine's self-confidence. She recalls:

She was clearly a woman (or rather, a person) I was not equipped to deal with on an equal level, and I spent a lot of time adjusting my stance toward her so as to engender the least personal conflict between us. While the relationship with Lorraine was frustrating, and in many ways destructive to me, I still held on to it. What I never realized was how threatening I was to Lorraine—younger, better trained in research and in writing, and generally more knowledgeable. It was important for me to be in that position since I felt at the time that I couldn't achieve status on my own.

Changing Behavior Patterns

When Donna's relationship with Roy eventually collapsed under the weight of unspoken conflict, she finally made some decisions, as she puts it, "out of desperation." While she continued to work with Lorraine, that relationship became more openly conflictual—which surprised Lorraine. Ms. Fogel concedes it was probably very confusing to Lorraine when she first started objecting to work she formerly had accepted without complaint. She notes:

We were working on one project I felt didn't have much value, and I think Lorraine felt the same way, but the project brought in money. I finally spoke up and told her we shouldn't prostitute ourselves on this, just to get funds. She was very defensive; she said, "What's the matter with you? Don't you believe in what we're doing?"

Ms. Fogel recalls she was having trouble "separating long built-up feelings of resentment" from the issues causing friction, and consequently her first attempts to "fight back" were erratic:

It's hard to say how or why my relationship with Lorraine changed. In some ways it was a much more important relationship than the one with Roy, in terms of my growing up. My relationship with Roy was so vague with so many fears and desires unstated by both of us. I think that when Roy and I broke up, I was simply weary of continually adjusting my position to other peoples', of always looking behind me to make sure I hadn't left any traces of my own feelings about.

Ms. Fogel worked with Lorraine another year, but resentment was more clearly evident. She still views her relationship with Lorraine as "very difficult," and since leaving the position has seen her only infrequently. She explains:

Seeing Lorraine opens too many old wounds and stirs up a lot of conflict in me. Importantly, though, I no longer feel permanently tied to her and dependent upon her whims. I'm beginning to feel as if I have something of my own now.

PART II

ABSTRACT

With the prodding of friends, Donna Fogel leaves her doctoral studies to enter graduate business school. During her first year, while searching for summer employment, Ms. Fogel encounters some of the complications her age and experience in other fields will present to her as a newcomer to the business world. However, she eventually obtains a desirable summer position in a Wall Street firm, and returns for the second year of her MBA program, still unsure of the course she would like her business career to take.

Entering Business School

According to Ms. Fogel, by the time she ended her relationship with Roy she had been influenced by the women's movement to the point of considering new career possibilities for herself, if only for the fact that she was a woman.

After talking to some friends who were graduate business students, she was taken with the idea of becoming a businesswoman. It would mean switching horses in midstream, however, and with a substantial investment already made in her doctoral work, Ms. Fogel was uncertain about facing another two years in school. The idea of entering the business curriculum became more enticing as her Ph.D. work became more tedious. Within a year, Ms. Fogel left her doctoral studies and entered graduate business school. She explains:

In many respects, the decision to go to business school was an impulsive, almost desperate one. In other respects, however, it was a rational choice which has given me more determination and direction. It was the one decision I clearly made myself, for myself, in the years since I left college. It's the one choice I've made which I've not been able to hold others responsible for, and thus it has been an important step for me in accepting responsibility for many aspects of my life.

Job Interview

During her first year of business school, Donna Fogel began searching for a summer job. Her first interview, she relates, was unsatisfactory, but a learning experience nonetheless. The interviewer was a younger man who was inexperienced at interviewing prospective employees. He knew little about the job being offered and told Ms. Fogel few details (such as salary). To her, he seemed very much taken with his own position in his firm. Moreover, in order to deal with a thirty-year-old woman whose background was more extensive and diverse than his own, he resorted to detailed technical questions. Ms. Fogel recalls:

All in all it was a frustrating and discouraging experience. At first, I blamed myself for coming off confused, unsure, and a little bit of a bitch. While the uncertainty is partly real, it wasn't until some days later that I realized that he also contributed to the conduct of the interview. He obviously didn't know what he was doing, couldn't tell me anything about the job being offered, and probably felt threatened by me. When I understood that, I was encouraged, because, for the first time, I had worked myself out of the trap of always seeing the fault in my own behavior.

Summer Employment

Donna Fogel eventually received a summer job in the prestigious Wall Street firm of Barrett & Banks. She was one of four professional women in a department of about forty people, and while she was generally regarded as student help for the summer, she was nevertheless treated with respect—primarily because she was an MBA candidate. She found herself often asked to make more substantial input in the conceptual aspects of the data collection projects.

The male professionals were not anxious to initiate any interaction with her. While they were open to questions and conversations about their jobs and about the firm, it was Ms. Fogel who had to make the first move in order to learn. In some cases she was rebuffed, but generally she found the senior people in the department friendly, open, and interested. As difficult as it was at first, Ms. Fogel soon found herself adapting. She began talking to more people, moving around the firm making contacts. Assessing the summer experience, Ms. Fogel notes:

Working on Wall Street is a seductive experience. One gets the sense of being surrounded by power and wealth. I found myself imagining my role in that structure. By that time, however, I had achieved enough maturity and confidence to be aware of the price to be paid for a career in Wall Street finance. I was attracted by the monetary and status rewards but repelled by the trade-offs required in terms of one's personal life. I found myself in the same old position, i.e., success vs. emotional security. This time, however, I was able to make a choice that was informed by knowledge and self-awareness, and knew I did not want to pay the price of a Wall Street career.

Ms. Fogel, now finishing her MBA studies is concentrating on job-hunting. She is again going through the interviewing process, but now she says she is learning "to set myself on an equal level" with the interviewer. She observes:

The business world is clearly not the glamorous utopia I've been waiting for all these years. On the other hand, I feel that I am able now to reconcile my desires for status and professional success with my emotional needs. I am aware of the trade-offs involved and am capable of taking responsibility for whatever decisions I may make in those two areas of my life. I also feel now that I have tangible and marketable skills, that I am a credible professional, and these things have given me a measure of personal confidence I've heretofore been unable to achieve.

Donna Fogel hopes to find a position in the financial community. During this period, Ms. Fogel returned to campus to seek advice from a professor. Recalling the interview, the professor observed:

She is not worried about getting a job; she feels a woman of her age and experience should be desirable to many firms. She is concerned, however, about finding work that will be satisfying and enjoyable. I don't think she wants to follow the traditional accountant's route, i.e., receiving relatively low pay and doing audits for two or three years. She does not want to do what many people have suggested she is perfectly qualified for, educational administration. She is more likely to enter the finance department of a firm. She is still ambitious and anxious to do well financially, but I feel she's aware of the limitations of finding identity in only one aspect of life.

6
Mary and George Norton

ABSTRACT

This case examines the experience of a middle-aged couple who work together in the ladies' accessories field. Mary and George Norton find their talents often complement one another, but there are also tensions which put a serious strain on both their business and marital relationships.

Entering the Business

In the mid 1960s George Norton, a Harvard Business School graduate then in his late forties, purchased the Crown and Crosby Company, an established wholesaler of ladies' accessories. The firm, then with an annual sales volume of $3.3 million, was known for its diversified line of scarves which attracted buyers from Sears to Saks Fifth Avenue. George Norton, a veteran of the heavier textile industry, became Crown and Crosby's president.

Mary Cooper Norton, then in her thirties, held a degree in Industrial Engineering from Penn State, where she had been one of only three women in the program. During college she edited the Engineering School's magazine and, upon graduation, was employed as an editor for a widely sold technical magazine. After two years of work Mary Cooper, then married to her first husband, resigned during her first pregnancy.

When, in 1958, Mary Cooper was widowed, she sought employment in the engineering field, registering with several professional employment firms. However, her prolonged absence from the job market, her unfamiliarity with innovations in the field, and the unequal status of

44

women in engineering made it difficult for her to find a position. Not financially bound to work, and unwilling at her age to begin in another field, Mary Cooper abandoned her search after four months.

In 1961, when Ms. Cooper married George Norton, she had still not returned to work, but filled her time with her two children and extensive volunteer work. By 1963, when George purchased Crown and Crosby, she was again contemplating a return to the job market. She recalls:

My children were older and in school all day, and I didn't see any real need to remain at home. The PTA and my other volunteer organizations were not enough to keep me satisfied. I felt, especially after being president of an organization, that I had organizational ability that could be used in a more financially productive manner. Then one day I was at the office waiting to go out to lunch with George, and I complained to one of the vice presidents that some of the scarf designs were really terribly dull. He asked if I could do any better, and I took him up on the challenge.

Early Work Experiences

Mary Norton began her work with the company on an informal basis, with the understanding that her status there would be more clearly defined if she continued. Both husband and wife found the arrangement convenient at first, since it allowed them to delay dealing with certain fundamental differences. George recalls:

I didn't think Mary was serious about this work, which was just as well, because I wasn't sure whether I wanted a working wife. I also didn't think it was a good idea to make it a family business, for either me, Mary, or any of our employees. But as I said, I didn't think it would last, so I didn't want to argue about it.

Contrary to Mr. Norton's expectations, Ms. Norton took the opportunity seriously and began working on a full time basis, though she was still unsalaried. The position of Fashion Coordinator was vacant, and Mary Norton gradually assumed many of those duties, exercising considerable influence on the 1965 Fall fashion line. Mary recalls:

I didn't mean to walk in and change the line, but I felt instinctively that the public was much more educated and sophisticated in their tastes than ever before. I was sure that the time was right for our company to trade up to a fine and more expensive taste level, and I think I've been proven right by our sales. We now do well over $7 million annually, and the fact that we relied heavily on our quality line shielded us somewhat from the recessions in the early 1970s.

After four months with the company, Mary Norton was formally named to the position of Fashion Coordinator (later raised to Vice President, see Exhibit 1). She recalls:

George did not make it easy for me at first. He made a point of saying I knew nothing and reversing my decisions. It was clear he was uncomfortable that I was working there. When I was made Fashion Coordinator, things changed somewhat since I felt I had a right to be there, but it opened up other problems.

Work and Home Relations between Mary and George Norton

Workplace friction between George and Mary was, according to one long time employee, evident from the first. However the employee noted:

It's not as intense as it used to be. I think they've learned how to handle one another, and more importantly, the staff has gotten used to it. Fighting between them used to upset the whole office; now it doesn't matter much.

Mary Norton relates:

When it became clear I would stay with the firm, and when I really began to know my way around, George and I began to fight about all sorts of things, both related to the office and not. If we had a bad day at work, we'd argue at home— over disciplining the children, or over repairs to the house. If things were bad at home, we'd bring it to the office.

After a while, and after our children and employees started complaining, we made a conscious effort to discipline ourselves—no fashion fights brought to the dinner table, and rules like that. In addition, when I got myself more organized on the job, I found that I could get my work done in less than a full day. Now George goes to the office by himself at 8:00 A.M. and I come in about 10:00–10:30 A.M. which gives me time to run personal errands. It also gives us a break from each other.

Although workplace disputes are now less frequently translated into domestic stress, office disagreements remain a major difficulty.

During the casewriter's observation of Crown and Crosby, several disagreements between Mary and George resulted from Mary's attempts to make suggestions or criticisms outside the realm of fashion design. Although Mr. Norton spends approximately 80 percent of his time on financial and administrative matters, he also, by choice, handles all personnel problems within the small firm.

Tensions between the Nortons were most clearly visible when Mary made suggestions relating to personnel or relations with suppliers and retailers; she never volunteered advice on financial dealings. Mary Norton confirmed this observation, noting:

Basically, if I offer suggestions in front of a third party, I know I'm in for trouble. When we are alone, he usually receives my suggestions without comment; if someone else is present he will often make a curt remark and leave the room. I used to take offense, and we'd fight all day over one incident. Now I say nothing, and half an hour later he's back without the slightest trace of anger, and occasionally having taken my advice. I know he's President, and I don't think I consciously try to undermine his authority. I stay out of the financial end of the business. But when it comes to the way he treats the employees, I just have to intervene. George has no tact, and yet he insists only he can handle personnel. George refuses to compliment people. He's afraid it will cost him money—they'll think they're good and ask for more.

Relations with Employees

Tensions between Mary and George Norton over personnel issues are heightened by Mary's self-described "maternal" attitudes towards her female employees. The three young women who work under Ms. Norton in the fashion design department jokingly refer to her as "Mom," particularly when she offers unsolicited advice about their personal lives.

One twenty-two-year-old female employee comments:

Mary works on the same level as we do and values our opinions, making it feel like a group effort. It's nice that she's also concerned with our personal problems.

However, an older female worker observed:

She's a bit maternalistic, but mostly friendly and family-oriented, which is good. But when she is in a bad mood she's very business-like towards others and snappy with us.

In one incident observed by the casewriter and said to be typical by office employees, Amy, the younger woman, was sent to a supplier to collect fabric samples. The supplier refused to give them to her without payment and used her as a conduit for some rather unpleasant messages to the Crown and Crosby management. Amy returned to the office clearly upset, and Mary Norton took it upon herself to comfort her. Ms. Norton then called in her husband, and the following conversation ensued:

Mary: Did you hear what they did to Amy over at the Smith-Hacker? They've got a lot of nerve treating our people that way. Why don't you call the President, take him to lunch, and tell him you'll cancel our orders if his man doesn't apologize to Amy.

> *George:* Don't tell me what to do. I know how to handle people. And anyway, we can't do that. They're cheaper than the others.
> *Mary:* Well I don't like the way they treated Amy. She's upset.
> *George:* It's none of your business! I *know* how to handle things. (Left room, slamming door.)

One senior male employee observed:

George is profit-oriented and Mary is people-oriented. One employee wanted three days off to attend a funeral out of town, and he was hesitant to ask George, so he went to Mary first. That really irked George and hurt his feelings.

Mary Norton tries to speak frequently with the company's seventeen sales representatives, all male, receiving, reviewing, and often implementing their fashion and marketing suggestions. In an effort at informality, she has established an open door policy, with only moderate success. She explains:

My attitude towards all who work for our company is to build loyalty and cooperation. I believe in a certain informality that breeds teamwork. But many of the salesmen still think of me as the boss's wife and are very formal. And they're scared to tell me anything for fear it will get back to George.

Because of her status as "the boss's wife," many suppliers, Ms. Norton believes, tend to regard her "as less of a businesswoman." She observes:

I'm sure it happens to all women, but there's a tendency on the part of our suppliers to think of me as a pretty lady who "helps out" around the office. One very charming young representative of a minor supplier used to bring me flowers. But when he delivered his orders late, twice in a row, I told him we wouldn't use him any more. He was so taken aback. He just looked at me and said, "But I thought we were friends."

Within the office there is a tendency on the part of senior officers to regard Mary Norton as in some way special.

Steve Morrow, Executive Vice-President in charge of Sales and Merchandising, told the caseworker:

Mary's a sensitive gal. I try to shield her a little. Sometimes if a favorite scarf of hers isn't selling well, I'll hide the fact from her. What good would it do to tell her? And George doesn't need an unhappy wife on his hands.

Mary Norton observed:

I'm really an office wife with three or four husbands. The vice-presidents identify with George and try to handle me as they would their own wives. In some ways that makes it easier to work with them. But I also make it a point to demand of myself good businesslike performance. I've learned how to say what I feel with conviction and support it with facts. This is important for women of my generation who were taught to place a higher value on the opinions of others. During meetings with George or Steve or a few others, I sit there with a pad and pencil taking notes and outlining points I want to make. It used to drive them crazy wondering what I was writing.

Salary Dispute and Continuing Problems

When she received the initial appointment, Mary Norton was budgeted for only a "token" salary which George, who handles all the family finances, would cash with his own. According to Mary Norton, this has become an issue of some importance in their relationship and presents one of the most serious threats to its stability. After ten years in fashion design, she has become a respected professional and has received salary offers of as high as three times her current pay. Ms. Norton notes:

I'm a middle-aged woman with a responsible position, and I would like to feel I have some financial independence. We're not getting any younger, and should something happen to George, I would have no line of credit, no checking accounts, no cards, nothing of that sort in my own name. Everything, including our savings, is in his name, and my desire for my own account has become quite an issue around here. Fortunately, we've never had major financial difficulties, and neither George nor I is a spendthrift, though he's much tighter with money. But we're both busy, and it's often convenient, as well as a little trying, to ask him for money.

George Norton was at first reluctant to discuss the issue but later observed:

I don't really see why it should be such a problem. We have gotten along this way for ten years, and I think it's silly to change now. Look, my wife is too old to start acting like a women's libber. Besides, if anything happened to me, my policies would take care of Mary.

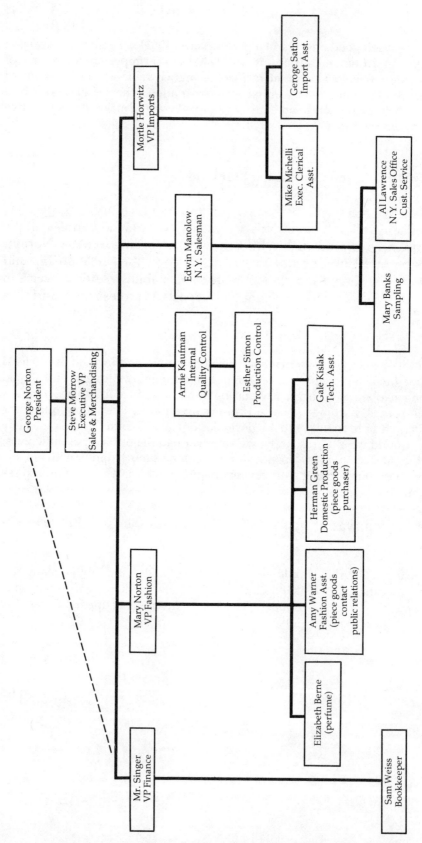

Exhibit 1. Organizational Chart—Crown and Crosby

Exhibit 2

Cowen, Michaels, Dunn and Dunn, Inc.
Certified Public Accounting

Crown and Crosby: Financial Highlights - By Fiscal Year

	NET SALES AFTER RETURNS ALLOW. & Dis-counts	PRE-TAX PROFITS	NET INCOME (AFTER ALL TAXES)	NET WORTH
	(000)	(000)	(000)	(000)
7 Mos. to May 31, 1964	$3,330	$ 92	$ 53	$136
Year to May 31, 1965	5,716	103	62	198
1966	6,393	216	106	284
1967	6,378	166	74	358
1968	5,864	(33)	(30)	328
1969	7,400	198	81	409
1970	7,781	242	105	514
1971	5,755	(478)	(245)	269
1972	4,847	(27)	(27)	241
1973	6,548	75	39	280
1974	5,239	(213)	(186)	83
1975	5,618	10,000	NA	NA
1976	7,200 (est.)	NA	NA	NA

NA=not available

7
Woman's Medical College of Pennsylvania

PART I

ABSTRACT

The Board of Corporators of Woman's Medical College of Pennsylvania met in September 1969 to decide whether to admit male students. Disagreement had developed concerning the impact of any integration decision on: (1) the mission of the College, (2) the quality of education offered, (3) future fund raising, and (4) who should have what voice in the decision.

The academic community debated whether reverse discrimination was possible or moral. Could an institution devote itself to serving a deprived minority exclusively without discriminating against the majority? Specifically, had Woman's Medical unfairly discriminated against men by excluding them?

Introduction

In 1848 Geneva College awarded the degree of Doctor of Medicine to Elizabeth Blackwell who thus became the first woman so recognized in the Western Hemisphere. Encouraged by this event, some Quaker physicians braved the disapproval of their colleagues to obtain a charter for the Female Medical College of Pennsylvania. On October 12, 1850, the first women's medical school was opened in Philadelphia. Two years later it graduated its first class of eight women. Its name was later changed to Woman's Medical College of Pennsylvania.

Nineteen similar schools were formed later. By 1895 all had disappeared; the last lost its identity through merger, leaving Woman's Med as the only all-female school in the Nation.

By 1968 Woman's Medical had about three thousand graduates, half of them living. It also ran a nursing school, a 365-bed teaching hospital, and small graduate, radiology, and medical lab technician programs. Space and facilities were regarded as inadequate for the number of students and patients. The College had never been successful in raising a significant endowment fund and so operated on a hand-to-mouth basis, sustained by Federal and Commonwealth grants, tuition, and alumnae and foundation gifts.

On October 4, 1968, on the recommendation of President G. E. Leymaster, M.D., the Chairman of the Board of Corporators appointed a Committee on Admission Policies chaired by Board member Mrs. John T. Brugger. The Brugger Committee, as it came to be known, was charged to advise the Board and the President "regarding procedures for further investigation of the desirability of the Woman's Medical College becoming coeducational."

The Brugger Committee was particularly concerned with whether the College was in violation of the spirit or letter of existing civil rights legislation in excluding men, and what effect admission of men would have on fund-raising efforts. A basic issue was the loss of the unique character of the institution as the only women's medical school in the country. Would the opportunities for women in medicine be reduced if limited seats in the College's program were assigned to men?

The Board Chairman selected a committee of twelve members from among the Board, the faculty, the alumnae, the administration, and the student body. Beginning in November 1968, monthly meetings were held. Mrs. Brugger appointed subcommittees on Joint Education, Cost and Facilities, Fund Raising, and Trust Funds, which were active in developing information regarding educational policy, estimates of cost, impact on funding, and legal implications on restricted trust funds. In December 1968, a letter announcing the formation of the Committee was sent to State and accrediting agencies, and to members of the faculty, staff, Nursing School, and all alumnae. The letter was regarded as a courtesy by the Board of Corporators anticipating public announcement; its intent was informational, but responses were invited.

In May of 1969, the Committee submitted its report. It recommended that male students be accepted, and that the name of the College be changed. Since all students lived off campus, no additional operating costs were attributed to the decision to admit men in place of women. Some trust funds, tied to continuing as an exclusively female school, were probably impaired, but their value was considered to be negligible.

The report recognized the importance of maintaining the continuity of the College in terms of purposes and standards, but felt that it was necessary to demonstrate a "capacity to adapt to rapidly changing circumstances." The report cited the College's primary purpose of excellence in the education of physicians with special emphasis on the education of women and concluded that this mission could "best be achieved in conjunction with the education of men." It recommended that coeducation be achieved by the addition of male students rather than by the supplanting of women. To this end, it further recommended a substantial increase in the size of classes as soon as supporting funds could be obtained.

The Committee was heavily influenced by Dr. Leymaster's opinions that faculty and house staff recruitment and morale would be favorably affected, and that the attitude of medical educators and the profession toward the College would greatly improve.

The recommendations of the Committee were not unanimously supported. A minority report was filed by (then) Alumnae President E. Cooper Bell, M.D., supported by student member Lourdes Corman. (See Exhibit 1.)

Mission

Woman's Medical College had been founded to afford women the opportunity in medicine from which they had previously been barred. While it was generally agreed that women had been discriminated against in the past, it could not be demonstrated that medical schools favored male students. It was evident that only a small number of women were being admitted to medical schools, but national records revealed that the same proportion of men and women were chosen from among the applicants of each sex.

Marion Fay, Ph.D., had served as Dean and President of Woman's Medical from 1946 to her retirement in 1963. She had previously been a member of the faculty for twenty-eight years. She continued to serve on the Board of Corporators and had served as Acting President for the past two years after Dr. Leymaster's resignation to accept another post. Discussing the issue of discrimination, she observed that "the prejudice against women in medical schools can be very subtle. Some schools have quotas; a few others take two women so one won't be lonesome." She also pointed out that since income tax laws allowed no childcare deduction, this also discriminated against mothers in school and in practice.

Dr. Lourdes Corman had been an officer of the College's junior class and a student member of the Brugger Committee. At the time she was interviewed, she was interning at Woman's Medical and planned to do her residency there in internal medicine, where her boss would be "a chauvinist, but a charming man, who wants the school to be just like other medical schools." She and others argued that the College was obligated to make a positive statement concerning the opportunities for women in medicine.

In a way, we need 'unequal opportunity.' The women applying for medical education are superior. They have to be because men are given more encouragement. I'm not saying I'm really being fair, but a student poll proved that a lot of girls who were qualified for medicine wouldn't be admitted if we didn't exist.

Recent civil rights legislation had raised the question whether the College's exclusion of male students was legal. At stake was the possible cancellation of the school's Federal subsidies and research grants, representing about one-third of the budget. See Exhibit 2 for background on a similar issue at the University of Michigan.

Quality of Education

Although a small school, with limited resources, Woman's Medical students had placed twelfth overall in the examinations administered nationally to the students of most of the 102 U.S. medical schools. Noting the inadequate teaching facilities, the accrediting committee had placed the College in the lowest quartile by this measure of quality.

Dr. Walter Rubin, a young member of the College's faculty, conceded that prejudice against women in medicine was real but argued:

A woman is only 60 percent of a man because she is less likely to practice. Further, she will probably have children and thus be prevented from taking a residency or going directly into practice. When she does get back to medicine, she's out of date.

Records at WMC showed the proportion of its graduates staying in medicine was higher than the national average for women doctors. Dr. Fay thought this was partly due to the fact that they hadn't been coddled at the College.

Dr. Rubin went on to say:

We all want the institution to grow and improve. Segregation must limit the quality of the student body. Any limitation on applicants accepted on any basis but ability results in a second-rate student body. We certainly wouldn't compromise on faculty quality to get women; so why students?

He also argued that women need association with medical men during training, since this is what they would experience in practice. He felt that married women were happy at Woman's Medical, but that single ones were not because of the limited social life.

Finally, he submitted that good men and women were less likely to apply for positions on the faculty of an all-women's school since it could not be the best school. Several departments, such as surgery, always suffered because of lack of interest in these specialties on the part of the women students.

Fund-Raising Problems

It cost about $13,000 a year to educate a medical student in 1969. Operating on a $4 million annual budget, inevitably complicated by its intertwining with the larger hospital budget, Woman's Medical was dependent on Federal and Commonwealth funds, tuition, and alumnae and foundation gifts. (The last portion of the small, unrestricted endowment was cashed and spent to balance the 1970 budget.)

Mr. Charles Glanville was Vice President for Planning and Development. A member of the Brugger Committee, he filled in much of the background on the School. He commented on the difficulty in obtaining grants from foundations:

They're not allocated to a monument; we're a relic. Money goes to innovative schools. The ideas developed with such funds must be exportable, useful to others; they won't be from a girls' school. Rather than debate the issue of advantages versus the disadvantages of coeducational medical education, foundation executives are more likely to make token contributions instead of generous grants.

The Commonwealth of Pennsylvania subsidized medical schools in the state in proportion to the number of students enrolled. The four other Philadelphia schools had 50 to 80 percent Pennsylvania students. Woman's Medical couldn't fill its classes with women from within the state, even if it had wanted to; so it had only 30 percent Pennsylvanians. The state was unwillingly subsidizing nonresidents. Dr. Fay noted that:

Several members of the Board were concerned that the Legislature would cut off this subsidy; it had been proposed but not considered seriously. The proposer died recently; a judgment perhaps.

Dr. Fay explained that fund raising was a special problem for women's schools. Even noted women's schools like Barnard, Wellesley, and Bryn Mawr had always had trouble getting funds. Women most often made gifts and bequests to their husbands' colleges. Alumnae gave to their undergraduate schools, where the happy memories were. She had wondered whether it was possible to use an offer to admit men to pry money from the people who had been critical in the past of the exclusion policy.

The Decision Process

Several of the people interviewed commented on the way the Board of Corporators and the Brugger Committee had handled the integration issue. According to Mr. Glanville:

The battle of 1850 is over. Why beat a dead horse? We're having trouble recruiting Board members. Our new governor, Milton Shapp, resigned from our Board, probably because we move so slowly. The Brugger Committee was dominated by the establishment point of view. There was insufficient ventilation of the issues. Discussion was cut off, and there weren't enough meetings. The report was not redrafted to get any consensus.

Dr. Fay felt that the Board of Corporators was divided on the problem of integration. The issue had been considered on many occasions in the past and had always stalled in committee.

I was on the fence. For years I heard the usual "Why don't you girls get generous?" jokes. The Brugger Committee probably moved too fast. The alumnae were solicited by mail for advice—but doctors never read their mail.

Dr. Corman felt that she was chosen for the Committee because she had originally openly favored integration. Only the year before had the student body finally been granted membership on such committees. Although the Brugger Committee had wanted opinions from the student body, they were unwilling to give any feedback. Dr. Corman had conducted a poll of the students. (See Exhibit 3.) After much debate the results were released to the students. All the meetings of the Committee were closed to nonmembers.

On the decision-making process, Dr. Corman volunteered:

I think Dr. Leymaster was a terrible public relations man, terrible. At first I was convinced we should go coed; I was waiting for them to tell me why. The Committee wasn't appointed to determine whether, but rather, when, and how we should integrate. The Board was just soothing a few factions. The Committee was very upset because things didn't go as smoothly as expected. They tried to suppress any minority report, pressing for a unanimous position. If the deliberations were emotional, it was mostly on my part. My ideas were ignored as being outside of the Committee's charge. Their whys just didn't match mine. The results of the student poll changed my mind. Lisa, the other student member, and I polled the students with a questionnaire. We had tried hard to get a fair response. Many of our students are married (about 30 percent), with children; they expect understanding of their problems. They thought that they would be less likely to get it if we went coed.

Dr. Corman suggested that the integration issue should have been made a matter for open discussion. She thought that "they shouldn't have pretended to examine an issue when the decision had already been made."

PART II

ABSTRACT

The decision to integrate the school and change its name poses a major threat to alumni fund raising activity.

The Board of Corporators of Woman's Medical College of Pennsylvania voted to admit men students in September 1969. The decision was made that at least sixty places would be reserved for women in each class and that at least 50 percent of every entering class would be women. This decision was to be reconsidered in two years.

Three men were enrolled in the 1969 Fall class. The men accepted had slightly higher grade point averages and admission test scores than the typical student. In 1969 there were six applicants for each place in the entering class; for the 1970 class there were eleven applicants per slot; preliminary estimates indicate twenty for 1971.

Paul Siegel, M.D., was appointed to chair a Mission Planning Council. The Council affirmed the Board's plans for the make-up of subsequent entering classes. The working draft of a "Statement of Mission" is attached as Exhibit 4.

Commenting on the Council's deliberations, alumna Lourdes Corman, M.D., said:

If the Council decides on a fifty-fifty ratio now, I think that things will change enough that there's no guarantee that in ten years this School won't be 90 percent male.

Dr. Siegel:

Our mission is "expanded" to also educate men; this meets all priority needs: national, ours, integration. With perhaps fourteen hundred to two thousand women due to graduate nationally in future years, whether we admit sixty more women is irrelevant to the future of women in medicine. Our people should be evangelists to recruit women into medicine. Why do ten times as many men apply as women? Medicine is no more demanding than any other profession if you're going to do it right. Another benefit of integration, we can now pick up men from foreign schools to fill third-year dropout slots. There's no future for a small school in medicine.

In February 1970, the Board of Corporators voted to change the name of the School to the Medical College of Pennsylvania (MCP) effective in July. Suggestions for the new name had been solicited in the alumnae magazine. Just prior to the effective date, the Alumnae President, Phyllis Marciano, wrote a letter to all alumnae urging they send telegrams to the

School rejecting the name change, arguing the new name was poor, that no change was needed to appease the few male students, and that the change was being made too fast and without consultation. The letter further suggested that future alumnae donations be placed in a trust fund and not administered by the School.

Dr. Marciano's arguments in summary:

I'm not a feminist, and I'm not against coeducation. We gave up before we started. Our name identifies our past and our commitment. Harvard and Vassar didn't change theirs. Neither did Episcopal Hospital when it admitted Catholic interns. We need a place where women are more equally appraised on their qualifications. Why does the word "woman" make anyone feel intimidated? In Africa, Woman's Med meant something; MCP means nothing. You can't be truly coed without discriminating against women. As I see it, every time you admit a man and turn away a qualified woman, you've discriminated against that woman.

In closing, Acting President Marion Fay said:

It's too soon to see improvement in fund raising. Private funds were peculiarly tied to the female nature of the school in the past. What do we use now? There's not enough feedback from the alumnae to their representatives on our Board. We received only a negative response on the name change. My phone rang for days. We should have waited and changed the name after the men's admission policy was assimilated, perhaps when the first men graduated. Our commitment to women may be further served by developing part-time internships and residencies and by tying our admissions ratio to the policies of other schools regarding women.

Exhibit 1

April 3, 1969

Board of Corporators
The Woman's Medical College of Pennsylvania
Philadelphia, Pennsylvania 19129

Dear Members:

As a member of the Committee on Admission Policies and as an alumna I respectfully submit the following opinion.

The *purpose* of the Woman's Medical College has been and should continue to be the training of women to become physicians.

The *challenge* facing this institution is to continue in excellence in its training.

The *challenge* facing our nation is to increase the number of physicians especially in the area of clinical medicine. To help meet this national need Woman's Medical College should increase its number of students. Since Womanpower in the United States is underutilized in the medical profession I believe this institution can best serve the nation by increasing its student body with more women students. Please compare our percentage as shown in the following tabulation:

Per Cent of Women Physicians to Total M.D.'s
in Selected Countries, 1965

Country	Per Cent
Philippines	24.7
Finland	24.2
Israel	24.0
Thailand	23.8
Germany	20.0
Italy	18.8
Austria	17.4
Scotland	17.0
Denmark	16.4
South Korea	16.1
England and Wales	16.0
Sweden	15.4
Hong Kong	14.5
Switzerland	13.6
France	12.8
Australia	12.6
Netherlands	12.5
India	12.0
Norway	12.0
New Zealand	10.1
Republic of South Africa	10.0
Japan	9.3
Canada	7.6
Brazil	7.1
Republic of China	6.7
UNITED STATES	6.7
South Vietnam	6.1
Madagascar	4.6
Spain	2.5

Replacement of women students by male students at Woman's Medical College will doubtless reduce the percentage of women physicians in the United States.

As evidence let me remind you that 93 (of 128 students who answered the questionnaire) of our current student body were accepted only by Woman's Medical College in spite of the fact that they made an average of 4.9 applications. In view of the fact that our institution accepts about 1 in 4 applicants I believe it should not be concluded that we have an inferior pool of applicants from which to choose. Moreover, our present freshman class is described as a superior group of students, so it must be conceded we are attracting good students.

Second, let me tell you that Dr. Marvin Dunn, in recent personal interviews with members of admissions committees of 25 medical schools, reported as follows:

Two encourage the acceptance of women; three claim absolute neutrality; 19 prefer to take men to the extent that a woman must be clearly superior, not equal, for them to accept *any more* than they now take.

Third, Dr. Glen Leymaster has stated that, until more teaching facilities are available, the admission of male students would necessitate a reduction in the number of female students admitted.

Finally, the fate of women applicants to Woman's Medical College rests with the Student Admissions Committee. I note with regret that three members of our current Admissions Committee have written statements favoring coeducation at Woman's Medical College. None of these three is alumnae of this institution. In fairness I wish to add that one member said she favors "a policy of retaining our identity by the institution of *active* programs related to their special needs (institution of a day-care center, part-time residency programs, etc.)." She further states that to retain this identification with women it will be necessary to impose a quota. She favors "a fifty-to-fifty quota as the optimum."

For the above reasons, if coeducation is adopted, I believe that the number of female students admitted in the immediate future to Woman's Medical College will be decreased, and since the admission policies of other medical schools have shown no recent change in the 7-10 percent enrollment of female students, the percentage if not actual number of female physicians will decrease in the United States.

One of the chief arguments offered for adopting coeducation at Woman's Medical College is the increase in money obtained from state and Federal Governments. However, I wish to remind you that Dr. Marion Fay has said that "today there are some five of the older medical schools that are in financial difficulties." Obviously coeducation has not prevented the financial difficulties at these schools.

Second, Dr. Marvin Dunn has stated that to garner needed state financial support Woman's Medical College will have to provide the promise of more Pennsylvania students. He listed the following facts:

(1) Pennsylvania has more places for first-year students/population unit than all other states excepting California and New York.
(2) Pennsylvania ranks 15th in numbers of students graduating from college/population unit among the states (the number of medical school applicants parallels this quite closely).
(3) The absolute numbers of applicants (male and female considered separately also) from Pennsylvania is inadequate to justify and fill the number of first-year places available within the state.
(4) The projected increases in Pennsylvania applicants for the next five years is less than the projected increases in plans for first-year students in the state.

Dr. Dunn concluded as follows: "To me this leads to a single conclusion: we would have one heck of a time trying to boost our present enrollment of 20 percent Pennsylvania residents even to the low of the other schools (60 percent at the University of Pennsylvania, not well received by the legislature) with no other changes being made than the admission of men."

The second major reason given for adopting coeducation is the enlistment of better qualified teaching and resident staff. This is undoubtedly a valid reason at the present time. However, if the institution is sufficiently endowed financially, this argument will not hold. If salaries are sufficiently attractive the sex of the students will be of minor importance to the professors.

I have no objection to the admission of male students *per se,* but until other medical schools accept female students on the basis of *equal* qualifications I believe there is a need for an institution such as Woman's Medical College to protect and provide a place for women desiring a medical education.

Instead of coeducation I urge that this institution accept as its goal the conversion of the Woman's Medical College to a *National Institute* for the undergraduate education of women physicians and the postgraduate training of those women physicians who need it. With the present national shortage of physicians and the underutilization of women in medicine I believe a strong appeal to state and federal bureaus as well as private and industrial sources would be favorably received. As one alumna has noted, since we are now practicing *reverse* discrimination in both public and private areas it is reasonable to suppose that public and private agencies might be influenced to support women in medicine if the proper publicity and propaganda are forcefully utilized.

The men and women who founded Woman's Medical College recognized the need for educating women in medicine. They met the challenge! The unique institution founded by them has survived for 119 years. Are we less visionary or courageous than they?

There still is, in the opinion of many, a need for a special institution for the education of women physicians. Like the late Dr. Martin Luther King, "I have a dream!" I hope you, the members of the Board of Corporators, have the same dream—a National Institute for the education of women physicians at Woman's Medical College.

Sincerely yours,

E. Cooper Bell, M.D.

P.S. I hope you will read certain letters, such as those of Dr. Maria Kirber and Dr. Virginia Lautz, which list problems and possible solutions.

Exhibit 2

Sex Discrimination: Campuses Face Contract Loss over HEW Demands[*]

The women's liberation movement has a new ally: the Department of Health, Education, and Welfare. HEW is demanding that colleges and universities, under threat of losing all federal contracts, stop discriminating against women students and employees. Furthermore, HEW is demanding that female employees be compensated for financial loss suffered because of discrimination over the last two years. The government is currently withholding new contracts from the University of Michigan and at least three other campuses, pending compliance with HEW demands.

The HEW action, begun last spring (Science, 1 May 1970), is authorized by Executive Order 11246, which prohibits discrimination by federal contractors. The Order, amended by President Johnson in 1968 to include sex discrimination, requires contractors to survey their own labor practices and submit an affirmative action plan for correcting deficiencies. HEW is charged with regulating all federal contracts to educational institutions.

[*]"Sex Discrimination," Bazell, R. J., Science, Vol. 170, 20 November 1970, pp. 834–835, Copyright © 1970 by the American Association for the Advancement of Science.

The sex discrimination provisions of the order have been largely ignored and still would be, but for the efforts of Bernice Sandler, a staff member for the House Education Committee, who founded Women's Equity Action League (WEAL). WEAL, a Washington-based group with a membership that includes several congresswomen, sent letters to women's groups at campuses across the country advising them of the potential power of Executive Order 11246. WEAL offered to assist the groups in filing complaints against their respective campus administrations. So far WEAL has presented HEW with over two hundred complaints, including, according to Dr. Sandler, charges against the entire college and university systems of New York City, New York state, and California. Because of a shortage of staff, HEW is investigating the complaints a few at a time, but HEW officials insist that all the complaints will be thoroughly investigated. HEW's eagerness to clamp down on sex discrimination is partially explained by the political pressure that WEAL presented along with the demands; feminism is currently a popular cause with several members of Congress.

Ann Arbor FOCUS on Equal Employment for Women, a group of students and university employees, filed the specific complaint against the University of Michigan, charging, among other things, that the university has only a small percentage of women faculty members (5.3 percent excluding the School of Nursing), few female administrators, and quotas on the admission of female students. The complaint also charged that women employees with degrees were assigned as clerk-typists but were expected to perform administrative duties for which men are paid higher salaries.

HEW's demands of each institution differ, depending on the types of complaints and HEW's subsequent investigation; but the demands for Michigan (see box) illustrate the nature of the requirements for an affirmative action program. HEW officials expect some negotiation of the exact terms of the demands, and certain campuses, notably the University of Illinois, are quietly working toward an acceptable affirmative action plan, although none are yet complete. But Michigan and certain other institutions not identified by HEW officials have chosen to resist. Calling the demands "totally unreasonable," Michigan officials circulated copies to several other university administrations in an attempt to gain support.

Appendix: HEW's Demands for Michigan.

The following are excerpts from HEW's nine requirements for an affirmative action plan for ending sex discrimination at the University of Michigan.

The university must:

1) Achieve salary equity in every job category in the university.

2) Compensate, through the payment of back wages, each female employee who has lost wages due to discriminatory treatment by the university. Payment must be retroac-

tive to 13 October 1968 (the date President Johnson amended Executive Order 11246 to include sex discrimination).

3) Achieve a ratio of female employment in academic positions at least equivalent to availability as determined by the number of qualified female applicants.

4) Increase ratios of female admissions to all Ph.D. graduate programs.

5) Increase the participation of women in committees involving the selection and treatment of employees.

6) Develop a written policy on nepotism which will insure correct treatment of tandem teams.

7) Analyze past effects of nepotism and retroactively compensate (to 13 October 1968) any person who has suffered discrimination.

8) Assure that female applicants for nonacademic employment receive consideration commensurate with their qualifications. The university must also ensure that the concept of male and female job classifications is eliminated through changes in recruitment procedures.

9) Assure that all present female employees occupying clerical or other nonacademic positions and who possess qualifications equal to or exceeding those of male employees occupying higher level positions be given primary consideration for promotion to higher level positions.

—R. J. B.

Exhibit 3

WOMAN'S MEDICAL COLLEGE OF PENNSYLVANIA

Philadelphia, Penna. 19129
Founded in 1850

February 10, 1969

To: Members of Committee on Admission Policies
From: Lisa Luwisch and Lourdes Corman
Re: Students' Response to Questionnaire on Admission Policies

Total response was 128 students or 55 percent of the student body. These students applied to an average of 5.8 schools and were accepted to an average of 1.4 schools. Ninety-three students applied to an average of 5.7 schools but were accepted only to WMC.

Table I

	% response	Average number of applications per student	Average number of acceptances per student
Class of 1969	28%	4.90	1.68
Class of 1970	47	5.80	1.31
Class of 1971	57	6.15	1.40
Class of 1972	75	5.90	1.26
No class listed	6 students	5.10	1.30

For 47 students WMC was their first choice, while for 81 it was not. Seven students of the 47 who chose WMC did so because of its segregated nature, while for 36 of the 81 students who did not choose WMC, the reason was its segregated policy. Eighteen of the 47 students (or 39 percent) for whom WMC was their first choice attended an all-women undergraduate school. On the other hand, 23 of the 81 students for whom WMC was not their first choice (or 28 percent) attended an all-women undergraduate school.

Table II

		A		B
	WMC was 1st choice	*percent attended segregated colleges*	*Other school was 1st choice*	*percent who attended segregated colleges*
Class of 1969	7 students	28%	9 students	11%
Class of 1970	10 students	20%	13 students	38%
Class of 1971	12 students	33%	22 students	45%
Class of 1972	14 students	50%	35 students	20%
No class listed	4 students	75%	2 students	0%

Thirty-nine percent of the students who answered felt that the environment of both segregated and nonsegregated schools were equally beneficial to their education. Twenty-two percent of the students answering felt a segregated environment such as WMC was *more* beneficial, while 31% felt that the *more* beneficial was a nonsegregated environment. Eight per cent of the students answering did not reply to this question.

Forty-three per cent (or 56 students) felt that women physicians have to "prove themselves" to male physicians. And of these, 57 percent felt that WMC was preparing them to do so.

Assuming equal standards of admission, 72 students (or 57 percent) would like to see WMC accept men. However, of these students only 34 (or 47 percent) would favor admitting men without increasing the size of the entering class. For 50 percent of the students who answered the questionnaire, the acceptance of men would be acceptable only if the size of the entering class is increased.

Of these students (73) who would favor a change in admission policy, 47 (or 64 percent) believed that the number of male students should be limited by a quota and suggested quotas ranging from 10-50 percent, and including a percent equal to that by which the size of the entering class would be increased. Twenty-three students of the 47 favoring a quota (or 48 percent) suggested 50 percent.

Sixty-two students (or 49 percent of the total number who answered) chose to comment. The comments were varied in both content and length, and we were not able to decide on a method to include them in this report without introducing a bias. We are open to suggestions from the members of the committee.

Exhibit 4

Statement of Mission

THE MEDICAL COLLEGE OF PENNSYLVANIA

The Mission of the Medical College of Pennsylvania is twofold:

—to teach those arts and sciences related to the preservation of human health and the prevention and treatment of disease, and to advance the body of knowledge in these areas.
—to continue its commitment to the education of women physicians and to develop and maintain programs which will expand the opportunities for women in the medical professions.

MCP proposes to carry out its mission by:

1. Operating effective educational programs in medicine, in related sciences, and in allied health professions.
2. Providing high quality health services to individuals and to community groups, responsive to the changing needs of modern society.
3. Pursuing vigorous programs in basic and applied research.
4. Encouraging coordination of the educational, service, and research activities to obtain the maximum benefit from all three.
5. Committing substantial portions of its resources to all aspects of the education of women in medicine.
6. Developing as rapidly as resources permit from a medical college with associated activities into a health sciences university with a comprehensive medical center.

8
Sue Garson

ABSTRACT

Sue Garson enters medical school only to find that the "solo woman" problem can be particularly acute for a woman in medicine. She encounters her greatest difficulties during the medical "rotation" period, when training doctors live in the hospital while they learn all aspects of ward life. The stress of the situation begins to take its toll, as this case recounts.

A paper prepared at The Wharton School that discusses the problems of the woman who finds herself alone in a professional peer group made up of men has had wide circulation among women students in a number of professional schools.[1] It reached Sue Garson, a third-year medical student, at a particularly opportune time. She had had several disturbing experiences that year and was beginning to wonder seriously about her choice of vocation.

Always an excellent student, Sue Garson had had no particular problems in college or in the first years of medical school. Oriented toward medicine and encouraged by her physician father, she had had no doubts about her choice of study, but had only been afraid that she would not be accepted by a medical school. She commented, recalling her anxiety:

When I was applying to med school, I would come home on vacation and tell my parents, "Gee, it's terrible. Millions of people are applying and I'm never going to get in. There are so few women accepted and why should they take me? Look at me—I look like I'm twelve years old and they'll say I'm not serious." But my father would say, "You just apply, you're going to get in. You've got everything it takes, don't worry." He really instilled confidence in me to keep going. Not that I didn't realize he was biased in my favor, but the fact that he had respect for me was very important.

Interestingly enough, he had certain biases about women himself. He kept telling us—I have a brother and two younger sisters—that he was very reality-oriented and wanted us to know the score, the way the world was, not necessarily the way he'd like it to be. So he'd tell me, "You may be smart, but the fact is that in our world beauty is a woman's most important commodity, and you'd better take off five pounds." And then he'd tell me that the time to get married is when I graduate from college, that the ideal time to find the greatest concentration of bright young men was at college. He certainly had that traditional attitude that of course I would get married.

Asked about her mother's role in the career decision, she said:

Well, she always stayed in the background. She was very proud of me and pleased with my achievements but she never said anything about my becoming a doctor. She never voiced an opinion about what I should do. She's active in community affairs and manages her home beautifully and does the kind of thing women in her peer group do. After I got into medical school she confessed to me that she had always wished that I would become a writer and that she was very surprised that I had gone to medical school.

I grew up in a small town and the only place that I had support for my aspirations was at home. When I mentioned it at school, the teacher would say, "A doctor? Don't you want to be a nurse?" And even when I talked to the other doctors in the community and mentioned that I wanted to go to medical school, they would say, "That's an awfully hard life to have ahead of you. Oh, you're going to want to get married." I think my father was unusual for his group.

She did marry during her first year of medical school, commenting that she may have chosen that time subconsciously to please her father. Both she and her husband were students in a prestigious Eastern medical school. In the first two years, students concentrated on scientific background courses even though they were introduced to some patient care in the second year. A series of twelve-week rotations through the various medical and surgical specialties in what were known as "clinical clerkships" made up the third year. She had completed her rotations through what were considered by the students as "minor" specialties—pediatrics and obstetrics—when her turn came for the rotation to "medicine." This referred to internal medicine and embraced the bulk of medical problems encountered by the physician. As Sue Garson described it:

The medicine rotation determines the largest part of the grade for medical school. It's the time when you're given the greatest challenge of learning and handling situations—greater than any other time in medical training. And you're also put under a lot of pressure both to take on patient care and stand up to the interrogation of your teachers.

The people teaching you will question you to find out what you don't know and point it out to you and let you know that you should go out and learn it. It's fine except that they're dealing with highly motivated, compulsive students who are trying to excel and it all leads to a sense of tension and fear. The students are very hyped up and trying very hard. And then a teacher will make you feel that you have failed in your duty if you don't do something right. "You blew it, you mismanaged this patient. What do you mean, you didn't learn that? How can you call yourself a doctor?"

You know they don't really expect you to be able to answer every question but those comments can be quite abusive. So you try to be on your toes all the time. You just don't stop to breathe because the minute you do you'll not have read about the very disease they'll ask you about and you'll be on the spot.

She was a little taken aback to find that she was the only woman student in the group of twelve. Until then there had always been at least one other woman in each of her classes, and she had found that she usually spent quite a lot of time with the other woman (or women) even if they had not been particularly friendly earlier.

By the end of the course we'd end up liking each other because I don't know exactly why, but there were certain things which we were going through that we needed to talk about. The women were able and willing to talk about things we couldn't discuss with men. We'd end up meeting for lunch or we'd work together as much of the time as we could, and it was really quite important to me.

She was not particularly concerned at her peculiar situation, however, not having experienced it before. Also, her husband was taking the course at the same time, and she felt that she could, of course, talk about things with him quite freely.

The medicine rotation period came in midwinter, a difficult time of year in hospitals when the patient load is generally heavy. The interns, who begin their first year as doctors in July, are midway in a stressful learning situation of their own, meanwhile acting as the principal teachers of the clinical clerks. The residents, out of medical school for one or two years, supervise the interns and are in turn checked by the professors of the medical school who take turns visiting the various wards of the hospital. In a teaching hospital, the intern has primary responsibility for his patients and must be able to report to the resident and to the visiting professor the exact details of the patients' diseases and the course of treatment he advises. The clinical clerks observe these "presentations" and are in turn called on to "present" patients of their own. Comments and/or grades, depending on the medical school, are entered in their records by the residents and professors.

Sue Garson began her first month's assignment on a ward where there were three interns and residents, all men. Each of the three months spent on "medicine" would be on a different ward:

I was assigned to an intern, which really means that you eat, drink, sleep, work, and breathe with your intern. You have to have that kind of close relationship because the intern is so busy so much of the time that you've got to be by his side if you're going to pick up anything from him. He's not going to take out fifteen minutes to sit down with you and talk or teach you. You have to be together, but unfortunately the intern I had just couldn't or wouldn't talk to me. He literally was running away from me for a month. He left me without any support or supervision about my patients and zero teaching.

So that was my first month, coming into this stressful environment where I was being questioned constantly and tested and challenged, and yet I didn't have my intern supporting me and showing me the way through all this. It was a terrible experience. One of the worst things I've ever experienced in my life.

Discussing those first weeks and her reaction to them later, she explained that the intern was "on," meaning on duty, for thirty-six hours at a time so that he would be available at night if needed. The intern was then given twenty-four hours off duty. The clinical clerk was expected to have meals with the intern, to follow him as he made "rounds" (going from one patient to another), and ideally to share sleeping quarters, so that any free time between duties could be used to discuss the various patients' problems. It was also advantageous to be on hand at night because the intern was invariably called for problems that arose then. A woman student was at an immediate disadvantage in this hospital, Sue Garson found, because the women's sleeping quarters were several floors removed from the men's, and the intern would not bother to call and waken her as he rushed to respond to his own call:

As I think about the situation now, it occurs to me that the intern I was stuck with, although very competent, must have been somewhat depressed. His one goal seemed to be to get through his duties and get off the ward. Any time he spent with me was a time he wasn't getting his work done and getting out of there. That's my conclusion now, but at the time I just thought, "Boy, I must be really stupid. Why am I so lost all the time, why don't I know what's going on? Why can't I get anywhere?" That was the first week, and the second week I was thinking to myself, "Gee, I'm not learning very much here," but it didn't occur to me to say it to anyone else.

By the end of the third week, though, I was going out of my mind with frustration. To be given responsibility for taking care of people and to have no one backing you up and telling you you're doing it right or not, and constantly thinking, "My God, am I doing the right thing, is my patient losing out?" is simply awful.

I was finally helped by the resident who reviewed one of my patients and asked me some questions about why I hadn't suggested this or that, and I said,

"I just didn't think of it." He was very surprised and wondered why I hadn't talked about it with the intern, and then I told him that the intern hadn't discussed the case with me. I said, "He hasn't discussed any cases with me. In fact, he never talks to me." The resident was very nice about it and said he'd try to see me through the rest of the month and said he was sorry it had happened. He did his best and was very helpful, though of course he has a lot of beds to supervise, and it wasn't the same thing as having the intern on hand.

The resident had urged her to open up and make more of an effort to let people know her. She was surprised at the comment because relating to people had not been a problem:

I realized that my anxiety over the situation had made me so uptight that my reaction at first was to be very quiet, really a zero, a nonentity as a total defense manuever. I've discovered since that it's a fairly classic reaction. And when I was a zero, it made me more of a puzzle to the men. When you're not joking, you're not talking, you're not doing any of the little things that make you a person, it adds to other peoples' frustration and aggravation as well as to your own.

When the second month's rotation began, she found herself with an intern who again did not seem comfortable with her, although his attitude was a considerable improvement over the first man's:

I could get him to sit down long enough to teach me something or talk about a patient, but when we went to lunch together, he made a tremendous effort to find someone else he knew that we could sit with so that he wouldn't be stuck with me. I had never felt like a shy wallflower before but I could feel myself shrivelling.

And then another incident arose that I suppose is kind of funny, though it didn't seem like it then. I found that, as in the first month, the intern wasn't waking me when he got up to see patients at night. That separate room for the women on the opposite side of the hospital was the problem again. So this time I said to the intern, "Look, this is stupid, me sleeping way over there and never learning anything. Why don't I—do you mind if I sleep in the bottom bunk in the intern's room on the ward?" I mean, he knew I was married. He was very uptight about it and said, "No, no, I think it would be better if you sleep in the women's quarters." He went on to explain that the professor had had a lot of pressure from the women students about having their own room to sleep in and that he thought we'd better not change anything. It was clear that he didn't want me there and that I was enough of an intrusion on his existence as it was, so I slept in the women's quarters and didn't get called!

With her change in ward assignment, Sue Garson also had a new supervising physician for whom she had to "present" her case each morning. She found this professor's manner difficult to deal with:

He put me under a lot of pressure, firing questions at me during that ten minute presentation. You know, it's sort of the moment of glory or doom. I don't respond well at all to being badgered. I was tense and couldn't relax enough to think and to present my cases. And doing it well was very important. Your future reputation depends on what the supervising physician thinks of you. This time I decided to go to the resident for help before too much time had elapsed, and I was lucky again. He was an exceptionally nice guy, very supportive. He talked to me and gave me tips about how to present. The others would just say, "Well, you've got to do better," but this guy actually took the time to tell me how to do better. I improved quite a lot after that.

Remembering the advice of the first resident, she tried to overcome her depression and to make the effort he had advised.

I would initiate towards the men. I would make little jokes, I would start the conversation, I would say, "Well, another day on the job. You look really tired from last night." And I'd do all the little supportive womanly things that you do, saying, "Gee, you look tired, you need a doughnut." All those things that I would never before have stooped to. I was really desperate to get some sort of relationship going. I would just say nice things to the interns, anything. You know, it was really kind of pathetic when you think about it. I was acting in that comforting role that the nurses adopt, now that I think about it, and I'm not sure I want the men to see me in that role. The male doctors often treat the nurses worse than they would servants, with total disrespect, treat them like children, and I will never be treated that way.

Asked about the interaction between women medical students and the nursing staff, she commented,

Well, I really like the nurses quite a bit, and of course they aren't all alike in their attitudes, but one thing I've found as a general rule is that the nurses are very curious, inordinately curious, about my marriage. I'm asked innumerable questions about how I manage with my husband, how do things work out. My first reaction was to resent it and to think, this is ridiculous, they'd never ask these questions of a male medical student. But then I thought that maybe they saw me as more accessible, more approachable then some of the other women in medicine and that I ought to be willing to answer them. So we'd talk about whether my husband minded if I wasn't home for the night, that kind of thing. I enjoyed talking to them and I found them usually very sensitive in discussing the patients.

When her third month's rotation occurred, she again brought up the subject of the sleeping arrangements with the intern in charge and this time was not rebuffed:

He was much more relaxed about my being a woman than the others had been and allowed me to sleep in the same intern's room with him. This meant that I was on call when he was, and it worked out really well. One night there was a person with massive internal bleeding, and he was called a number of times. Finally he was so tired that I was the first to answer the phone. He was too exhausted to get out of bed each time, so when the phone rang I would wake him up, and he would tell me what to do. While he got a little sleep, I helped take care of the patient all night, which made me feel good because at last I was part of what was going on.

I was doing some of the work as opposed to being just a superficial person there. And I was learning and helping him which meant that we would both feel better about him helping me. We didn't really develop a close relationship, but it was much better than the other two.

That business of not being relaxed with each other really interfered with the learning situation. The men were not relaxed enough to ask me to do things. It's a funny thing, but if someone is your buddy, you're willing to ask him to do you a favor. I suppose getting stuck with too much routine work is bad—the male students are always complaining about that—but I think not being included in the work of the ward so that you don't feel needed or useful is much worse. You're not given the opportunity to do as many things so you don't learn, you don't develop a skill.

I noticed that the other house officers* would think nothing of handing their students—male students—a list of things to do or of asking them to help in doing procedures. In contrast, I often asked for things to do and was told that there wasn't anything for me to do.

Asked what else might have been done to improve matters, she commented:

Well, I think now that what happened was not deliberately mean, not intentional. The men were just not comfortable with me. To go through the trials and the tensions and the demands that a doctor goes through in that thirty-six hours on duty, and to have to have a shadow with you eating meals with you and sleeping in the same room—you really have to be comfortable with each other. I was the wrong sex to be a shadow, to be seen as their younger selves. They were on their guard, they censored their language, they censored their jokes. They were unsure of how I was taking things or what I wanted or what I meant, and as I said before, I became silent and uptight.

I think that if I had ever been able to say—which I wasn't able to do—"What the hell are you doing, you're not teaching me a damn thing, you're not doing your job. Shape up, mister, or I'm going to report you to the Chief of Medicine" maybe things would have been better, but I wasn't able to do it, thinking it all my own fault.

At the same time that she was uncomfortably trying to accommodate herself to the teaching situation, she was faced for the first time with direct contact with the death of a patient she had known. Among the in-

---

*Interns and residents.

formal duties of the clinical clerks was the expectation that the students would familiarize themselves with the functioning of the hospital ward, learning what they could and contributing to the life of the ward through contact with all the patients, not only the ones they had been assigned directly. She had come to know a middle-aged woman patient who had widespread cancer. She would often visit the patient at night:

When I walked by her room at night I'd sometimes see her sitting up, unable to sleep, and I would go in and say, "Good evening, Mrs. X, is there something wrong?" She would shake her head—she knew she was dying and she, well, I guess she just couldn't sleep. I'd say, "Well, why don't you lie down and try to sleep?" and I'd sit by her bed and hold her hand and just sort of be there. We wouldn't say much. We had a sort of quiet, out of the way relationship in that I wasn't working on her case but I had this contact with her.

And then one night I happened to be there when the resuscitation team rushed into her room. Well, I know intellectually what all the machines are for and that they're necessary and often successful in prolonging life for another six weeks, but the first time you see it done, well, it's a shock, and it seems like an assault on the dying person. Every machine known to medical science is brought to bear on the problem by the best technicians. And to see the masses of EKG paper* and syringes all over the place and people pumping and squeezing and pounding, it's really quite a scene—even if you don't know the person, but especially so if you do because the person is unconscious the entire time and all these things are being done to them.

I watched the death scene and the sort of persistence of life after death. And finally it was decided that she was dead. And all the fervor that had been brought to bear suddenly ended, and everyone dispersed. They just leave the room and usually no one says anything to anyone else, they just leave. We had all witnessed a death and yet the community didn't get involved in the death, didn't communicate about it verbally or really comfort one another in any way. The nurses do some comforting among themselves, and occasionally if the patient has been very special to one of the interns or residents and the rest of the staff knows it, they'll give some support. But in many cases that isn't so and so people just leave.

I was just left there with my feelings about the lady and her death and the manner of it. And the message was quite clear that no one wanted to talk about it and that was very hard.

The medical students have a meeting once a week with the psychiatrist on the staff, and that's really an excellent session. I brought this up at the next session a few days later because it had gotten to a point where I just had to talk about it.

Surprisingly, the male students just didn't respond at all the way I did. They just couldn't relate to it at all. They related to it in the way that I've seen house officers do: "Well this patient's died. We did everything we could." And then they, the male doctors, will say they have six other patients to care for, and they can't get too involved in emotionality because they have work to do and have to

*Measurements of electrocardiogram machine, recording the patient's heartbeat.

go on to the next patient. And they go. Well, that's a useful, functional attitude, but I think that at some point you have to stop and deal with feelings. Maybe not just at that moment but some time you have to work out the feelings you had at the deathbed. I was really surprised.

The group of men students were all at basically the same point in their training as I was, and yet they reacted differently. First of all, they didn't identify with the dying patient at all or with her death experience. It wasn't a person, it was someone who had died, and that was the end of it. And to me it wasn't quite the end, that the living still had some relationship to the dead person if only in memories. Secondly, the students didn't want to talk about it. Every one of them was asked to comment and it seemed to me from the way they avoided it or talked around it that they didn't want to be depressed by the sad topic or to experience those feelings. They talked about how the patient died, what the EKG machine showed, how the pulse changed, what drug they injected—all the technical things about the death but nothing about the person dying. It was all intellectual, technical. And I was saying that if that was how they wanted to deal with it, fine, but there is some emotional impact, especially for those of us just starting to see suffering and death, and it isn't necessary for everyone to have to react the same way.

I got the unspoken message then and afterward that mine was not the way you're supposed to react. I think the male student sees the male interns and the male residents treating the death in a male way. And then a female comes into the group and responds to the death as a female, and it's just not done. You're not supposed to cry or get all upset that a patient who was going to die has died. You just don't cry.

It's allowed for the nurses, the community of women who are there. They'll cry among themselves, hold each other and comfort each other, but a woman medical student is in limbo. You're not a nurse, and that's made very clear. You have to relate to the nurses as a doctor and you really cannot go to the nurses' community for comfort. Right now there's no group we can go to if we have to stop and deal with our feelings. The male doctors deal with it as, "Onward and upward, that's too bad, but you have to go on."

Asked if her husband's reaction had been the same as that of the other male students, she replied:

Well, we had been on duty at different times, and there was no chance to talk to him about it alone. He was in the psychiatric discussion group when I first brought it up, and he was more willing to talk about it than the other men were, but even he said at a certain point, "You know, I've really had enough of talking about death. It's just enough. I'm really sick of talking about death. Can't we talk about something else?" I know he's very sensitive in a lot of respects and would be willing to talk about it later, but he does have his limits of tolerance. There was a very heavy silence after he spoke.

I'm aware that the men feel they have to guard against breaking down, and that they have their defense mechanisms well in order and don't want them disturbed. The trouble was that knowing it was no help to me, and I was beginning to have terrible doubts about being able to function well as a doctor. It was just about at this point that someone gave me a copy of the Wharton School paper, and I realized that the problems I had had were usual ones, that other women had withdrawn and become depressed at the hostility they felt in a male group, that the fault didn't lie in me alone but was part of the group process going on. (See article by Wolman and Frank, pp. 246–55.) Just reading that made a tremendous difference to me, and I found I could relax a little and begin talking to people about things that bothered me without being so self-conscious about it.

She sought out the resident supervising her ward and told him about her unsatisfactory discussion with her fellow students and about her reactions to the death of the patient.

When I finished talking he thanked me and said, "Well, you know, we lose sight of all that when we're working so hard, and yet it's important. You know, I think the medical students have something to offer the house officers in renewing their feelings about patients as living people." And then he went on to say, "I wish you had talked to me sooner and I wish you would talk to me more often about the things that you're feeling and that you see going on here because we really are blind to them a lot of the time." He thought that often the interchange between students and house officers was one-sided, with the teachers asking questions and giving information involving the technicalities of patient care because there's so much to learn . . . and that the human experience of being a doctor is not discussed as it should be.

I was very pleased with the relationship I had with him, and I don't think it would be a bad thing if we were able to make the house officers stop what they're doing for the moment and look at the student as a person and not just as "the clinical clerk for February." Right now, to make them see you as a person and be aware of your feelings is very hard because discussion, open discussion, of feelings is really taboo.

Later in a conversation with another woman student she mentioned her need to show her feelings at times:

She told me she was very involved with her own patients, and that sometimes when things didn't go well she would have some tearful reactions. And once in a while a male staff member would be present and would tease her about it. She finally told him she didn't intend to have to leave in order to hide her feelings, and that after that he seemed to accept her as she was. We agreed that women tend to hide their feelings because we're already being seen as weak. The men are already reluctant to let you do things and will see you as even weaker than you are.

At the end of her three-month rotation on medicine, she was scheduled for a meeting with Dr. Arthur Grau, the professor who this year was the administrative head of the student program. Among his duties was the assembly of comments from the house staff and the grading of the students. He scheduled a meeting with each student in order to explain and discuss the grade that had been given. It was a relaxed session, and Sue found Dr. Grau unexpectedly warm and interested, somewhat in contrast to his more formal manner when she had had contact with him on the wards. She found herself telling him about her uncomfortable experience as the only woman in the course, and she showed him the Wharton School study that had so impressed her:

I was still upset and I put it all in somewhat strong, heated terms. And it was a surprise to him. Of course in the distant past they had had no women students, and recently when there had been a few, there were usually at least two on rotation at a time. He realized, however, that even when more than one took the course they were likely to be separated and sent to different floors where they again became solo women. He asked to borrow the study and said we would talk about it again after he'd read it carefully. He commented that no one else had complained and said, "I can't believe that none of them have this problem." I didn't think it was unique either, and I explained that if I hadn't been reinforced by the study I had shown him and if we hadn't happened to have had this meeting, I never would have complained either.

I had never gone to him or to anyone else about the difficulty with the interns. First, it took me a long time to realize it wasn't my fault. And I was hesitant to get someone into trouble, and also, like many other women, I didn't want to seem like a complainer who's blaming other people for her problems.

But when I read that paper, I saw my whole experience there. It wasn't just that I was uptight, there were reasons why I was uptight. Although I normally relate quite well to men, and have good relationships, I think that I was overwhelmed with the stressful experience of the medical rotation and wasn't able to overcome the interpersonal barriers the way I normally do.

Another reason why I think the female students would not voice any complaints is that they're trying so hard to fill a role that stresses competence, they don't want to verbalize any inadequacies. That is true of the men as well, but the men are getting support from the other men. Not the kind of verbal support of saying, "It's all right, I know it's tough," but the support of being with them, close by and accessible, in touch with what they're going through. The women are completely isolated.

Anyway, when I saw Dr. Grau again, we discussed what could be done about the women students. I suggested trying to put two women together at least during the first month so that they would have mutual support during the worst period. They could separate after that if they wanted to. With more women coming into medicine these days, that ought to be possible to arrange. Dr. Grau said he would talk to the house officers about this and try to sensitize them to the problems of isolation among the women students. I certainly felt better after talking to him.

You know, when I entered medical school, I planned to become an internist and thought I would spend about 60 percent of my time doing psychotherapy.

This was my image of practicing internists. But the doctors I met during my medical rotation were not at all like that. Most were part-time researchers who were more interested in the physical and technical aspects of medicine than in the psychological. It seemed to me that the psychological experience of the patients was clearly de-emphasized.

It was during my rotation in psychiatry that I realized how strong my interest in it really was. I found it a powerful experience, intellectually challenging and emotionally demanding. I felt that all my faculties were being used, and none stultified. My supervisors were very excited by my work and so was I. It seems the logical choice of specialty for me now.

Notes

1. Wolman, Carol and Frank, Hal: "The Solo Women in a Professional Peer Group," chapter 26 in this book.

9
Susan Bronson

PART I

ABSTRACT

At twenty-nine, Dr. Susan Bronson is completing the final year of a residency in cardiology at the Stanford Medical School hospital. During these first years of professional experience she candidly admits she has "followed her instincts" when dealing with colleagues and staff. The result has often been frustration and interpersonal problems which, Dr. Bronson says, she did not anticipate when she began her residency. Her relations with the nursing staff have been strained by her attempts to solve her difficulties with ward LPNs herself, instead of working through nursing supervision. Dr. Bronson has become isolated from other residents as a result of her refusal to join them in a work stoppage at the hospital.

Background

Sue Bronson's early career aspirations reflected her determination to acquire independence and status as an adult, a determination which sprang from the economic realities she faced during childhood.

Dr. Bronson was born into a middle-class household; her father was an accountant, her mother a housewife. When Susan was eleven, her father died, leaving only a small amount of money in insurance benefits. Her mother supplemented this income by working part-time as a clerk, but the salary was not sufficient to restore the family to its previous level of financial security.

Sue remembers:

My mother had never thought in terms of supporting a family before Dad died and had never acquired any marketable skills. She worked as a clerk to help pay

80

the bill for my father's night school tuition before I was born. But nobody wanted a middle-aged woman who had been out of the job market so long. During those years, I must have promised myself a thousand times that I would never allow myself to be financially dependent on anyone. I wanted a skill, and wanted it at a young age.

Susan Bronson also felt it was important to acquire status on her own. The drastic change in the emotional stability and social position of her family, she recalls, made a deep impression on her:

As a child I had a very idealized view of both my parents. Suddenly, I had lost one parent totally and lost my innocence about my mother, all at the same time. I learned that my mother was not a very strong person emotionally without her husband; his death seemed to sap her self-esteem. Over the years I believe she had grown more dependent on him, which I suppose is natural in most marriages. And to make matters worse, society suddenly did not accord her as much status or respect without a husband. Her friends stopped inviting her to dinner parties, unless they had some man they wanted her to meet, which was not often. Most of my parents' social relationships had been formed around a nucleus of the men my father worked with; the women were on the periphery. And these friendships quickly died out. Quite frankly I resented the loss of status my mother's widowhood brought all of us. Widowhood was almost treated like a social disease, and I was an infected offspring. I learned a great deal in those days about the status of women.

Although Susan Bronson's esteem for her mother had suffered a serious blow, she was not without inspiring female role models. She remembers her female school teachers as "my intellectual standard-bearers," and found them "interesting, vital" people who seemed to enjoy life. Yet Dr. Bronson found these spinster teachers being ridiculed and sarcastically addressed as *"Miss* Smith" or *"Miss* Jones." Dr. Bronson recalls:

One of the things which first appealed to me about medicine, as opposed to law or another profession, was that I would be addressed as "Dr. Bronson."

Susan Bronson attended an all-girls' high school in San Diego, where she found the atmosphere conducive to the development of leadership abilities. She remembers, however, being disturbed by neighborhood and community co-ed activities where the same girls played only supportive roles. At the University of California at Los Angeles, she sought no leadership roles, but remained strongly motivated.

Despite personal and financial problems through the years, Susan Bronson has pursued her medical degree with single-minded determination. During her years of internship and residency, however, she has found that her ability to work with and supervise other professionals—as well as her own aptitude and concern—is crucial to the welfare of her patients. She admits she is often disturbed by the methods she has developed to deal with male colleagues, though she claims some of the methods are necessary:

As a last resort, one can always flirt or be coy, if that's what it takes, to get what you want. When dealing with someone who is above you in the hospital hierarchy, you can always coax and make him feel like a "big man" doing you a special favor. I realize it's very unprofessional, and it's a habit I've tried to break. I certainly dislike it when I see other women using it. Occasionally, though, being a coaxing feminine woman is the only way I can control men who have authority over me, and if that's what it takes to help a patient, or to help myself for that matter, then I'm going to do it.

Ben Tomkins, the chief resident at the hospital, notes however that Dr. Bronson is capable of "pulling off the leadership bit" when necessary. Tomkins entered medical school after spending two years as a public health worker among Apache Indians, a substitute for serving in the armed forces. He graduated from medical school a year before Susan Bronson, and his position as chief resident puts him in a confidant/advisor role with other residents. Ben Tomkins says Susan Bronson is "quite firm" with subordinates:

Susan's found out she has to be more of an authoritarian than most men would be, dealing with subordinates. Frankly, I think she's probably right, but sometimes she can be unsympathetic, too, and that gets her into trouble.

However, Dr. Bronson believes that she must be blunt if she is dissatisfied with the performance of those over whom she has some seniority. She never "kids around" with these men, she explains, because it allows them to avoid taking her criticisms seriously. She notes:

In many situations in a hospital, one isn't really in a position to issue a direct order since we are all professionals. However, there are certain men who by unspoken protocol should be following my directions and, occasionally, one will simply choose to ignore me and subvert the process, placing me in the uncomfortable position of having to pull rank, which is a difficult thing to do within this understood hierarchy. In certain cases I find it necessary to confront them with the fact that they are ignoring my authority and charge them with sexism. Usually this comes as a surprise to the men and really shakes them up. But it's an effective technique. However, it only works if I make sure they understand that I am not joking.

The most difficult situations to handle, Dr. Bronson believes, are those in which an associate does not openly challenge or ignore her authority but very clearly indicates that he resents it. Such an individual, Dr.

Bronson believes, is clearly aware of the implications of his behavior. She explains:

He usually gets the message across by trying to put you down in a sexist fashion, or by trying to turn a professional interaction into a social situation. He tries to exert authority over you as a man by telling you, "you have nice legs," or "I really like you." I suppose behavior like that irks me more than any other, because I don't like being on the defensive, and I find myself going on the offensive.

Two Career Marriage

During her senior year as an undergraduate, Susan Bronson was married to a third-year medical student. At first, both Susan and George, her mate, were wrapped up in their respective studies and found each other supportive and the marriage convenient.

As Susan Bronson began her fourth year of medical school, however, George was settling into the routine of being a doctor and was openly dissatisfied with their relationship. He wanted to establish a life-style similar to that of other young physicians and their spouses but found that Susan's hectic schedule, including months of clinical work in which she lived at the hospital, made this impossible.

Ben Tomkins, recalling George's discomfort when he was unable to secure a position as prestigious as Susan's, observed:

George just didn't like it in San Francisco—that's where he got a job. It's nearby, but Susan had landed a better residency. I think it rankled . . . Susan getting such a good position, I mean. He didn't really feel comfortable with her "crowd"—me, my wife, or our other Stanford friends.

By mutual consent, Susan Bronson and her husband obtained a divorce during her first year of internship. Ms. Bronson retained her maiden name. She now believes:

The ability to maintain both a marriage and a career varies dramatically from couple to couple. I am aware of middle-aged and young women in the professions, mainly law and medicine, who do have families, and do have domestic responsibilities, who also have careers. But very often those careers are limited, and no matter how much a woman has achieved, it's less than she would have achieved had she been single, or a man. The reason that men can excel, and they do, is that they can be single-minded about what they're doing. If you're worried about caring for children, or about domestic duties, then it's inevitably going to take something out of you, and you won't be able to concentrate as intensely on career-related responsibilities.

Into the Profession

Through her last year of medical school, Susan Bronson had remained unsure of how committed she could be to the medical profession, and what specialty would best complement her abilities and life-style. Still very conscious of status, she had ruled out family medicine and was not attracted to psychiatry or pediatrics, two areas traditionally considered attractive to women. When she graduated from medical school, Dr. Bronson was still undecided, so she served a one-year general, or rotating internship. During that year she recalls:

I often felt depressed that I was not able to work beyond the point of exhaustion to the point at which one gets a second wind, which I observed many men were able to do. Whether because of superior physical conditioning or out of some sheer inner drive, they would keep going past the point where I was ready to say "enough, you're pushing us too hard."

Dr. Bronson, a petite woman who has never been attracted to athletic activities, tends to believe that the deciding factor in maintaining the exacting physical pace required is often psychological:

Most women might, on a philosophical level, be consciously willing to make the same sacrifices and put out the same effort as a man, but their conditioning is not as strong. They stop and think about whether the sacrifices are worth it, or necessary, while many of the men automatically make them, without questioning. And there's where the men have the edge.

During this period, Dr. Bronson's duties often required her to handle emergency situations on the cardiac care ward. Despite the rigors of the specialty, she had been considering entering cardiology and discussed the possibility with Ben Tomkins. While Dr. Tomkins had not discouraged her, he recalls being skeptical:

Susan's a tireless worker and always wrapped up in ward work. But I just wasn't sure she'd handle cardiology well. A lot depends on the physical stamina of the doctor. Susan's a small woman, but she's certainly determined.

Dr. Tomkins recalls one emergency room incident where Dr. Bronson was attempting to revive a heart attack victim:

When I got there, to check up on some other arrivals, I saw Susan working on this middle-aged man—a big man. She looked over at me, but she went on trying. It didn't look to me like she was applying enough pressure—you know, pumping on his chest. The mechanical equipment (to jolt cardiac arrest victims into breathing) wasn't there, so I moved her over and started on him myself. I'd done it once with one hand when I'd broken my wrist horseback riding and had a cast on. There was an old Apache who had an MI (myocardial infarction), and I leaned on that one hand and pumped away, and it worked.

As Susan Bronson's choices narrowed, she seriously considered applying for a surgical residency, but rejected it, as well as the extremely lucrative field of radiology, partly because it "would have limited the kind of ongoing contact with one patient that makes medicine an absorbing profession."

Dr. Bronson believes the practice of medicine is emotionally exacting on a woman:

I think women on the whole are more aware of the responsibilities one is assuming in inflicting pain upon people. They are more aware of the process happening to them, which conditions them to care less about, and become less involved with, their patients, and they are more apt to rebel against it. In the end, though, I would say that most of them do learn to adopt that professional role that is required.

PART II

ABSTRACT

During her residency, Susan Bronson has difficulty in her dealings with other staff members. She refuses to participate in a newly formed doctors' organization and later clashes with the head nurse.

Conflict With Colleagues

Eventually, Susan Bronson decided to enter a residency in cardiology. At about this time several members of the medical staff were organizing a doctors' association which eventually entered into union activities. Their first major effort at bargaining with hospital management came on the issue of continuous call hours. Dr. Bronson did not join in their meetings, or their activities, and began to feel herself isolated from the rest of the staff. However, according to Ben Tomkins, Susan Bronson was surprisingly unaffected by her distance from her peers. Tomkins observes:

I think she's in her own world, and it's a world of hard work and a certain aloofness. Maybe that's good for her, right now, on her own again after the divorce. She is concentrating on the job of being a doctor, not on the less obviously beneficial contacts with the other staff doctors. And she's one of our more efficient ones, too.

Eventually the nascent doctors organized a work slowdown to protest working conditions such as long hours and low pay scales. Part of their effort involved refusing to fill out Medicare and Medicaid forms, which, they declared, should be performed by administrative personnel. Dr. Bronson, however, unsympathetic with their stand, considered it her responsibility to perform this duty as usual. When the other doctors finally became aware that Susan was not, as they put it, "cooperating," a group of interns approached her to ask why. Ben Tomkins describes the situation:

Susan's a gutsy person. She listened to them explain what they were up to, and I think she was genuinely surprised that they were so insistent. They wanted her to join them, and they told her she was sabotaging them because she wasn't participating. Susan finally had enough of it, and she told them, "Get off my back. You don't have any right to try to tell me how to conduct myself on the job. Besides, you aren't very well attending to *your* jobs now, are you, when you take time out to confront me on work time?" Of course, that didn't do much to improve her relations with the other staff doctors, but they couldn't fault her for lack of backbone.

At the same time, Dr. Bronson was experiencing some difficulties with a nursing staff supervisor, Ms. Chin, who had recently been promoted to head of the cardiology nursing staff. Ms. Chin had established a regular reporting system to route residents' complaints about the performance of the nursing staff. Where previously these complaints were handled on an informal doctor-to-nurse basis, Ms. Chin insisted all problems be brought to her, or in her absence, to the charge nurse. Dr. Bronson, however, objected to this procedure and openly ignored it. She recalls:

Once I asked a charge nurse to accompany me on rounds, but she was not too helpful. . . . in fact, she made several mistakes in ordering medication that I thought were sloppy and inexcusable. I tried to talk to her about it, but she kept insisting we had to go see Ms. Chin first. A few days later, I had another problem with the same nurse and thought that in the interest of getting along more smoothly, I'd just talk it out with her. Her performance had to improve, but I didn't want to get her in trouble.

As tensions between Dr. Bronson and Ms. Chin intensified, Ben Tomkins called a conference with the two women. Dr. Tomkins recalls:

Ms. Chin was unhappy about Dr. Bronson's refusal to route complaints the right way, and Susan was just as unhappy that she was not "permitted" to solve disputes on the spot. Susan feels her patients don't get her full attention when she has to wait for days to settle what she sees as simple, day-to-day difficulties that shouldn't take up so much time. This time, Ms. Chin was right. We'd already had too many flare-ups handling problems the way Susan wanted to, so we had to stick by the rules.

Future Prospects

As she was completing the final months of her residency, Dr. Bronson reflected on the decisions she has made and her future:

I had been seeking money and status, and I had gotten a taste of them both. But over the years money had become the much less important of the two. Even as an intern, I was, by the standards of my childhood, doing well financially.

It was in one sense a compromise. Yes, it involves total commitment and often unpredictable hours, but it's not that constant expenditure of one's physical resources which surgery would require. Much of my time will be devoted to office hours, but there are ample opportunities for research. I'd like to be associated with a university and perhaps go into teaching, which is an elite area usually closed to women. Cardiology is well-paying and respected. According to the standards of a child who wanted status and money, I've done rather well for myself.

10
Northside
Health Care Center

ABSTRACT

Dr. Regina Neal, an experienced pediatrician, finds herself the director of an expanding community health facility. Torn between increasing administrative responsibilities and her desire for patient contact, Dr. Neal faces challenges to her leadership from her staff.

Northside Child Health Care Center

A few years ago comprehensive health care facilities for children from low-income families were established by grants from the federal government. While the primary objective of the program was the provision of health care to children, individual centers had the prerogative of adding other activities. Exhibit 1 summarizes the objectives for the Northside Center at its founding. The government required that the agency supply one-third of the funds and that the center director be a board-certified pediatrician. No administrative experience was required.

The Northside Center was organized to provide a facility and extend services to an estimated 5,000 children in one area of the city. Exhibit 2 illustrates the organization structure. The center director, Dr. Regina Neal, is an extremely intelligent, aggressive pediatrician who is totally dedicated to improved health care for children. She sees health as including education, housing, employment of parents, day care, and the many other variables which affect the physical and mental health of children.

Exhibit 1

Northside Child Care Center: Initial Objectives

A. Objectives established by federal government
   1. Comprehensive health care to children and youths from low-income families in major cities, to include:

      a. Promotion of health
      b. Medical care
      c. Case finding
      d. Preventive health services
      e. Diagnosis
      f. Treatment
      g. Correction of defects and aftercare
      h. Dental care
      i. Emotional care

   2. Better methods for delivery of care
   3. Improved quality of health services
   4. Reduction of preventable and disabling illness
   5. More efficient coordination of health services to children

B. Subobjectives established by the center
   1. To develop better procedures and mechanics for the delivery of comprehensive medical care
   2. To coordinate existing health services for children, to bridge gaps, and to avoid duplication
   3. To increase efficiency of the delivery of service
   4. To reexamine concepts of pediatric care—Can excellence and continuity reside in a health team, rather than in a doctor-oriented service?
   5. To determine to what extent medical health professionals or other newly defined health workers can provide services traditionally given by the physician.

She had been in private practice for a number of years and was actively engaged in the health rights movement.

Dr. Neal has definite opinions regarding ways in which services could be improved. She states that patient care is a team effort of pediatrician, nurse, and paraprofessional workers. For staff members who are accustomed to traditional health care systems, she provides a stimulating environment in which to work. For example, she maintains that nurses can assume many of the responsibilities for well-child care, which comprises 80 percent of a pediatrician's work load. Costs could be reduced by hiring fewer pediatricians and adding paraprofessional workers to take on the routine managerial and technical duties.

Dr. Neal insists on treating patients two or three days a week in the pediatric care walk-in clinic. In effect, she acts as center director, Pediatric Section head (because this position was never filled), and physician. She is a whirlwind of energy and an inspiring person. Nonetheless, some staff complain about her tendency to utilize favored personnel rather than those on duty. For example, she will bypass the duty nursing supervisor to communicate normal doctor's orders directly to the director of nursing services. Some registered nurses especially complain that Dr. Neal treats them according to the old stereotype of the nurse as doctor's handmaiden rather than as professional colleagues.

The center has been quite successful in treating children brought to the clinic. However, many staff are dissatisfied for two reasons: (1) they aren't seeing all the children they should because some aren't being brought in and (2) some illness is so family related that treatment of the child requires family treatment (for example, one child was treated several times for an infection of unknown origin; in fact, it was caused by a chronic disease afflicting her mother of which the center knew nothing).

Consequently, the center has decided to expand its services to include adult care. Dr. Leonard Warren, an internist, has recently left a lucrative suburban practice to accept a position as adult care director and co-director of the center. He in turn is engaging various physicians and staff technicians. A walk-in adult clinic service is to be provided (although it has not been decided yet whether or not this should be physically separate or integrated with the child care clinic). In addition, the staff feel they must do more than just wait for patients to come in; they want to get out into the community; therefore a new section of Social Work and Community Services is being established. Social workers and psychologists from the new section, along with nurses from the Nursing Services Section, are supposed to cooperate to locate illness and encourage treatment. More important, they hope to educate families to modify conditions and behavior that support illness.

A government community medicine consultant suggests that the center organize family health teams composed of a physician, a community health nurse, a family social worker, and several paraprofessional aids. These teams could become intimately familiar with specific families and their problems. They could draw on the specialized physicians, psychiatrists, and dentists when necessary. Many staff physicians don't like this proposal because they fear they will waste much precious time traveling outside the clinic center. The medical records administrator wonders if she must maintain records for the new adult care section and family care activities without new clerks. The Dental Section director is similarly concerned. The director of nursing services is worried about whom the proposed teams would report to, how they would be controlled, and how she could supply nurses to the teams as well as the new adult care clinic. Dr. Neal feels that the teams could simply report directly to her, so she would be sure of cooperation from the physicians.

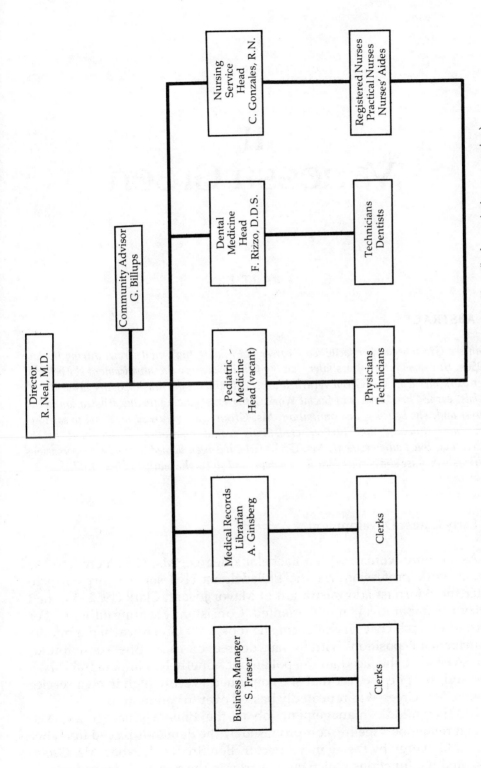

Exhibit 2. Northside Child Health Care Center: Organization Chart (before mission expansion)

91

11
Vanessa Green

PART I

ABSTRACT

Vanessa Green began her social work career in Philadelphia's civil service during the late 1950s. But some fifteen years later, having failed to achieve the advancement she believed her work merited, Ms. Green returned to school, and despite unsupportive academic officials, earned her Masters of Social Work. After experiencing further frustration in her career and, she believes, discrimination, Ms. Green again returned to school to earn her doctorate, thinking that further credentials would guarantee advancement in the profession. Such advancement, Ms. Green feels, has been denied her on several occasions variously because she is black, she is a woman, and she is the mother of five children.

Early Career Development

As a young woman with a Bachelor's degree, Ms. Green entered the social work profession via the Philadelphia civil service corps which, after the reformist administration of Mayor Joseph Clark (1952–56), had become comparatively merit-oriented. Consistently scoring either first or second on each civil service exam she took, Ms. Green reached a middle management position with a fair degree of ease. She soon found, however, that she faced an unspoken but nonetheless impenetrable barrier and, despite the fact that she continued to score high in civil service exams, Ms. Green was repeatedly passed over for promotion.

On that middle management job in the Philadelphia agency, Ms. Green remembers feeling compromised by the demands placed upon her time and energy by the agency director, Ben Brooks. Further, Ms. Green resented the functions which her superior in the social service agency expected her to perform, and his frequent absences from the office. She recalls:

The director (her supervisor) was too frequently gone from the office on personal business, and I was the one who had to make excuses and cover for him. I felt compromised. When I think back, it is amusing, the range of things I did. While he often asked personal favors that were annoying or trivial, he relied on me so heavily that I also performed many of his most important administrative functions—like counseling my fellow workers and devising training programs. It was an odd situation and a no-win one for me so I decided to move on.

Personal Factors

But while resentful of Mr. Brooks, Ms. Green never refused any of his requests. Both her early reluctance to assert herself and her subsequent decision to return to school were, Ms. Green observed recently, in line with her personal philosophy for "coping" developed early in life and reenforced by socialization experiences. Ms. Green explained:

There were two notions of how to lead a good life which Momma (actually her aunt) went to great pains to pass on to me. One was a deep respect and love for books, intellectual pursuits, and excellence almost for its own sake. The other, which seemed far more practical at the time, was how to handle men. And Momma was far from the only female relative who warned me, "You are smarter than any man, but you must let men think they are smarter. You're a pretty girl and you can catch more flies with honey than you can with vinegar." In short, the conventional wisdom of her generation, and I suppose mine too. But that is not to put it down, you understand.

While Ms. Green's aunt was herself a full-time homemaker, the niece found the two concepts applicable to a professional career, as well as valuable in her roles as wife and mother. According to Ms. Green:

I never had to feel guilty about being too "scholarly" or serious because those were virtues for a woman. Competence was totally compatible with femininity, but telling a man off, or refusing to help him, or bothering him with your complaints was not. So instead of confronting men with their own prejudices and discriminatory practices, I took the burden off them. I assumed that if I became even more qualified and got all the proper degrees, they would have no choice but to promote me. It would just be so obvious that I deserved a better job they couldn't rationalize keeping me down, and I wouldn't have to force myself into confrontation.

However, recent experiences, a separation from her husband, and changing societal attitudes to discrimination, have caused Ms. Green to begin questioning, though not radically reforming, her methods of handling such situations. She observed in an interview:

Maybe the times are changing, and maybe I'm just not the cute young thing I once was, but the old methods just don't seem to work as well. And I'm too busy raising a family and working to worry about making everybody happy.

The Return to School

Ms. Green applied for graduate school, but was refused. The Dean informed her at the time that with five small children to care for, she would not be able to stand the rigors of a graduate program. Determined to earn her Master's Degree, but not willing to challenge the Dean directly, she quietly enrolled in night classes. At this point, Ms. Green was managing her home and a full-time job, as well as attending night school. After maintaining an 'A' average for two semesters, she reapplied for full-time graduate status and was accepted. Ms. Green recalls:

I didn't get angry or fight the Dean. I acted as if I would accept their judgment. You might say I didn't show my hand until I could come back with a full house— high marks in their own courses.

After successfully completing the Master of Social Work program, Ms. Green again returned to the labor market, this time finding employment at an educational institution in a social counseling role. After several years, the position of Social Services Director became vacant, and Ms. Green found herself in competition with another woman who was young, white, and had less administrative training, although she had been with the school slightly longer. Ms. Green's memory of this incident is, she commented, somewhat "bitter":

The administration was very gracious after denying me the job I deserved. They told me I was so much more mature, and the other woman could not have taken the disappointment, and that other opportunities would come along. But I'm convinced her whiteness had a lot to do with her getting the job. When we were competing for the position, the way she acted was inexcusable. She played politics and screamed and maneuvered, and, believe it or not, she even cried. Those are things one just does not do in a professional setting. Certainly I would never make a fool of myself that way to win a job.

Ms. Green quietly resigned her position with the school and matriculated at the University of Pennsylvania as a doctoral candidate.

Repeat Experience

During her first year as a doctoral student, Ms. Green's field placement was as an administrative assistant to the Director of a large unemployment office, a placement which her advisors said would give her an opportunity to participate in top-level management. Ms. Green was quickly disenchanted with the placement, however, and saw it in many ways as simply an extension of that first "personal assistant" relationship she had developed with Mr. Brooks back in the civil service. Ms. Green explains:

I was doing for the director, Mr. Smith, about the same things I had done ten years ago for another boss. And I think I was even worse off with Smith because he was, or thought he was, so damn considerate that he didn't want to overwork me, which meant he was careful not to ask me to shoulder his workload. I did, however, find myself doing many of the same personal chores which always offended my sense of being a professional. All I did was hold Mr. Smith's hand and give him his heart pills. It was a depressing experience, and it also made me wonder whether that doctorate was really the key to doors I had thought it would be.

Mr. Smith was acutely aware of his own administrative shortcomings, and held Ms. Green responsible for critiquing office procedures and suggesting new approaches on a regular basis. Despite the fact that Mr. Smith himself had requested these reports, Ms. Green reports that he was self-conscious about accepting them and went to what she considered artificial lengths to assure her that he did not consider her efforts to be in any way domineering. Towards the end of her placement, when the two had been working together for almost ten months, Ms. Green submitted a report suggesting the radical revision of client notification procedures.

Later that day, Mr. Smith approached Ms. Green and commented:

You know, Mrs. Green, we really are proud of the way you come up with these suggestions. I know you're accustomed to managing your time well—with the family and school—and it takes a strong person to do that. I just want you to know I think you handle it all gracefully. You're taking just the right amount of initiative on these office problems. You have real tact—more than the men have, sometimes.

Ms. Green, reflecting on the incident, said:

What impressed me about the whole thing was that he meant very well, and in a sense I was flattered. But what his comments also said to me was that he was very self-conscious about working with a black woman, and very bothered by the stereotype of the domineering black matriarch. Several times that year he insisted on talking to me about how he rejected the notion that black women had in some way harmed black men—the whole emasculation myth. I must admit I was almost as self-conscious in those discussions as he was, and sometimes I wonder whether my behavior is subtly affected by those stereotypes.

PART II

ABSTRACT

As a second year doctoral student, Ms. Green feels the time has come to speak up, and she confronts a white male supervisor. Later, she decides that a black supervisor presents the real difficulties in her work situation, but for several reasons she handles him in a far different manner.

New Placement

During the second year of her doctoral studies, Ms. Green's field placement was with a special social work education project in which she was the lead instructor. Ms. Green's superiors on the project were Mr. Eisen, the white director, and Mr. Wilson, the black coordinator, both retired administrators from more traditionally structured public agencies.

The project centered on social worker-client relations, particularly in urban areas, and, according to the project proposal, the primary responsibility for structuring the curriculum was to be in Ms. Green's hands. However, her pedagogic philosophy differed fundamentally from that shared by both superiors, which created the first of several disagreements. While her superiors favored bringing in "name" researchers and noted theorists to give guest lectures, Ms. Green was convinced that the most valuable speakers would be those currently involved in field work.

First Conflict

During the seminars, Mr. Eisen, invited to class to introduce guest speakers, often monopolized class time with commentary on his own social work philosophy, an intrusion that angered Ms. Green. Finally, Ms. Green sought the counsel of the Dean of Social Work, and, with the Dean's support, confronted Director Eisen. It was the first time she had taken such a direct stand. Eisen was apologetic and explained:

I hadn't realized you felt so strongly about class format. It's your prerogative as the instructor to conduct seminars as you see fit, although I still feel the students would benefit from a more theoretical base and more directed dicussion. But, quite frankly, I'm annoyed that you went over my head to the Dean without first talking with me. But I suppose that I am so accustomed to running things my own way that I can seem overbearing.

From then on, Mr. Eisen did in fact refrain from interfering with classroom procedure, though relations between the two were described by Ms. Green, as "somewhat cooler." Ms. Green noted:

He always did treat me as if he thought I was somewhat imcompetent. I think there's an element of racism in his attitude. He just can't trust the abilities of a black woman.

Administrative Considerations

Though Mr. Eisen was the titular head of the project, he was involved in several different concerns and usually deferred administrative responsibilities to Mr. Wilson, who had a more complete knowledge of day-to-day operations. In planning her programs, Ms. Green reported to and received almost daily direction from Mr. Wilson, who informed her at the outset of the program:

I've worked up some long-term guidelines here for the project, and I will be expecting the approach from your end (curriculum development and instruction) to dovetail into this. I'll need to know each week what problems you're having lining up materials, speakers, and class schedules.

Ms. Green observed:

In principle, I agreed with his desire for a well-organized program. But weekly reports really weren't enough for him. He would always be popping in and out of my office asking for this form or that and demanding to know when something would be done. His interference limited the flexibility of not only the program's curriculum, but my own workday. I think I spent more time assuring him that work would get done than doing it.

Towards the midpoint of the semester, Ms. Green reported she was considering confronting Mr. Wilson, as she had Mr. Eisen, but was somewhat reluctant "because I have to work with him every day, and because of personal reasons."

Shortly afterwards, however, Ms. Green was hospitalized for a month with a serious heart condition. During her absence, Mr. Wilson personally supervised Ms. Green's students and maintained a personal interest in them after her return. Two months after she resumed work, Ms. Green commented:

When I returned to work everything was calm and relaxed. I was not physically or mentally prepared to confront Mr. Wilson. It's true that he maintains very close control now, but I just don't relate to him in a way that makes me want to fight. Mr. Eisen always made me nervous. He would race in and out of the office and be very abrupt. Mr. Wilson has an easy-going way about him even when he is constantly checking up on me. With Eisen, I suspected it was his racism which made me anxious to object. With Mr. Wilson (who is black) it's just the way he is. Still I think I'm far more capable than his treatment of me suggests, and I may have to speak up.

Both Mr. Eisen and Mr. Wilson were asked to evaluate Ms. Green's job performance. Mr. Eisen observed:

I think Mrs. Green is a very talented social worker, very good with people. But there's a general confusion about her, and her administrative style is so haphazard that I'm not sure she should go into administration. She seems to get things done though. I would rate her as an excellent field worker but an only fair potential project director.

Mr. Wilson commented:

Vanessa is so well-intentioned. She could be in the middle of writing a crucial report, and she'd stop everything she was doing if a student had a problem. I would like to see her adopt a more disciplined style of working and limit her activities some for the sake of her health. But I'm sure she will make it and be a real leader in the field, given the proper direction.

12
Evelyn Robinson

ABSTRACT

Evelyn Robinson, who has been working for an insurance company as an agent specializing in the college market, finds that being black and female makes one especially vulnerable to conflict in the company. Although she wins several prizes for her sales ability, many accounts default because of circumstances beyond her control, and she is fired.

Ms. Robinson, a student at the Wharton Evening School of the University of Pennsylvania, went to see one of her professors because she was failing his course. She has been taking courses at night for four years in order to satisfy the requirements for a bachelor's degree in business. This semester, very serious problems in her work situation are interfering with her schoolwork. She has been working for an insurance company for almost two years and has been losing increasing amounts of income each month because of defaulting policy holders.

Personal Background

Evelyn Robinson is a black woman, thirty-three years old, from a lower-middle-class family. She was married and divorced early, and has one son, age sixteen, who is enrolled at a private school because of a learning disability. She gets no alimony or child support from her ex-husband, and she is buying the house she lives in. Her responsibilities include two pure-bred Afghan hounds which she shows.

Since 1971, Ms. Robinson has been attending classes at the Wharton Evening School of the University of Pennsylvania, and received the

A.B.A. in May of 1975. Additional courses were taken at two other local colleges. She is a Notary Public, belongs to the University Real Estate Society, the National Association of Life Underwriters, and has been active in several other clubs and societies. She had worked full time since 1962, first as a head cashier, then a Hertz representative, a department manager, and an annuity benefits supervisor. She applied for her present position of insurance agent because of the challenge and earning potential the job seemed to offer.

Entering The Insurance Business

The position for which Ms. Robinson applied was listed with the University Placement Center as "Financial Planner." Upon her inquiry, however, she was told that she was not qualified for it because she did not yet have her B.S. degree, but was encouraged to submit her resume so she could be considered for other jobs. A week later she received a call from the Aetna Life Insurance Company and was granted an interview.*

The interviewing process was a very extensive one. She was given several tests over a period of five weeks and was told that the position she was being considered for was that of insurance agent specializing in the college market. At the end of five weeks, and after she had successfully taken the State examinations for life and health insurance, she was offered the position of College Marketing Representative. (See Exhibit 1.) She spent one week at the home office in Hartford, Connecticut, in a training program, then started on the job working out of a "career agency" with eleven other agents. Her four coworkers in the section to which she was assigned were all men.

Compensation

Insurance agents are paid on a commission basis. Commissions range from 30 to 55 percent of the annual premium of new business depending on the kind of policy sold. Life policy commissions are higher than those on health policies and annuities. Those on renewal premiums are considerably less, ranging from 2 to 14 percent over a period of ten years.

Since she had no previous selling experience, Evelyn was put on a salary contract, which ran for two years to $600 per month. This amount would increase or decrease according to the value of annual premiums of policies which were put in force by the firm. First year premiums had to

*The author makes no claim concerning the correctness or incorrectness of statements made by Ms. Robinson about the policies and practices of the Aetna Life Insurance Company.

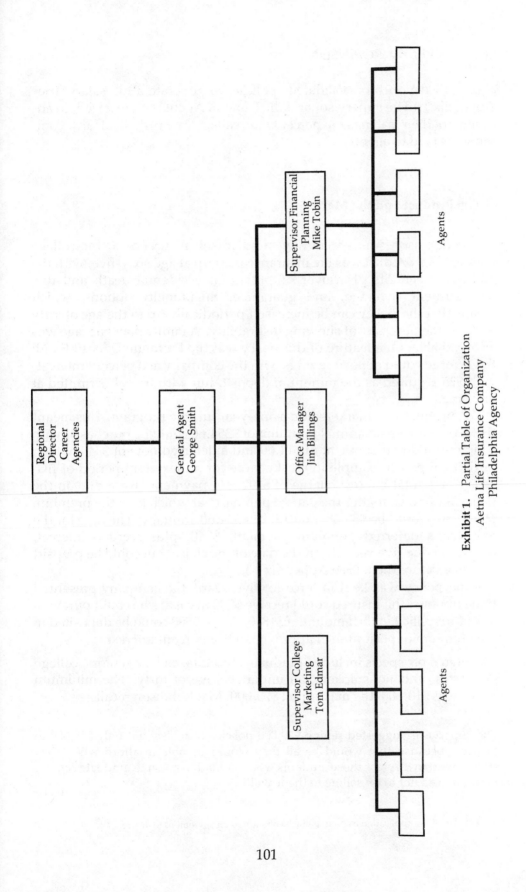

Exhibit 1. Partial Table of Organization
Aetna Life Insurance Company
Philadelphia Agency

101

equal $1500/month on validated* policies to generate a full salary. (See Appendix 1.) The supervisor and the General Agent both received, in addition to their salaries, a percentage, called "override," of any commissions paid to agents.

The Product and the Market

Ms. Robinson was specifically hired to sell insurance to the college market. Her product was life insurance paid up at age sixty-five, with the additional benefits of waiver of premium, accidental death and dismemberment coverage, and guaranteed insurability options, which means that the policy can be increased periodically up to the age of forty without the necessity of showing insurability. A family plan package was also available. One feature of this policy was the Premium Deposit Fund: the insured could deposit savings with the company at 8 percent interest, with $25 required as the minimum deposit, but withdrawal permitted at any time.

The product was marketed on a one-year finance program. This meant that a policy with an annual premium of $354.60 could be purchased with a minimum down payment of $14.60 and a deferred note of $340, which carried a 6 percent simple interest charge for a maximum period of five years, or a total interest charge of $102. No payments were due on the policy for one year after the date of purchase, at which time the premium payments would be $30.28 monthly or $354.60 annually. The note for the first year's deferred premium payment, $340, plus accrued interest, would fall due five years from the date of purchase, but could be prepaid any time before then. (See Appendix 2.)

If the policy was kept in force for five years, the company presented three options: the insured could receive $500 in cash; s/he could purchase a paid up policy in the amount of $1840; or the $500 could be deposited in the premium deposit fund at approximately 8 percent interest.

Evelyn's prospects included graduate students, college seniors, college graduates, and nonsmokers, all under the age of forty. The minimum policy was $10,000, the maximum, $25,000. Ms. Robinson recalls:

The supervisor suggested selling $20,000 policies to males, but only $15,000 to females, because that would be all they would be able to afford when they started working. As for those students who planned to go on to graduate school, I was advised not to try selling to them at all!

---

*Acceptance of the application by Aetna which constituted an agreement to insure.

First Year's Experiences

During her first six months with Aetna, Evelyn Robinson submitted applications totaling $610,000, which included three months of over $100,000 in business each. She received certificates of commendation for this feat and was encouraged to apply for membership in the Million Dollar Round Table (MDRT), an honorary society and nonprofit organization supporting various worthy causes. The main qualification to join was the ability to claim personal credit for $1,000,000 worth of life insurance sold on a minimum of fifteen policies between January 1 and December 31 of any calendar year. At the end of her first year, Evelyn's accomplishments qualified her for membership. Unfortunately, no one in her office knew the application procedures, and when the information was finally made available to her, the deadline was too close for her application to be considered. She had, however, no trouble securing information on applying to the Women Leaders Round Table, a similar but much less prestigious organization, which seemed, as she put it, "a little peculiar" in an office which had eleven males and only one female. Her application was successful, and she subsequently joined this organization.

The Regional Meeting

A very important incentive policy employed by insurance companies is the running of contests. Evelyn Robinson won several prizes; one of them was a four-day trip to West Virginia to attend an Aetna Regional Meeting. All expenses would be paid, including the stay at the Greenbrier Resort Motel. Children and guests could not attend under any circumstances, though spouses were welcome at the attender's expense. The transportation provided was by air on three small commuter lines, and a limousine to the final destination, but no allowance was promised the would-be attender who decided to travel by car. Evelyn did not like the kind of air travel provided but was unwilling to make the car trip by herself. She told her supervisor about her problem and asked whether she could bring a guest if she paid for separate rooms. Or, failing that, was there an alternative prize, since she could not use the one she had won? "After all," she said "not everyone is married!" Both the supervisor and the office manager doubted that anything could be done, but the office manager said he would see what he could arrange. "Unfortunately," Evelyn noted "the company stuck to its moralistic principles as far as guests were concerned."

George (general agent): Evelyn, I'm sorry. I did what I could. I thought they
   might go along with it if I said separate rooms, but they still said "no."
Evelyn: Thanks a lot for trying. Don't worry about it.
George: It's a shame you won't go. The Greenbrier is really a fantastic place. In
   the past, I personally knew some who attended who didn't go alone, but
   weren't married. How they did it, I don't know.

Recalls Evelyn:

With the last statement, I sat down and did some thinking. If others could do it,
why not me? If I had enough motivation, determination, and drive to sell
enough insurance to qualify for this trip, why should I be penalized for being
single? Who was to say I was married or single when I arrived at the Greenbrier?
Would they go around and ask for marriage licenses?

She decided she would go with a friend to whom she would pretend to
be married. After an eight-hour drive she arrived with her "husband"
Dennis at the Greenbrier. The office manager, Jim, had advised her to
keep all gasoline and toll receipts for possible reimbursement and had
also assured her that a room was still reserved for her. Upon her arrival
she was dismayed to find her room reservation cancelled. But the resort
quickly found new accommodations for her and her "husband," and she
joined the convention. George, the general agent, expressed surprise at
her sudden marriage but congratulated her. Noticing that she was the
only black agent present, and was being ignored by most of those there,
she asked him:

Evelyn: George, this is really poor representation for the blacks in the com-
   pany, isn't it? Where are they?
George: I didn't notice.
Evelyn: How could you not have noticed? Or are you acting like the rest of
   them?
George: I'm afraid I don't understand exactly what you mean.
Evenlyn: Well, you know the company has quite a few black agents. I guess
   they didn't qualify.

Ms. Robinson comments sardonically:

The same way George hadn't noticed was the same way I was noticed—like a
nonperson."

She did not, however, let this nontreatment prevent her and Dennis
from enjoying themselves. He spent his time at the miniature golf course
when she was at the business meetings in the mornings, and they spent
the afternoons together watching tennis matches, horseback riding, and
swimming.

Back at the office the following Monday, nothing was mentioned about her "marriage." She turned in her receipts and was fully reimbursed for them a month later.

The Annuity Problem

Ms. Robinson had been in the insurance business for four months when a friend asked her about the possibility of purchasing a retirement program from her. She consulted her supervisor:

Evelyn: I was asked about an annuity. What are the rates, and do we have any literature?

Tom: There are a couple of ways this can be handled. An agent in the Financial Planning section can go out with you to explain the program. If the prospect buys it, the agent will split the commission with you. On the other hand, if you know the person well, I can get the information for you, explain it to you, and you can present the program yourself. If you sell it, I will submit it in my name and split the commission with you. The application can only be submitted by someone who is licensed to sell annuities.

Evelyn: Okay. You get the information, and I will present it. But tell me, what are the requirements for me to be licensed?

Tom: The company won't allow you to take the exam until you are out of the college market. The best thing is for you to give the business to another agent and split the commissions. You won't receive volume credit for it, because it'll be in the other agent's name. But you will get some extra dollars in your pocket.

Evelyn: That doesn't make sense. Why should I give away business I can write?

Tom: If you write the business, you will not get paid commissions until after your two-year contract is over. The money will be held for you in a separate account. Some agents don't make it in our business that long. Two years is a long time!

Evelyn: Sure it is. But if I can write the business and receive volume credit, I would rather do that. How is the money finally paid?

Tom: All money is paid in a lump sum. But it doesn't make sense to let it lay around that long.

Evelyn: That is your opinion. But I think receiving a sizable lump for the entire sum is much better than receiving half of the commission whenever I write a policy.

A few months later, a meeting was held to inform all agents that they were required to take an examination three weeks hence to be licensed to sell annuities by the Securities Exchange Commission. That is, they would not have to wait two years to be eligible to take the examination.

The Second Year

It was in the second year of her job with the company that Evelyn ran into serious problems. It will be recalled that agents were paid on a commission basis, but 10 percent of their earnings were subtracted and placed in an escrow account to reimburse the company for defaulting business. Any amount over that was deducted from the rest of an agent's earnings. (See Appendix 3.)

In the second year, monthly payments on the policies Evelyn had sold the previous year became due. Eight out of ten of these policyholders lived out of state. It was her responsibility to contact these clients at her own expense to remind them of their obligations. The home office would send out notices sixty days before the due date. If the premiums were two weeks overdue, another notice was sent out. If they still went unpaid, the policyholders would receive a letter from an attorney stating that they were legally obligated to pay back the note for the first year's premium. At this point Evelyn also was to contact her clients once more by telephone to get them to reinstate their policies, again calling at her own expense. In May of 1975, the persistency rate* in the college marketing area was so low that the company ruled that no policy that exceeded $15,000 could be sold on a note basis. Notes became due in full thirty days after the policies had lapsed, and the agent's escrow account was debited for the amount at that time.

The persistency problem was so great that three of the five college marketing agents quit their jobs. Evelyn confronted Tom, her supervisor, with the problem:

> *Tom:* I know all of you have been experiencing policy lapses. Rather than waste time running after people that let their policies lapse, go out and sell more insurance.
> *Evelyn:* What about the deductions being made from the escrow accounts?
> *Tom:* The deductions are not affecting your salary. You only have to validate your predetermined figure to get your paycheck.

But by this time Evelyn was on a straight commission basis, and her earnings were being affected by policy lapses. At one point, the deductions exceeded her earnings. She commented:

One of the things I could not understand was, if the company saw they were losing a great deal of money because of lapsed policies, why didn't they pull out of the college market altogether? Agents are bound to leave the company when monies are being deducted from their earnings, and when that happens the company can't possibly recover the money due to it.

*The percentage of policies kept in force by the insured.

Thinking that perhaps someone in the office would have better knowledge of company policy, she made an appointment to see the office manager, Jim:

> *Evelyn:* Jim, I've been experiencing quite a bit of lapses, so my persistency rate is decreasing. What can I do? Tom suggested forgetting about the lapses and going out to sell more insurance.
>
> *Jim:* Tom is very uninformed about company procedures and is not functioning properly in his capacity as supervisor if he instructed you to do that. He is thinking of himself. Don't forget, he gets an override on any business you sell!

Shortly afterwards the supervisor in question announced he was leaving the company. Evelyn contemplated resigning also, but it was explained to her that if an agent had been in the insurance business for two years, no New York-based company could offer him a salary contract; the only companies that could offer such an arrangement would be those in the debt business. This would mean that she would not receive any earnings for eight to ten weeks! She decided to stick it out and see what would happen, even though the office was in a shambles with the resignation of the general agent, the supervisor, and three of the five college market agents.

The Final Weeks

When the office had been without a general agent for six months, the home office finally appointed a replacement from the Atlanta office. After the introductory meeting called by the office manager, the new general agent, Joe Collins, met with each agent individually. Evelyn reported the following exchange:

> *Joe:* Well, Evelyn, I understand you've been with the company almost two years. How do you like the organization?
>
> *Evelyn:* It's all right, I suppose.
>
> *Joe:* Is this your first experience selling insurance?
>
> *Evelyn:* Yes, it is.
>
> *Joe:* Well, I've been in the business for more years then I care to remember. Been in the Atlanta office five years before coming here. Born and raised in Mississippi. Lived in a small town all my life. Not by chance, though. I'm just not a big-town man. Have two daughters in their teens. How about you?
>
> *Evelyn:* I have a teen-age son.
>
> *Joe:* Well, by George, I think that's really great! Say there, are you having any problems we may be able to help you with?

Evelyn: No, not especially. My biggest problem is with defaulting notes. There is really nothing much left to be done that I haven't already tried in collecting them.

Joe: Oh, yes, those college marketing notes. Heard about them. Other than that, is there anything else you would like to talk about that is bothering you?

Evelyn: No, not especially.

Joe: I'll be moving up here in a month, and when I do, I want to get this agency moving.

Discussing the new general agent with a black coworker, Edwin Jones, Evelyn and he agreed that the man was a middle-aged southerner trying to show how liberal he was, but they decided to wait and see how things would work out.

A month later, Edwin had occasion to go into the office one evening to pick up some forms he needed. He found Joe in the office hanging newly purchased pictures and rearranging the furniture. After some light conversation, Edwin picked up the forms, made a few phone calls, and left. Two days later, the locks on the front office door were changed. Jim, the office manager, announced that all agents would have to come in during normal business hours because they would not be issued new keys. This constituted considerable hardship because often agents could not get to the office during the day and would come in during the evening hours to complete reports, pick up policies, and phone for appointments.

When Evelyn went to the office to pick up the last paycheck of her contract, Jim, the office manager, wanted to see her. He handed her the paycheck and an unsealed envelope containing an interoffice communication addressed to her from Joe, the new general agent:

Exhibit 2

AETNA
Life & Casualty
INTEROFFICE COMMUNICATION

TO   Evelyn Robinson
FROM   Joe T. Collins, C.L.U., General Agent
DATE   November 12, 1975
SUBJECT   NOTE SELLING PRIVILEGES

The Home Office has notified me that due to substantial lapses on College Note business sold by you, they have suspended your note selling privileges effective November 1, 1975.

Additionally, you have a negative escrow balance of $5,458.98. Since you are responsible for the notes taken as settlement for the first year's premium on policies sold to your clients, it will behoove you to do everything within your power to conserve this business and assist in the collection of the notes that have been charged to your escrow.

In view of the reasons which necessitated the decision to suspend your note selling privilege, I also find it necessary to terminate your Agency Agreement with this Agency and Aetna effective November 15th, 1975. All sales materials and keys should be returned to the Office Manager.

I wish for you the best of success in your future endeavor.

Sincerely,

Joe T. Collins, C.L.U.
General Agent
JTC/ed

After reading the letter, Evelyn recalled:

I said to Jim that it was just as well, because there was no way I could stay with the company and have my earnings reduced to practically nothing because of the lapsed policy deductions. Jim understood and blamed the supervisor for misinforming the agents regarding company policy.

A week later, Edwin resigned. He also had notes that were defaulting.

Appendix 1.

Aetna Life And Casualty

INTEROFFICE COMMUNICATION

TO   GENERAL AGENTS
FROM   P. L. Slausen, Mgr., Manpower Selection & Compensation
DATE   April 19, 1974
SUBJECT   24-MONTH COLLEGE MARKET PLAN

My letter of March 1, 1974 announced the changes in the 24-Month College Market Finance Plan. An interpretation of the changes as it relates to the calculation of bonus, increases, and decreases might be helpful.

It is important to remember that increases will be granted only where the earned commissions justify it. Bonuses will be paid based only on earned commissions. The annualized validation schedule is used only to determine whether an agent has validated his current level. An agent would drop to the level that would result after using the highest of the annualized or earned commission schedule.

An example will help to explain these calculations.

Example No. 1 (15 Months)

Starting Training Allowance $600   ($600 x 15 Months) $ 9,000
Cash Commissions Credited   9,576 ($100 Health)
Annualized Commissions Credited   10,000
Total Earned Commission – Training Allowance Paid × $1/2$ = bonus payable

Step No. 1 is to determine whether the agent has validated his present level. This calculation is as follows:

$$\frac{\text{Total Earned Commission} - \text{Other Lines}}{\text{Earned Validation Requirement}} = \text{Training Allowance Level}$$

or

$$\frac{\$9,576 - \$100}{\$1,197} = \$792$$

Remember that only College Market Commissions will count towards validation. Once you have determined the agent has validated at least his present level, Step 2 is to determine whether cash commissions credited exceed the training allowance paid.

Step No. 2—

Total Earned Commission − Training Allowance Paid × ½ = Bonus Payable

or

$$\$9,576 - \$9,000 \times \tfrac{1}{2} = \$288$$

The agent is eligible for a payment of one half of the excess or in this example $288.

Step No. 3 is to determine the new training allowance level.

A.
$$\frac{\text{Total Earned Commission} - \text{Other Lines} - \text{Bonus Paid}}{\text{Earned Validation Requirement}}$$
$$= \text{Training Allowance Level}$$

or

$$\frac{\$9,576 - \$100 - \$288}{\$1,197} = \$768$$

B.
$$\frac{\text{New Training Allowance} + \text{Present Training Allowance}}{2}$$
$$= \text{New Level for Next Quarter}$$

or

$$\frac{\$768 + \$600}{2} = \$684$$

Please recognize that the dividing by the number of months that was announced in my March 1, 1974 letter has been eliminated. You should take the attachment to that March 1 letter and eliminate the portion of the third paragraph that states "divided by the number of months that he has participated in the training allowance plan."

Once again annualized commissions may not be used to increase levels.

Hopefully this clarifies the methods used to calculate the training allowance levels and bonuses paid. If there are any questions, please let me know.

P. L. Slausen

Appendix 2.

The Ætna College Plan*

A LIFE INSURANCE PLAN OFFERED BY THE ÆTNA LIFE INSURANCE COMPANY

NAME_____GRADUATION DATE_____

NAME OF SPOUSE _____MAJOR_____

DRAFT CLASSIFICATION_____ROTC_____

SOCIAL SECURITY NUMBER_____

1. Expected field of employment after graduation?_____

2. Anticipated monthly income? $_____

3. Do you agree a person should save money systematically?
   ☐ Yes   ☐ No

4. Are you in   ☐ Excellent   ☐ Good   ☐ Fair   ☐ Poor Health?

5. Do you engage in such activities as:
   ☐ Flying   ☐ Skin Diving   ☐ Auto Racing   ☐ Other

6. How has your education been financed?
   ☐ Scholarship   ☐ Loans   ☐ Parents   ☐ Self

7. Are you now in a position to make your own financial decisions for
   the future?   ☐ Yes   ☐ No.

*Reproduced by special permission, Aetna Life Insurance Company, Hartford, Connecticut.

Ætna
LIFE & CASUALTY

ÆTNA COLLEGE PLAN

PURCHASE AGE 21-M- $ 20,000 INSURANCE ESTATE   POLICY FORM 37662
                  GUARANTEED COST

PURCHASE PRICE   LIFE PAID UP AT 65   1. PROTECTION WITH LIFE
$ 256.00 ANNUAL   WITH   INSURANCE
$ 21.68 ACP MO   FIFTH ANNIVERSARY BENEFIT 2. ACCUMULATION OF CASH

```
┌────── GUARANTEED ESTATE COMPLETION ──────┐
│ IF DEATH OCCURS WHILE THE POLICY IS IN FULL FORCE │
│              THE BENEFIT IS:                       │
│                                                    │
│                                                    │
└────────────────────────────────────────────┘
```

END OF YEAR	*TOTAL CASH	*ANNUAL CASH INCREASE	PAID-UP INSURANCE	CASH VALUE	END OF YEAR
1	$ -0-	$ -0-	$ -0-	$ -0-	1
2	-0-	-0-	-0-	-0-	2
3	80	80	320	80	3
4	320	240	1240	320	4
5	540	220	2040	540	5
6	805	265	1020	280	6
7	1051	246	1780	500	7
8	1319	268	2540	740	8
9	1588	269	3280	980	9
10	1878	290	4020	1240	10
11	2164	286	4720	1500	11
12	2470	307	5440	1780	12
13	2778	308	6100	2060	13
14	3087	309	6720	2340	14
15	3416	330	7360	2640	15
16	3767	351	8000	2960	16
17	4120	352	8620	3280	17
18	4473	354	9180	3600	18
19	4848	375	9740	3940	19
20	5225	376	10280	4280	20
AGE 62	14157	491	18940	12400	AGE 62
AGE 65	15720	536	20000	13800	AGE 65

TOTAL PURCHASE PRICE TO AGE 65 $ 11264.00

```
THE FIFTH ANNIVERSARY BENEFIT OPTIONS ARE: OPTION A -- $ 500 IN CASH; OR, OPTION
B -- $ 1880 ADDITIONAL PAID UP INSURANCE; OR, -- LEAVE THE $ 500 TO ACCUMULATE
AT COMPOUND INTEREST IN THE PREMIUM DEPOSIT FUND.
*THESE COLUMNS ASSUME THE $ 500 FROM OPTION A WILL BE DEPOSITED IN THE PREMIUM
DEPOSIT FUND (OUTLINED IN THE POLICY), AND ADDED TO THE GUARANTEED CASH VALUE.
THE ANNUAL GUARANTEED COMPOUND INTEREST RATE FOR ACCUMULATIONS IN THE PREMIUM
DEPOSIT FUND WOULD BE AT LEAST 5% FOR THE FIRST FIVE YEARS, 4% FOR THE NEXT
TEN YEARS, AND 3% THEREAFTER. IF THE $ 500 FROM OPTION A WERE LEFT TO ACCUMU-
LATE IN THE PREMIUM DEPOSIT FUND AT OUR CURRENT RATE (NOT GUARANTEED) OF AC-
CUMULATION -- 8% COMPOUND INTEREST -- IT WOULD AMOUNT TO $10057 AT AGE 65,
AND ADDED TO THE GUARANTEED CASH VALUE WOULD EQUAL $ 23857.
```

IF THE FIRST ANNUAL PREMIUM IS HANDLED ON A DEFERRED NOTE BASIS, THE FIFTH
ANNIVERSARY PAYMENT WOULD BE APPLIED TOWARD PAYMENT OF THE NOTE (IF NOT
PREVIOUSLY PAID).
AT 65-20P $ 7090.32, AT 65+B $ 8386.99, AT 65+C $14027.11, ALL B.$ 345.60/$ 29.48

CM-202   Ætna Life Insurance Company, Hartford, Connecticut   SPS 18.3.23-1

Assets

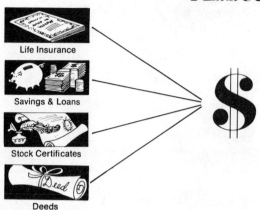

Life Insurance

Savings & Loans

Stock Certificates

Deeds

$

EMERGENCY

EDUCATION

OPPORTUNITY

RETIREMENT

TAXES

— P R O B L E M —

HOW TO ACCUMULATE MONEY THAT WILL BE AVAILABLE WHEN NEEDED

TEMPORARY	PERMANENT
_____ **Banks** . . .	_____ **Social Security** . . .
_____ **Credit Unions** . . .	_____ **Pension** . . .
_____ **Savings and Loans** . . .	_____ **Home** . . .

$ _____ / $ _____ Mo.

Asset

LIFE INSURANCE

☐ REGULAR PAYMENT BASIS — POLICY

PAID-UP INSURANCE	CASH VALUE
_____ 5th _____
_____ 10th _____
_____ 15th _____
_____ 20th _____
_____ Age 65 _____

☐ Pro Rata Ownership
☐ Money Accumulation
☐ Cash Distribution — Lump Sum . . . Life Income
☐ Insurance Options
  • Additional Insurance • Disability
        • Other

OTHER ASSETS

☐ CONDITIONAL SALES CONTRACT BASIS
—Home . . . Auto . . . Etc.
  • Market Conditions
   Determine Value

ASSET DISTRIBUTION

☐ POLICY

• Clear Title
• Proceeds To Named Beneficiary
• Income Tax Free
• Avoid Probate
• Creditor Proof
• Debt Free

☐ ESTATE

• Heirs Complete Payments
• Requires Probate
• Will To Specify Heirs
• Subject To Claims

BUILDING AN ESTATE—A PLANNED PROCESS

THE BENEFITS AND PURCHASE PRICE OF LIFE INSURANCE PROPERTY (POLICY) DEPEND UPON THE QUALIFICATIONS OF THE INSURED AND THE OPERATIONAL EFFICIENCY OF THE INSURANCE COMPANY

☐ Best Health
☐ Non Hazardous
☐ Income Potential

☐ Insurance Ownership
☐ Policy Size
☐ Persistency

WHY NOW

DESIGNED FOR TODAY — AS WELL AS TOMORROW — TAILORED TO FIT YOUR NEEDS

TODAY

☐ Youngest Age Group   ☐ Immediate Estate

THINK OF YOUR ESTATE IN REGARD TO:

YOUR PARENTS . . .
should you die

Based on estimates by Goverment Surveys and Educational Reports, your parents have already spent approximately $40,000 in raising you and helping you through college.*'As a result, you may feel a strong sense of obligation.

*U.S. Commission on Population & The American Future.

YOUR FAMILY . . .
minimum needs

At Age 25 With One Child — Age Two

A. $500 monthly 'til Child is age 18	$ 96,000
B. Thereafter, $150 a month to Wife for life (Wife age 25)	$ 61,020
C. College Fund	$ 6,000
D. Cash Fund (paying debts and settling estate).	$ 3,000
E. Mortgage or Rental Fund	$ 20,000
F. Emergency Fund for Family	$ 2,500
Minimum Amount of Money Needed by Family. . . .	$188,520

Assuming you would be eligible and fully qualified, there would be a total of approximately $90,000 provided by Social Security in the above example. Your estate would be called upon to furnish the balance of the *minimum* needs. In that regard, it is important to note that life insurance normally represents 87% of the estate left at death.

YOURSELF . . .
opportunities — retirement

In addition to the responsibilities you have to your parents and your family, you have an even greater responsibility to Yourself.

10% of earnings should be saved for your retirement. It must be paid for NOW with money & time or LATER with pride & charity.

TOMORROW

☐ Estate Tax   ☐ Retirement Income
                      • Favorable Income Tax Consideration

Waiver Of Premium Disability

(OPTIONAL)

YOUR MOST VALUABLE ASSET IS YOUR POTENTIAL EARNING POWER

The average college graduate can expect to earn **$1,125,000** during his lifetime*—**HOWEVER:**

$$
\text{your chances of disability at age} \begin{cases} 22 & 7.5 \\ 32 & \text{are } 6.5 \\ 42 & 4.0 \\ \text{\scriptsize Official U.S.} \\ \text{\scriptsize Govt. Figures} \end{cases} \text{times greater than death.}
$$

*U.S. Dept. of Commerce

REGULAR DISABILITY: If you become disabled through either illness or injury, the Company, after six months, will:

- ☐ Pay your premiums as long as you are disabled (retroactive).
- ☐ Continue your full insurance and any supplementary benefits in force.
- ☐ Guarantee that premiums paid for you NEVER have to be repaid.
- ☐ Increase your cash values just as though you had paid the premiums yourself.

SPECIFIED DISABILITY: The Company will pay your premiums whether or not you can or do engage in any occupation, should you suffer the irrecoverable *"loss of use or severance"* of:

- ☐ Sight (Both Eyes) or
- ☐ Both Hands or
- ☐ Both Feet or
- ☐ One Eye and One Foot or
- ☐ One Eye and One Hand or
- ☐ One Hand and One Foot

The specified disability will pay premiums on your present policy AND all future policies issued under the Guaranteed Insurability Option. This applies to any such disability beginning prior to age 65.

Guaranteed Insurability Option

(OPTIONAL)

REGULAR OPTIONS: You can add to your program at any time, provided you are in good health and your job is non-hazardous. However, the Guaranteed Insurability Option gives you the guaranteed right to acquire additional life insurance in the future at standard rates *regardless* of your health or occupation.

OPTION AGES	OPTION AMOUNT	TOTAL ADDITIONAL INSURANCE

ADDITIONAL OPTIONS: You can purchase additional insurance under these options on any of the following occasions, and these are *in addition* to your Regular Option privileges:

- ☐ MARRIAGE
- ☐ BIRTH OR ADOPTION

CREDIT: Premium Credit will be given on the first year's premium *every time* a Regular Option or an Additional Option is exercised under the guarantee.

$_____ **Option Amount Exercised**
(X) $5 per 1,000   **Premium Credit**

$_____ **Total Amount of Premium Credit on Additional Insurance**

ADDITIONAL FEATURES: ☐ PRE-OPTION INSURANCE   ☐ SPECIFIED DISABILITY
Up to 60 Days when requested   Maximum is $250,000 AD & D

Accidental Death and Dismemberment
(OPTIONAL)

Your greatest hazard is premature accidental death, since studies show that prior to age forty, 50% of all deaths are accidental.   BENEFIT AMOUNT $_____

ACCIDENTAL DEATH PAYS A TOTAL OF:

☐ **REGULAR:**   [3×] $_____   **FARE-PAYING PASSENGER:**   [5×] $_____
(Including Automobiles)   (Licensed Common Carrier—Land-Sea-Air)

ACCIDENTAL DISMEMBERMENT: LOSS OF —

☐ SIGHT (BOTH EYES) OR   [3×] $_____
BOTH FEET OR BOTH HANDS   cash
— OR —
☐ ONE HAND & ONE FOOT
— OR —
ONE FOOT & SIGHT OF   [2×] $_____
ONE EYE   cash
— OR —
ONE HAND & SIGHT OF
ONE EYE

ALL FUTURE PREMIUMS WAIVED

ON YOUR $_____ POLICY

PLUS   — AND —

FOR ALL POLICIES ISSUED UNDER THE REGULAR GUARANTEED INSURABILITY OPTIONS.

☐ ONE EYE OR ONE HAND OR
ONE FOOT   [1×] $_____
cash

☐ THUMB & INDEX FINGER
OF (EITHER HAND)   [½×] $_____
cash

ANY ACCIDENTAL DISMEMBERMENT LOSS WILL BE **DOUBLED** IF LOSS OCCURS WHILE A FARE-PAYING PASSENGER ON A LICENSED COMMON CARRIER.

Family Benefit

(OPTIONAL) This Complete Coverage on Family Provides:

1. COVERAGE ON WIFE (_____) Decreasing and Convertible Term to Age 60 ... $_____
age   (Reduces $50 per year)   Initial Amount

ACCIDENTAL DEATH*   EXAMPLE
Regular .... 3X   Wife's Age at Death_____
Fare-Paying Passenger .... 5X $_____
Fare-Paying Passenger (while riding
with Insured Spouse) .... 11X   X_____
*Based on the amount of coverage at time of death $_____

2. COVERAGE ON PRESENT INSURABLE CHILDREN TO AGE 25 (Conv. Term) ... $ **1,000**
All future children automatically insured without charge after 15 days of age for the full $1,000

3. ESTATE BUILDER FOR CHILDREN ... $ **25,000**
The $1,000 coverage can be changed to a $25,000 Insurance Policy at age 21, 22, 23, 24 or 25 regardless of health or occupation

4. IN EVENT OF HUSBAND'S OR WIFE'S DEATH, THE FAMILY BENEFIT ... **FULLY PAID UP**

5. IN EVENT OF HUSBAND'S DISABILITY, THE FAMILY BENEFIT ... **PAYS ALL PREMIUMS FALLING**
(Same benefit and qualifications as outlined in Disability Provision) **DUE DURING DISABILITY**

BASED ON WIFE'S AGE____ NEAREST BIRTHDAY $_____ /MONTH
(Contact the Company if you desire to apply for this benefit at a later date)

A COMPLETE AND TRUE PRESENTATION: CERTIFIED BY _____.
Licensed Representative

YOUR COLLEGE POLICY INCLUDES   MONTHLY PREMIUMS
☐ Basic Plan $25,000 $_____ /Mo.
☐ Waiver of Premium Disability $20,000 $_____ /Mo.
☐ Guaranteed Insurability Option $15,000 $_____ /Mo.
☐ Accidental Death & Dismemberment
☐ Family Benefit $10,000 $_____ /Mo.

BASED ON $_____POLICY   **$_____ANNUALLY**

```
┌─────────────────── CALCULATIONS ───────────────────┐
│                                                     │
│                                                     │
│                                                     │
│                                                     │
│                                                     │
└─────────────────────────────────────────────────────┘
```

DEFERRED PAYMENT PLAN

FIRST YEAR_____

You handle the first Annual Premium:

  By 10% or $_____ down payment, and a $_____Deferred Note
  through Ætna Life Insurance Company, Hartford, Connecticut.

SECOND YEAR_____

You make your second and future Premiums by paying annually direct to Ætna or having Ætna notify your bank to forward $_____ each month.

SCHEDULED NOTE MATURITY DATE_____

Your Deferred Note (made for the balance of the first Annual Premium) is not due for five years, *as long as your premiums are made on your policy.*

After premiums are made for five years,
your policy pays (5th Anniversary Payment) Option A $_____

  DEFERRED NOTE AMOUNT $_____

  PLUS_____% SIMPLE INTEREST $_____
    Interest is tax-deductible—pre-payment
    saves proportionately on interest.

          Total Payment $_____

          Difference $_____

```
┌─────────────────────────────────────────────────────┐
│ IF YOU LAPSE YOUR POLICY BEFORE THE FIFTH ANNIVERSARY,│
│      THE NOTE WILL BE DUE AS OF THE LAPSE DATE.        │
└─────────────────────────────────────────────────────┘
```

QUALIFICATIONS

The acquiring of life insurance depends on a person's:

	HEALTH	OCCUPATION	CHARACTER
PREFERRED	_____	_____	_____
A	_____	_____	_____
B	_____	_____	_____
C	_____	_____	_____
D	_____	_____	_____
Uninsurable	_____	_____	_____

CATEGORY

**IN ORDER TO DETERMINE HOW YOU WOULD QUALIFY,
THE COMPANY NEEDS TO KNOW YOUR INDIVIDUAL SITUATION.**

The benefits and privileges in the outline are subject to the terms and conditions of the policy.

ABSOLUTE GUARANTEED SAFETY
ÆTNA LIFE INSURANCE COMPANY

LEGAL RESERVE COMPANY
- Approximately 95% of the life insurance in force in the United States is provided by such companies, and the fact that these companies must maintain reserves as required by law is considered the strongest guarantee in the Financial World
- All leading Independent Insurance Reporting Services recommend the Company for its financial soundness
- Founded in 1853
- This policy and its benefits are offered by the Ætna Life Insurance Company which is an affiliated company of —

ÆTNA LIFE & CASUALTY

RANKED AS No. 1 U.S. Diversified Financial Company in Terms of Assets and Revenues
- 65 Billions of Life Insurance in Force
- Leading Writer of Individual Variable Annuities
- Ranked First Among Insurance Companies in Health and Group Premiums

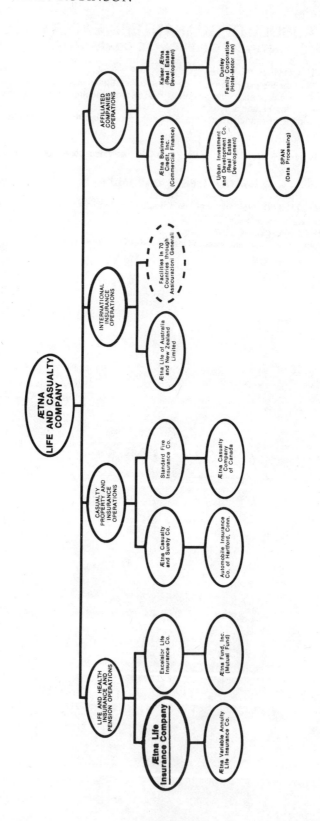

Appendix 3.

Aetna Life & Casualty
(extracted sections of Company policy)

E. *Level Adjustments on Training Allowance Payments*

1) Validation Requirements

A. The agent may validate on either a cumulative cash commission basis or an annualized commission basis (both before deduction for escrow) on College Market business.
B. The first qualifying period will be at the end of six complete calendar months after the starting financing date and quarterly thereafter. His progress will be reviewed monthly.
C. For the first six months, the training allowance will be at the initial rate.

2) Validation

A. At the end of the first six complete calendar months and at the end of each succeeding qualifying quarter, the agent's progress is reviewed in relation to attainment of the cumulative commission production required to validate his training allowance.
B. If the cumulative cash commission production of the agent exceeds the amount required to validate his training allowance, then his training allowance will be increased by 50% of the excess of the cumulative commission production over the amount required to validate his training allowance divided by the number of months that he has participated in the Training Allowance Plan.

Note: Any single increase will not exceed 50% of the current training allowance, and in no instance will the resulting training allowance be more than $1,200.

C. If the agent fails to validate his training allowance, then his allowance will be reduced to the larger amount that he has validated on a cash commission or annualized commission basis.
D. If the agent fails to meet the performance requirements for both [sic] an annualized cash commission basis for a level which is $200 per month below his initial training allowance level, he will be automatically terminated from the Plan.

Note: Commissions on Mutual Funds, Casualty Business written on the lives of the agent, his wife and his children, or dependents residing with him do not count toward validation.

F.   *Successful Completion of Program Requirements*
   1)   When an agent successfully completes the 24-month financing period, he will be "forgiven" an amount equal to the excess of the training allowance payments received over his earned commissions on all lines of business except for business described in 2-D Note above.
   2)   Earned commissions are defined to be equal to cash commissions less the required escrow deductions.
   3)   The difference, if any, between 20% of his paid annualized first year commissions and the excess forgiven will be paid in cash to the agent over a 12-month period in equal monthly installments.
   4)   The cash first-year and renewal commissions accruing after successful completion of the program on the business written during the financing period will be received by the agent as long as he remains with AETNA.
   5)   The Agent's service while under financing counts towards the service requirements for vesting under the respective agent agreements.
   6)   In return for the training allowance and for the forgiveness feature, the agent assigns to the Company his rights to commissions under the plan and to potential vesting.

   Note: If the agent [is] subsequently terminated as a full-time agent under the AETNA Career Agency Agreement or the AVAR Career Agent Contract, or as an employee, any commissions on business written during the financing plan revert to the respective companies.
   7)   Additional financing will not be permitted.

G.   *Non-Completion of Program*

   1)   *Agent Failure to complete the requirements:*

   If agent fails to complete the requirements under the College Marketing Finance Plan, the Aetna Career Agency Agreement, the AVAR Career Agents Contract and the College Market Supplementary Agreement are terminated.

a) All payments to the agent cease.
b) All deferred first-year and vested renewal commission subsequently accruing on business submitted during the financing period revert to the respective companies.
c) The training allowance does not constitute indebtedness under the plan.

July 1974

13
Ellen Leder

PART I

ABSTRACT

Ellen Leder, an English major from an Ivy League university, decides, contrary to her parents' expectations, to enter law school. There she finds few obstacles directly related to her sex, but during a summer's employment in a major law firm she discovers a far different climate outside academia. As she searches for a permanent position, Ms. Leder is careful to investigate the treatment of women by her prospective employers and finally accepts an appointment in the estates and trusts division of an established firm.

Personal History

Ellen Leder had been raised to think in terms of a career, though one more traditional for a woman than law. Although her mother did not work outside the home when Ellen and her two sisters were young, Ellen's father, a pediatrician, spent a considerable amount of time with his daughters encouraging them to be independent and to cultivate a wide range of interests. When Ellen entered high school, her mother returned to college to earn her Masters in Social Work and later took a position in a mental health center.

Although Ms. Leder's home orientation was strongly procareer, the suburban high school she attended was not supportive. According to Ellen Leder:

I was never really encouraged by my teachers to think of a career, for that was for the boys. It was considered very unfeminine to be assertive or show one's ambition.

As a result, Ms. Leder's career guidance came exclusively from the home, where the virtues of a career in education were stressed.

Ms. Leder enrolled in an eastern Ivy League college and majored in English with the intention of earning a teaching certificate. Ms. Leder now humorously recalls:

I heard my mother's words echoing in the background . . . "Ellen, be a teacher! It's a great occupation. You only work until 3:00, you have the summers off with pay, and the retirement benefits can't be beat. It is a good profession to fall back on after marriage."

After several education courses and field work in city schools, Ms. Leder decided she would not enjoy teaching. At the very last minute, she signed up to take the LSAT (Law School Achievement Test) in her senior year, and scored well on all portions of the exam. After graduating with honors, Ms. Leder enrolled in a prestigious eastern law school. Her recollections of her experiences there are generally positive.

By the time I entered law school, most of the barriers had been broken. The women had their own lounge, courses on sex discrimination were given, and that infamous professor who only asked women questions on rape cases was just a legend. On the whole, the law professors were courteous and showed an awareness of women's fight for recognition. However, not all of my fellow students were as enlightened. Law school is a competitive business, and some of my male colleagues were on the look-out for the female's threshold of weakness. It was obvious who they were, and that they felt threatened, since they were the ones who made remarks accusing the women of being unfeminine and even castrating. But this was not the norm, and it was more of a nuisance than anything else.

Summer Employment

In the summer between her second and third years of law school, Ms. Leder worked in a high caliber law firm in Philadelphia. It was Ellen Leder's first experience in a semiprofessional capacity, and it sensitized her to some of the potential trouble spots in her relations with others in a law firm.

Ms. Leder was most disturbed by her poor interaction with the firm's secretaries, all of whom were female. She recalls:

My relationship with the secretaries was a fiasco. I had to have my briefs handed in about one week ahead of time to make sure that they were typed up and ready on the specified due date, whereas my male coworker could hand his in perhaps one day ahead. When I first arrived at the firm, I felt very funny about asking them to type up my papers; however, as soon as the pressure came on, I really had no other choice. I later realized that they were trained professionals in their own right, and that I was projecting my own discomfort at being asked to type someone else's work. Still, the secretaries and I were not comfortable with one another, perhaps partly because I tried so hard to make sure I was not mistaken for one.

During that summer, Ms. Leder found a few of the firm's clients unwilling to have anything to do with a female lawyer. They, however, were in the minority.

A senior partner of the firm admitted, when questioned, that several clients were reluctant to accept Ms. Leder's assistance in the management of their legal affairs. He explained:

One elderly gentleman, who was revising his will and who has been a client of ours for years, was certain a woman could not be competent. He's set in his ways, and the work was very important to him, so we deferred to his wishes. Another man was going through some bitter divorce proceedings and wanted absolutely nothing to do with a woman lawyer. There were two others who simply stated flatly that they did not like or trust women lawyers. We are not at present prepared to lose clients over this issue.

Among her colleagues, Ms. Leder encountered a variety of reactions. Some of the young male lawyers jumped at the opportunity to work with her, others carefully avoided it. Ms. Leder considered many of the older partners "chauvinistic" in their attitude toward women lawyers in general, though they were grudgingly accepting the increased presence of women in the field.

Of those colleagues who seemed "too anxious" to work with her, Ms. Leder reflects:

At first I was flattered that some of the men were so anxious to work with me. But when I thought about it, I was not surprised. They would ask me to do more work than they would the male students, and when the work turned out well, they didn't feel obliged to share the credit. They also expected me to look up to them, and they seemed to enjoy the role of "teacher" to a young female. They fancied themselves Pygmalion-type heroes, and one of the men had "different" motives.

Several times that summer, Ms. Leder claims, she was treated as a "sex object," usually by clients. But, she explains, she had made at least one preparation for that possibility:

I purposely planned my outfits with great care, trying to minimize sexual differences. My summer wardrobe consisted of three or four conservative-looking pantsuits and two midlength skirts.

Commenting on her summer's work as a total experience Ms. Leder notes:

I was disturbed, even depressed, about some of the things that had occurred. I really hadn't anticipated either the subtle or not so subtle discrimination I ran into. But later, when I found out that my superiors at the firm had rated my work very highly, I had a real sense of accomplishment to have done so well in an essentially alien environment. It built up my confidence. But I can't deny that I feel a residue of bitterness when I remember that summer.

Interviewing For a Permanent Position

During her third year of law school, more self-assured and less self-conscious, Ellen Leder began job hunting. Several top-notch firms, with few or no female members, were anxious to interview Ms. Leder, and she actually found herself more sought after than male colleagues with comparable academic records. Despite the firms' desires to avoid any appearance of discrimination, Ms. Leder believes her interviewers made several sexist *faux pas*:

One of the first questions I was consistently asked was whether or not I was married or committed to someone. "Did I plan to have children?" they all wanted to know. They almost always prefaced the question with the remark, "When we hire a woman we usually like to know if she will be with us for a while." Apparently, it was unthinkable to them that I might choose to continue my career while raising children. And the interviewers naturally assumed I would be interested in domestic relations or trusts and estates.

In fact, Ms. Leder *was* interested in trusts and estates, primarily, she explains:

because it is an area in which, with the exception of wealthy people, the client often receives very poor legal advice. There's nothing wrong with wanting to see children and widows, or widowers for that matter, well taken care of.

During the search for an appropriate position, Ms. Leder made a point of asking to speak with female members of those firms she was seriously interested in joining. Generally, the firms were cooperative.

Ms. Leder recalls that she had mixed reactions to the women lawyers she met during this period:

Some of them I really admired. They had been through a lot, more than I would ever have to face, and they had come out on top. But a few of the older lawyers themselves had a very conservative view towards women. Either they had never married, or they hadn't worked while their children were growing up, and they resented the young women who wanted to deviate from that pattern. One lawyer I met was very aggressive and not at all friendly. Perhaps she had become that way to succeed in that firm, which was very competitive, but the prospect of becoming like her really unnerved me.

Ms. Leder spoke with one female lawyer from the firm she eventually joined, who told her:

I'm in criminal law, and really don't know too much about the way trusts and estates is run. In general, the young lawyers, male and female alike, do much of the research, while the older men argue the cases. They've been careful not to treat me any differently from other young lawyers, which is not too great. But that's the way it is in most of the large establishment firms.

Ms. Leder, impressed by the reputation of that firm, and the starting salary she was offered, accepted a position as junior counselor in the estates and trusts division.

PART II

ABSTRACT

In 1975, only a year after receiving her accreditation to practice law, Ellen Leder finds herself in serious conflict with the senior partners of a major New York law firm. She has become involved in the supervision of the firm's paralegal staff and antagonizes the senior partners with her open lobbying for the employees.

Professional Beginnings

Determined to learn from past experience, Ms. Leder set out to establish friendly relations with other women in the law firm. This time, she was more confident of her professional status and hence less worried about being identified as a secretary. She found most of the women, particularly the older secretaries, quite willing to treat her as both a professional and a friend when approached on an equal level.

The estates and trusts division was a bread and butter function of the firm. The minimum fee for drawing up a will was high, and often the firm served as executor of the trust or will, receiving generous payment for its services. Within the trusts and estates department, paralegals played a crucial role. The paralegals, in this case all women, were college graduates who had completed a special six-month course in estate law, and were generally as knowledgeable in this narrow field as the lawyers themselves. Although they could not legally notarize or execute a will, the paralegals often administered all the details of a client's will, while the lawyers reviewed their work and dealt with the clients.

When Ms. Leder entered the division, there were three male lawyers (one a senior partner), five female paralegals, and four female secretaries. Considerable tensions existed among the three groups. At first, however, Ms. Leder found she could maintain fairly amicable relations with all parties. She recalls:

I showed a great deal of deference to the secretaries, not to be conniving or condescending, but because they worked hard, were good at what they did, and deserved respect. I anticipated problems with the paralegals, since they were all around my age and knew as much as I did about estates, but didn't earn anywhere near as much. But they didn't blame me for the situation, which, quite frankly, was a bad one.

New Administrative Duties

Although the secretaries remained under the supervision of one of the male lawyers, and clearly preferred it that way, Ms. Leder was assigned to oversee the functioning of the paralegals. The assignment came after tensions between the paralegals and the young male lawyer who had been supervising their work reached an intolerable level, which interfered with the operations of the office. Ms. Leder took a cautious approach to her assignment:

I made it clear to the paralegal staff that I felt I was working with them, and any oversight function was a formality. I was extremely lucky that they did not force me into a situation where I had to play the heavy. Instead, I became increasingly sympathetic with the causes of their discontent.

The paralegals, like the lawyers, kept time charts, recording every quarter-hour devoted to a client's business. The firm billed clients $20 for every hour spent by a paralegal, and $75 per hour for the lawyers' time. In addition, there were minimum fee schedules which the firm charged for such services as drawing up a will. During Ms. Leder's first week of supervision, a paralegal approached her and said:

I don't know if you realize this, but we paralegals are under a good deal of pressure to overestimate our time so that the firm can justify its fee schedule. When the client gets his bill, my signature is on that time chart, and I don't like it when the hours are inflated. If the firm feels its fees are fair, then it should have the integrity to charge them without asking me to lie. For $9,500 a year, I figure I'm getting paid too little as it is, without being asked to compromise my honesty.

Ms. Leder was appalled by this revelation, since she herself had never been pressured to inflate her time chart hours.

She soon became conscious of another major complaint of the paralegal staff. Although often a paralegal would do all the work on a will or trust, the lawyers alone met with the clients. The time a lawyer would spend with the client usually decreased proportionately with the client's wealth. One paralegal complained to Ms. Leder:

There's one male lawyer in particular who takes very poor background material when he sees a client is not wealthy. He often misses a pertinent fact that could save the person money, which means I'm not doing as good a service for the client as I might be. But the firm's policies prohibit me from contacting the person myself for further details. It's almost as if the firm is keeping us hidden in the closet, afraid to admit how much of the work we do around here.

But the chief complaint of the paralegals was a financial one. Observed one paralegal:

I was a math major, which is why I'm so good at administering estates. Now, a little elementary school arithmetic says that at $20 an hour, billing a minimum of thirty hours a week (and I usually bill more), I bring in $600 a week, or $30,000 a year working fifty weeks. Now I don't happen to think I'm worth that much, but I'm sure worth more than $9,500 a year. I feel a certain sympathy for the client— we're both being ripped off.

Attempts at Direct Intervention

Ms. Leder, distressed over the dissatisfaction of the paralegals, made an appointment for herself and the senior paralegal to confer with the senior partner in the estates and trusts division, Mr. Barnes. Both Ms. Leder and the paralegal outlined the basis of the complaints for Mr. Barnes, who listened silently. After the explanation, Mr. Barnes thanked the paralegal, and then asked Ms. Leder to remain in his office for a moment. The following conversation ensued:

Mr. Barnes: This meeting was totally inappropriate and certainly not constructive, Miss Leder. While it is not your position to shape personnel policy, I would have been willing to discuss this matter with you in private, had I known you were so upset about it.

Ms. Leder: It's my understanding that the paralegals have spoken to you before.

Mr. Barnes: Yes, they have.

Ms. Leder: But their salaries remain inadequate. And considering the amount of revenue they bring in . . . .

Mr. Barnes: You're new with the firm and there are things about this situation which you don't understand.

Ms. Leder: Such as?

Mr. Barnes: If we were to greatly raise the paralegals' salary range, the girls in the secretarial pool would be very upset. And the paralegals are limited in what they can do.

Ms. Leder: I feel there's an element of sex discrimination involved. After all, none of the paralegals are men.

Mr. Barnes: I'm sorry that you feel that way, but you're wrong. And you've made the situation much worse by storming in and interfering prematurely. Frankly, I think you are out of line. Perhaps you were just trying to be helpful to the women of our paralegal staff, and perhaps you identify with them too strongly. But you're way out of line, Miss Leder.

News of Ms. Leder's meeting with Mr. Barnes reached the male lawyer who had previously supervised the paralegals, and he became even more antagonistic to Ms. Leder and the paralegals. Tensions between the paralegal staff and other employees heightened as the paralegals became more insistent in their demands, and, well aware of the country-wide shortage of paralegals, threatened to resign en masse. Meanwhile, Ms. Leder told a friend:

I'm not positive now I was right to approach it the way I did. But I'm convinced that the paralegals have a good case, and now that I'm in the fray, I'm not going to back down. That just wouldn't be fair to the paralegals. Things are very tense around the office. It's an unpleasant working situation, and one of the paralegals got so demoralized over her isolation from the rest of the firm, that she resigned. And who knows what my future in the firm is now.

At present, Mr. Barnes and the other senior partners have officially taken a revision of the paralegal wage scale "under consideration."

II
READINGS

14
Government in the Lead

MICHAEL H. MOSKOW

Discrimination in employment by federal government contractors and subcontractors because of race, color, sex, or national origin was prohibited by Executive Order 11246, as amended by Executive Order 11375. Under this order, the Office of Federal Contract Compliance was established within the Department of Labor to administer its provisions and to coordinate the activities of all federal contracting agencies. My discussion will cover the activities of the Office of Federal Contract Compliance, and I will generalize a bit about some of the parallels and contrasts between problems of minorities and problems of women.

The United States government purchases about $70 billion worth of goods and services each year from firms that employ an estimated one-third of the labor force, including all of the country's large employers. These are the contractors covered by the compliance program. For example, if we look at the banking industry, we find that the program covers all banks insured by the Federal Deposit Insurance Corporation, all banks that sell and redeem savings bonds, and all banks that have federal funds on deposit—and that virtually exhausts the banks in the United States.

The compliance program is very important because it gives the federal government immediate and powerful leverage to discourage discrimination in employment. There are certain procedures that have been established to use this leverage—such as conciliation, show-cause hearings, and consultations—but ultimately the federal government has the

Originally published in *Corporate Lib: Women's Challenge to Management*, edited by Eli Ginzberg and Alice M. Yohalem (Baltimore and London: The Johns Hopkins University Press), pp. 125–32. Copyright © 1973 by The Johns Hopkins University Press.

power to refuse to do business with someone. It can cancel, terminate, or suspend existing contracts, or it can bar a contractor from receiving future government contracts. These are very powerful economic weapons to discourage employers from discrimination and to encourage them to take affirmative action to employ minorities and women.

The Office of Federal Contract Compliance is a unique organization in the federal government. The government could have organized all persons involved in federal contract compliance into one agency which would have dealt with all contractors and subcontractors. Instead, it was thought that more effective results would be obtained if compliance officers were part of the contracting agencies themselves, so that they would work as a part of the regular contracting process. The only exception is in the case of universities with federal contracts whose compliance is supervised by the Department of Health, Education and Welfare, regardless of the contracting agency.

The bulk of the compliance staff, then, is in the contracting agencies. The Office of Federal Contract Compliance is responsible for coordination of contracting agency activity, for issuing rules and regulations, and for monitoring the contracting agencies and the compliance officers. From our point of view, this division of responsibility makes much more sense than having one central agency, since it permits the question of equal employment opportunity to be considered as part of the entire contracting process.

Here are some figures that give an idea of the magnitude and growth of this program. In fiscal 1969, the Office of Federal Contract Compliance had only 26 people on its staff, and a budget of $600,000. This fiscal year the staff has risen to 119 people and the budget is $2,500,000. In the contracting agencies, in fiscal year 1970, there were 643 people and a budget of $7,000,000 and this fiscal year there will probably be over 1,500 people and a budget of $21,000,000.

Order Number 4 was issued by the Department of Labor to delineate the criteria to be used by federal contractors in developing plans of affirmative action to increase employment opportunities for minorities. Affirmative action requires the government contractor to go beyond refraining from employment discrimination. The contractor is required, as part of the contracting process, to analyze his work force and to determine whether there are deficiencies in the utilization of minorities. If there are deficiencies, the contractor then must formulate written corrective measures, including goals, timetables, and a plan of action for their elimination. These written corrective measures are required to be established for each job classification. Together, they comprise the contractor's affirmative action plan.

Generally, a "job classification" is a job for which the wages, functions, and opportunities are the same. If several jobs are related in these respects, they can be combined into a single job classification for which one set of goals and timetables is sufficient. If they are not so related, there must be separate goals.

The contractor's affirmative action plan is kept on file and it is subject to periodic review by the compliance agencies. The Office of Federal Contract Compliance has developed an analysis form, called form A, which the contractors use to expedite their analysis of their work force. This will also provide a data base for use in measuring overall progress or lack of progress.

In 1970, certain guidelines were issued to cover sex discrimination. These guidelines were a stopgap measure to make the commitment of the federal government to equal employment opportunity apparent, while buying time in which to develop a detailed affirmative action program for the employment of women.

According to the guidelines, employers with women employees have to provide them with various facilities, such as locker rooms and rest rooms, and cannot refuse to hire women on the basis of the nonavailability of these facilities. A second guideline stipulates that employers cannot refuse to hire women because of restrictions existing in the so-called state protective laws. The federal government regards all these laws as preempted. Third, employers must make certain accommodations for female employees, such as allowing a reasonable period of leave for childbearing.

A revised version of Order Number 4 was issued in December 1971, presenting criteria for the utilization of female workers, since the original order had applied only to minorities. In effect, the revision extended the mandate for affirmative action to women. This revision was developed after consultation with employers, women's groups, compliance agencies, minority groups, etc., and it tailored the principles and procedures dealing with the underutilization of minorities to the problems of the underutilization of women.

Contractors are required to revise any existing written affirmative action programs to include changes embodied in the order. They are also required to communicate to employees and to prospective employees the existence of their affirmative action programs and to make available the essential elements of their programs to allow the employees and prospective employees to avail themselves of the benefits.

When a contractor undertakes an analysis of his work force, Order Number 4 requires that he take the following criteria into consideration in determining female utilization.

First, he must consider the size of the female unemployment force in the labor area surrounding the facility. Second, he must look at the percentage of the female work force as compared to the total work force in the immediate labor market area. Third, he must consider the general availability of women having requisite skills in the immediate labor area. Fourth, he must ascertain the availability of women having requisite skills in an area in which the contractor could reasonably recruit, outside of his immediate labor market area.

Next, he should inquire into the availability of women seeking employment in his labor or recruitment area. He must also note the availability of promotable *and* transferable female employees within his own organization. He should have some idea of the anticipated expansion, contraction, and turnover of the work force—its growth or lack of growth. Finally, the existence of training institutions capable of training persons to develop the requisite skills and the degree of training which the contractor is reasonably able to undertake as a means of making all job classes available to women are important considerations. The contractor then must arrive at goals and timetables for the employment of women, based on these criteria.

The criteria for women are similar to those for minorities, modified to meet the particular problems attendant to sex discrimination. Where deficiencies are found, the contractor is required to establish separate goals and timetables for women and separate goals and timetables for minorities. The order provides that if it comes to the attention of the director of the Office of Federal Contract Compliance, or the compliance agencies, that there is a substantial disparity in the participation of different minority groups, then separate goals and timetables can be required for each of those minority groups, such as for Spanish-Americans, for Indians, or for Orientals. If substantial disparities are found in the employment of men and women of a particular minority group, separate goals and timetables can be required for males and females of those groups. We plan to monitor these figures for minority and sex subgroups very closely to insure that problem subgroups are separately treated.

In terms of implementation, a search for evidence of sex discrimination is included as part of the general compliance review that is made of a contractor. The person making the review looks at the distribution of the work force by sex as well as by race, religion, and national origin.

The general compliance review is automatically conducted for any supply contractor with a contract of more than a million dollars before the contract is awarded. Other contractors are chosen for a general compliance review based on apparent underutilization of minorities or women revealed in part by the Equal Employment Opportunity Commission annual compliance reports. Specific individual complaints are referred to the EEOC for investigation.

To give some idea of the number of general compliance reviews, in fiscal 1969 there were approximately 8,000 of these reviews. In this fiscal year we estimate that about 44,000 general compliance reviews will be completed. Next year we expect that number to increase to about 60,000. In our potential universe there are probably 250,000 contractors.

My own view is that Revised Order Number 4 represents a very significant change in public policy. No longer are we simply going on record against sex discrimination, although that was certainly a necessary preliminary step. Now we are requiring tangible evidence that meaningful steps are being taken to improve the employment prospects of women. This order goes beyond merely prohibiting discrimination against women to stimulating the recruitment of women. The great strength of the order is in the use of the federal government's compliance apparatus to put some teeth into the effort.

It will no longer be sufficient for a government contractor merely to refrain from overt acts of discrimination against women. Instead, he must present evidence that he has made a viable plan for finding and employing women who are potentially qualified for his work force.

There are parallels and contrasts between public policy regarding discrimination against minorities and against women. Let us look at some of the parallels. First, the obvious similarity is that the provisions of the Executive Order and of Order Number 4 now apply both to minorities and to females. Another parallel is that mere enforcement of equal pay for equal work will not suffice to bring about equality of opportunity for either group. Women, like blacks and other minorities, suffer not only from low wage rates relative to others in the same job but also from being denied entry into prestigious, well-paid, and challenging occupations. Both groups suffer from unequal opportunities for advancement and promotion, which means that an activist policy requiring affirmative action is a necessity.

Let me mention two contrasts between the situations of women and minorities. In the past, the status and income available to a married woman has depended primarily on the success of her husband, and she has found it in her interest to support his cause, although this may conflict with her own career interests. I do not think that minorities find it in their interest to support the interests of whites in that way.

The primacy of the husband's career interests operates as a constraint on the equal opportunity movement, as many married women are content either to play the traditional role of the housewife or to engage in labor market activity from a disadvantaged position. However, both male and female attitudes toward the appropriate role of married women are changing rapidly; over time this voluntary barrier to equal opportunity may be lifted.

Another difference between women and minorities is that there is really no approximation among the latter of the particular situation resulting from childbearing. Clearly, here is another area where attitudes are changing on the part of both men and women. Nevertheless, childbearing often continues to involve a long interruption in the work experience of women. By long interruption, I do not mean a month or two month's leave, but five years or more, until the children are in school.

When the female is off the job for five years, her male counterpart is on the job. He is learning and building up human capital, as the economists, would say. When she returns after a five-year break in her employment, the woman will clearly be at a disadvantage. She is not going to have the same skills or the capital that he will have built up in that five-year period.

This has an important policy implication. If that type of break in the career of a female is to be eliminated or greatly reduced, is the development of improved day care facilities on a massive scale a prerequisite? We have already seen some steps in this direction. An attempt was made in the last session of Congress to pass a child development bill which would subsidize the child care expenses of poor and near-poor women. Another start in this direction is the proposed Family Assistance Plan. Here, child care would be provided specifically to facilitate the employment of welfare mothers in an attempt to help them leave the welfare rolls. It is a job-oriented type of child care service.

Both the extent and the type of child care to be provided for poor women are still under debate at this time. I mention it because I think it is one policy that attempts to ease the entry of women into the work force on a large scale.

Hopefully, the emphasis on affirmative action will facilitate the achievement of equal employment opportunity for women. In the battle against job discrimination, the compliance program of the federal government should be an effective complement to existing legislation. The compliance weapon enables us to reach about one-third of the U.S. labor force. Although it cannot have an immediate impact on the entire labor force, we believe that this effort will have a substantial impact and will significantly advance the equal opportunity movement.

15

U.S. Laws against Discrimination on the Job*

ASSOCIATION OF AMERICAN COLLEGES

	Executive Order 11246 as amended by 11375	Title VII of the Civil Rights Act of 1964 as amended by the Equal Employment Opportunity Act of 1972	Equal Pay Act of 1963 as amended by the Education Amendments of 1972 (Higher Education Act)
Effective date	Oct. 13, 1968	March 24, 1972 (July 1965 for non-professional workers.) (Employers with 15-24 employees were not covered until March 24, 1973.)	July 1, 1972 (June 1964 for non-professional workers.)
Which employers are covered?	All employers with federal contracts of over $10,000.[5]	All employers with 15 or more employees.	Most employers.[8]
What is prohibited?[1]	Discrimination in employment (including hiring, upgrading, salaries, fringe benefits, training, and other conditions of employment) on the basis of race, color, religion, national origin, or sex. Covers all employees.	Discrimination in employment (including hiring, upgrading, salaries, fringe benefits, training, and other conditions of employment) on the basis of race, color, religion, national origin, or sex. Covers all employees.	Discrimination in salaries (including almost all fringe benefits) on the basis of sex. Covers all employees.

*Prepared by Project on the Status and Education of Women, Association of American Colleges, 1818 "R" Street, N.W., Washington, D.C. 20009.

Exemptions from coverage	None.	Religious institutions are exempt with respect to the employ- ment of individuals of a particular *religion or religious order* (includ- ing those limited to one sex) to perform work for that institution. (Such institutions are not exempt from the prohibition of discrimi- nation based on sex, color, and national origin.)	Some retail and service establishments, certain seasonal establish- ments, some farm workers, all household employees.[8]
Who enforces the provisions?	Office of Federal Contract Compliance (OFCC) of the Depart- ment of Labor has policy responsibility and oversees federal agency enforcement programs. OFCC has designated agencies that control grants and contracts as Com- pliance Agencies to enforce the Executive Order and to conduct reviews in various in- dustries.	Equal Employment Opportunity Com- mission (EEOC).[6]	Wage and Hour Divi- sion of the Employ- ment Standards Administration of the Department of Labor.
How is a complaint made?	By letter to OFCC.	By a sworn complaint form, obtainable from EEOC.	By letter, phone call, or in person to the Wage and Hour Division of- fice.
Can complaints of a pattern of discrimi- nation be made as well as individual complaints?	Yes. However, indi- vidual complaints are referred to EEOC.	Yes.	Yes.
Who can make a complaint?[2]	Individuals and/or or- ganizations on own be- half or on behalf of ag- grieved employee(s) or applicant(s).	Individuals and/or or- ganizations on own be- half or on behalf of ag- grieved employee(s) or applicant(s). Members of the commission may also file charges.	Individuals and/or or- ganizations on own be- half or on behalf of ag- grieved employee(s).

Time limit for filing complaints?[3]	180 days.	180 days.	No official limit, but recovery of back wages is limited by statute of limitations to two years for a nonwillful violation and three years for a willful violation.
Can investigations be made without complaints?	Yes. Government can conduct periodic reviews without a reported violation, as well as in response to complaints. Pre-award reviews are mandatory for contracts over $1,000,000.	No. Government can conduct investigations only if charges have been filed.	Yes. Government can conduct periodic reviews without a reported violation as well as in response to complaints.
Can the entire establishment be reviewed?	Yes. The Compliance Agency may investigate part or all of an establishment.	Yes. EEOC may investigate part or all of an establishment.	Yes. Usually the Wage-Hour Division reviews the entire establishment.
Record keeping requirements and government access to records	Employer must keep and preserve specified records relevant to the determination of whether violations have occured. Government is empowered to review all relevant records.	Employer must keep and preserve specified records relevant to the determination of whether violations have occured. Government is empowered to review all relevant records.	Employer must keep and preserve specified records relevant to the determination of whether violations have occurred. Government is empowered to review all relevant records.
Enforcement power and sanctions	Government may delay new contracts, revoke current contracts, and debar employers from eligibility for future contracts.	If attempts at conciliation fail, EEOC or the U.S. Attorney General may file suit.[7] Aggrieved individuals may also initiate suits. Court may enjoin respondent from engaging in unlawful behavior, order appropriate affirmative action, order reinstatement of employees, award back pay.	If voluntary compliance fails,[9] Secretary of Labor may file suit. Aggrieved individuals may initiate suits when Department of Labor has not done so. Court may enjoin respondent from engaging in unlawful behavior, order salary raises and back pay, and assess interest.
Can back pay be awarded?[4]	Yes. OFCC will seek back pay only for employees who were not previously protected by other laws allowing back pay.	Yes. For up to two years prior to filing charges with EEOC.	Yes. For up to two years for a nonwillful violation and three years for a willful violation.

Affirmative action requirements *(There are no restrictions against action which is non-preferential)*	Affirmative action plans (including numerical goals and timetables) are required of all contractors with contracts of $50,000 or more and 50 or more employees.	Affirmative action is not required unless charges have been filed, in which case it may be included in conciliation agreement or be ordered by the court.	Affirmative action, other than salary increases and back pay, is not required.
Coverage of labor organizations	Any agreement the contractor may have with a labor organization cannot be in conflict with the contractor's affirmative action commitment.	Labor organizations are subject to the same requirements and sanctions as employers.	Labor organizations are prohibited from causing or attempting to cause an employer to discriminate on the basis of sex. Complaints may be made and suits brought against these organizations.
Is harrassment prohibited?	Employers are prohibited from discharging or discriminating against any employee or applicant for employment because he/she has made a complaint, assisted with an investigation or instituted proceedings.	Employers are prohibited from discharging or discriminating against any employee or applicant for employment because he/she has made a complaint, assisted with an investigation or instituted proceedings.	Employers are prohibited from discharging or discriminating against any employee because he/she has made a complaint, assisted with an investigation or instituted proceedings.
Notification of complaints	Notification of complaints has been erratic in the past.	EEOC notifies employers of complaints within 10 days.	Complaint procedure is very informal. Employer under review may or may not know that a violation has been reported.
Confidentiality of names	Individual complainant's name is usually given to the employer. Investigation findings are kept confidential by government, but can be revealed by the employer. Policy concerning government disclosure concerning investigations and complaints has not yet been issued. The aggrieved party and respondent are not bound by the confidentiality requirement.	Individual complainant's name is divulged when an investigation is made. Charges are not made public by EEOC, nor can any of its efforts during the conciliation process be made public by the commission or its employees. If court action becomes necessary, the identity of the parties involved becomes a matter of public record. The aggrieved party and respondent are not bound by the confidentiality requirement.	The identity of a complainant, as well as the employer (and union, if involved), is kept in strict confidence.[10] If court action becomes necessary, the identity of the parties involved becomes a matter of public record. The aggrieved party and respondent are not bound by the confidentiality requirement.

For further information, contact	Office of Federal Compliance Employment Standards Administration Department of Labor Washington, D.C. 20210 or Regional DOL Office	Equal Employment Opportunity Commission 1800 G Street, N.W. Washington, D.C. 20506 or Regional EEOC Office	Wage and Hour Division Employment Standards Administration Department of Labor Washington, D.C. 20210, or Field, Area, or Regional Wage and Hour office

(A similar chart, "Federal Laws and Regulations Concerning Sex Discrimination in Educational Institutions," is available from the Office for Civil Rights, HEW, Washington, D.C. 20201.)

1. A bona fide seniority or merit system is permitted under all legislation, provided the system is not discriminatory on the basis of sex or any other prohibited ground.

2. There are no restrictions against making a complaint under more than one antidiscrimination law at the same time.

3. This time limit refers to the time between an alleged discriminatory act and when a complaint is made. In general, however, the time limit is interpreted liberally when a continuing practice of discrimination is being challenged, rather than a single, isolated discriminatory act.

4. Back pay cannot be awarded prior to the effective date of the legislation.

Executive Order 11246 as amended by 11375:

5. The definition of "contract" is very broad and is interpreted to cover all government contracts (even if nominally entitled "grants") which involve a benefit to the federal government.

Title VII of the Civil Rights Act of 1964 as amended by the Equal Employment Opportunity Act

6. In certain states that have fair employment laws with prohibitions similar to those of Title VII, EEOC automatically defers investigation of charges to the state agency for 60 days. (At the end of this period, EEOC will handle the charges unless the state is actively pursuing the case. About 85 percent of deferred cases return to EEOC for processing after deferral).

7. Due to an ambiguity in the law as it relates to public institutions, it is not yet clear whether EEOC *or* the Attorney General will file suit in all situations which involve public institutions.

Equal Pay Act of 1963 as amended by the Education Amendments of 1972 (Higher Education Act)

8. The following are exempted from coverage of the Equal Pay Act: (a) employees of a retail or service establishment which makes most of its sales within an individual state and the volume of whose annual sales is less than $250,000 (covered hospitals, nursing homes, laundries, dry cleaners, and educational institutions are not subject, however, to this exemption); (b) employees of certain seasonal amusement or recreational establishments, motion picture theaters and certain small newspapers, and switchboard operators of telephone companies which have fewer than 750 telephones; (c) farm workers employed on small farms; (d) household employees; (e) students employed in educational institutions receiving federal funding.

9. Over 95 percent of all Equal Pay investigations are resolved through voluntary compliance.

10. Unless court action is necessary, the name of the parties need not be revealed. The identity of a complainant or a person furnishing information is never revealed without that person's consent.

16
Guidelines on Discrimination Because of Sex*

ABSTRACT

This is a reprint of Guidelines on Discrimination Because of Sex recently issued by the U.S. Equal Employment Opportunity Commission (EEOC). It is a clearly written document detailing what does and does not constitute legal discrimination in hiring, provision of benefits, and other considerations relating to employment. It should be carefully read by all prospective managers.

Authority: The provisions of this Part 1604 are issued under Section 713(b), 78 Stat. 265, 42 U.S.C., Sec. 2000e-12.

Source: The provisions of this Part 1604 appear at 37 F.R. 6835, April 5, 1972, unless otherwise noted.

By virtue of the authority vested in it by section 713(b) of Title VII of the Civil Rights Act of 1964, 42 U.S.C., section 2000e-12, 78 Stat. 265, the

*U.S. Gov't GPO 940-312

Equal Employment Opportunity Commission hereby revises Title 29, Chapter XIV, § 1604 of the Code of Federal Regulations.

These Guidelines on Discrimination Because of Sex supersede and enlarge upon the Guidelines on Discrimination Because of Sex, issued by the Equal Employment Opportunity Commission on December 2, 1965, and all amendments thereto. Because the material herein is interpretive in nature, the provisions of the Administrative Procedure Act (5 U.S.C. 553) requiring notice of proposed rule making, opportunity for public participation, and delay in effective data are inapplicable. The Guidelines shall be applicable to charges and cases presently pending or hereafter filed with the Commission.

Section 1604.1   General Principles.

(a)   References to "employer" or "employers" in Part 1604 state principles that are applicable not only to employers, but also to labor organizations and to employment agencies insofar as their action or inaction may adversely affect employment opportunities.

(b)   To the extent that the views expressed in prior Commission pronouncements are inconsistent with the views expressed herein, such prior views are hereby overruled.

(c)   The Commission will continue to consider particular problems relating to sex discrimination on a case-by-case basis.

Section 1604.2   Sex as a Bona Fide Occupational Qualification.

(a)   The Commission believes that the bona fide occupational qualification exception as to sex should be interpreted narrowly. Labels—"Men's jobs" and "Women's jobs"—tend to deny employment opportunities unnecessarily to one sex or the other.

(1)   The Commission will find that the following situations do not warrant the application of the bona fide occupational qualification exception:

(i)   The refusal to hire a woman because of her sex based on assumptions of the comparative employment characteristics of women in general. For example, the assumption that the turnover rate among women is higher than among men.

(ii)   The refusal to hire an individual based on stereotyped characterizations of the sexes. Such stereotypes include, for example, that men are less capable of assembling intricate equipment; that women are less capable of aggressive salesmanship. The principle of non-discrimination requires that individuals be considered on the basis of individual capacities and not on the basis of any characteristics generally attributed to the group.

(iii)   The refusal to hire an individual because of the preferences of coworkers, the employer, clients or customers except as covered specifically in subparagraph (2) of this paragraph.

(2)   Where it is necessary for the purpose of authenticity or genuineness, the Commission will consider sex to be a bona fide occupational qualification, e.g., an actor or actress.

(b)   Effect of sex-oriented state employment legislation.

(1)   Many states have enacted laws or promulgated administrative regulations with respect to the employment of females. Among these laws are those which prohibit or limit the employment of females, e.g., the employment of females in certain occupations, in jobs requiring the lifting or carrying of weights exceeding certain prescribed limits, during certain hours of the night, for more than a specified number of hours per day or per week, and for certain periods of time before and after childbirth. The Commission has found that such laws and regulations do not take into account the capacities, preferences, and abilities of individual females and, therefore, discriminate on the basis of sex. The Commission has concluded that such laws and regulations conflict with and are superseded by Title VII of the Civil Rights Act of 1964. Accordingly, such laws will not be considered a defense to an otherwise established unlawful employment practice or as a basis for the application of the bona fide occupational qualification exception.

(2)   The Commission has concluded that state laws and regulations which discriminate on the basis of sex with regard to the employment of minors are in conflict with and are superseded by Title VII to the extent that such laws are more restrictive for one sex. Accordingly, restrictions on the employment of minors of one sex over and above those imposed on minors of the other sex will not be considered a defense to an otherwise established unlawful employment practice or as a basis for the application of the bona fide occupational qualification exception.

(3)   A number of states require that minimum wage and premium pay for overtime be provided for female employees. An employer will be deemed to have engaged in an unlawful employment practice if:

(i)   It refuses to hire or otherwise adversely affects the employment opportunities of female applicants or employees in order to avoid the payment of minimum wages or overtime pay required by state law; or

(ii)   It does not provide the same benefits for male employees.

(4)   As to other kinds of sex-oriented state employment laws, such as those requiring special rest and meal periods or physical facilities for women, provision of these benefits to one sex only will be a violation of Title VII. An employer will be deemed to have engaged in an unlawful employment practice if:

(i)   It refuses to hire or otherwise adversely affects the employment opportunities of female applicants or employees in order to avoid the provision of such benefits; or

(ii)   It does not provide the same benefits for male employees. If the employer can prove that business necessity precludes providing these benefits to both men and women, then the state law is in conflict with and superseded by Title VII as to this employer. In this situation, the employer shall not provide such benefits to members of either sex.

(5)   Some states require that separate restrooms be provided for employees of each sex. An employer will be deemed to have engaged in an unlawful employment practice if it refuses to hire or otherwise adversely affects the employment opportunities of applicants or employees in order to avoid the provision of such restrooms for persons of that sex.

Section 1604.3   Separate Lines of Progression and Seniority Systems

(a)   It is unlawful employment practice to classify a job as "male" or "female" or to maintain separate lines of progression or separate seniority lists based on sex where this would adversely affect any employee unless sex is a bona fide occupational qualification for that job. Accordingly, employment practices are unlawful which arbitrarily classify jobs so that:

(1)   A female is prohibited from applying for a job labeled "male," or for a job in a "male" line of progression and vice versa.

(2)   A male scheduled for layoff is prohibited from displacing a less senior female on a "female" seniority list; and vice versa.

(b)   A seniority system or line of progression which distinguishes between "light" and "heavy" jobs constitutes an unlawful employment practice if it operates as a disguised form of classification by sex, or creates unreasonable obstacles to the advancement by members of either sex into jobs which members of that sex would reasonably be expected to perform.

Section 1604.4   Discrimination Against Married Women

(a)   The Commission has determined that an employer's rule which forbids or restricts the employment of married women and which is not applicable to married men is a discrimination based on sex prohibited by Title VII of the Civil Rights Act. It does not seem to us relevant that the rule is not directed against all females, but only against married females, for so long as sex is a factor in the application of the rule, such application involves a discrimination based on sex.

(b)   It may be that under certain circumstances, such a rule could be justified within the meaning of Section 703(e)(1) of Title VII. We express no opinion on this question at this time except to point out that sex as a bona fide occupational qualification must be justified in terms of the peculiar requirements of the particular job and not on the basis of a general principle such as the desirability of spreading work.

Section 1604.5   Job Opportunities Advertising

It is a violation of Title VII for a help-wanted advertisement to indicate a preference, limitation, specification, or discrimination based on sex unless sex is a bona fide occupational qualification for the particular job involved. The placement of an advertisement in columns classified by publishers on the basis of sex, such as columns headed "Male" or "Female," will be considered an expression of a preference, limitation, specification, or discrimination based on sex.

Section 1604.6   Employment Agencies

(a)   Section 703(b) of the Civil Rights Act specifically states that it shall be unlawful for an employment agency to discriminate against any individual because of sex. The Commission has determined that private employment agencies which deal exclusively with one sex are engaged in an unlawful employment practice, except to the extent that such agencies limit their services to furnishing employees for particular jobs for which sex is a bona fide occupational qualification.

(b)   An employment agency that receives a job order containing an unlawful sex specification will share responsibility with the employer placing the job order if the agency fills the order knowing that the sex specification is not based upon a bona fide occupational qualification. However, an employment agency will not be deemed to be in violation of the law, regardless of the determination as to the employer, if the agency

does not have reason to believe that the employer's claim of bona fide occupational qualification is without substance and the agency makes and
maintains a written record available to the Commission of each such job
order. Such record shall include the name of the employer, the description of the job and the basis for the employer's claim of bona fide occupational qualification.

(c) It is the responsibility of employment agencies to keep informed
of opinions and decisions of the Commission on sex discrimination.

Section 1604.7   Pre-employment Inquiries as to Sex.

A pre-employment inquiry may ask "Male _____, Female _____"; or
"Mr. Mrs. Miss," provided that the inquiry is made in good faith for a
non-discriminatory purpose. Any pre-employment inquiry in connection with prospective employment which expresses directly or indirectly
any limitation, specification or discrimination as to sex shall be unlawful unless based upon a bona fide occupational qualification.

Section 1604.8   Relationship of Title VII to the Equal Pay Act

(a) The employee coverage of the prohibitions against discrimination
based on sex contained in Title VII is co-extensive with that of the other
prohibitions contained in Title VII and is not limited by Section 703(h) to
those employees covered by the Fair Labor Standards Act.

(b) By virtue of Section 703(h), a defense based on the Equal Pay Act
may be raised in a proceeding under Title VII.

(c) Where such a defense is raised the Commission will give appropriate consideration to the interpretations of the Administrator, Wage
and Hour Division, Department of Labor, but will not be bound thereby.

Section 1604.9   Fringe Benefits

(a) "Fringe benefits," as used herein, includes medical, hospital, accident, life insurance and retirement benefits; profit-sharing and bonus
plans; leave; and other terms, conditions, and privileges of employment.

(b) It shall be an unlawful employment practice for an employer to
discriminate between men and women with regard to fringe benefits.

(c) Where an employer conditions benefits available to employees
and their spouses and families on whether the employee is the "head of

the household" or "principle wage earner" in the family unit, the benefits tend to be available only to male employees and their families. Due to the fact that such conditioning discriminatorily affects the rights of women employees, and that "head of household" or "principal wage earner" status bears no relationship to job performance, benefits which are so conditioned will be found a *prima facie* violation of the prohibitions against sex discrimination contained in the Act.

(d)   It shall be an unlawful employment practice for an employer to make available benefits for the wives and families of male employees where the same benefits are not made available for the husbands and families of female employees; or to make available benefits for the wives of male employees which are not made available for female employees; or to make available benefits to the husbands of female employees which are not made available for male employees. An example of such an unlawful employment practice is a situation in which wives of male employees receive maternity benefits while female employees receive no such benefits.

(e)   It shall not be a defense under Title VII to a charge of sex discrimination in benefits that the cost of such benefits is greater with respect to one sex than the other.

(f)   It shall be an unlawful employment practice for an employer to have a pension or retirement plan which establishes different optional or compulsory retirement ages based on sex, or which differentiates in benefits on the basis of sex. A statement of the General Counsel of September 13, 1968, providing for a phasing out of differentials with regard to optional retirement age for certain incumbent employees, is hereby withdrawn.

Section 1604.10   Employment Policies Relating to Pregnancy and Childbirth

(a)   A written or unwritten employment policy or practice which excludes from employment applicants or employees because of pregnancy is in *prima facie* violation of Title VII.

(b)   Disabilities caused or contributed to by pregnancy, miscarriage, abortion, childbirth, and recovery therefrom are, for all job-related purposes, temporary disabilities and should be treated as such under any health or temporary disability insurance or sick leave plan available in connection with employment. Written and unwritten employment policies and practices involving matters such as the commencement and duration of leave, the availability of extensions, the accrual of seniority and other benefits and privileges, reinstatement, and payment under any health or temporary disability insurance or sick leave plan, formal or informal, shall be applied to disability due to pregnancy or childbirth on the same terms and conditions as they are applied to other temporary disabilities.

(c)   Where the termination of an employee who is temporarily disabled is caused by an employment policy under which insufficient or no leave is available, such a termination violates the Act if it has a disparate impact on employees of one sex and is not justified by business necessity.

17

The Sources
of Inequality

JUANITA KREPS

Inequality between the sexes is currently the source of so many inquiries that the researcher is being drowned in a mass of documentation. This complaint comes with ill grace, I realize, from one who has contributed to the statistical overload. Yet I do sense the need these papers express— the need to reach for perspective rather than for additional evidence of discrimination, to remind ourselves, once again, what it is we want to establish. It is said that Gertrude Stein, who was known to repeat herself occasionally, was still perplexed by it all when on her deathbed. With her remaining strength she inquired of her lifelong friend, Alice B. Toklas, "Alice, what's the answer?" After some thought, came the reply, "Gertrude, I don't know." And after another pause, Gertrude persisted, "Then, Alice, what is the question?"

What are the questions we are now raising? Are they the ones we ought to pursue under the rubric of "Women's Challenge to Management"? One might, incidentally, question whether women are in fact offering a challenge to the business world; our present job status in industry would certainly not seem to lend strength to any such call to arms. In any case, if we are to examine the poor showing of women in the higher ranks of American industry, we clearly do not need further data showing that we have had only limited access to these positions. Rather, we need to ask and keep asking why the access is so limited, or why, at least, women perceive it to be so limited. And we ought to raise a second, quite different set of questions: To what extent are women eager to move into the executive ranks given the demands of that lifestyle? Do the family commitments women have traditionally made allow them the luxury of such ambition? Are there prior, intrafamily decisions to resolve before married women can compete effectively for the most consuming and demanding careers?

By everyone's agreement, business leadership has been an exclusively male calling and women have not been invited, tolerated, or even seriously considered. It helps but little to note in passing that just as women have been excluded, so, too, have practically all men; only the most aggressive, or talented, or lucky, or well born—sometimes all of these—have made it to the top. Still, I stress this set of credentials, not to excuse a discriminatory system, but to remind ourselves that freedom of access is a necessary but not a sufficient condition for executive leadership.

Why have men in industry been reluctant to admit women into their higher ranks? Have the performances of those few women who have tried to climb the ladder been poor? Is the threat of her dropping out for childbearing and childrearing the major deterrent to placing a young woman in an executive training program?

The first question is one that industry itself has to answer, and there may be too few cases to permit generalization. In assessing the value of women's contribution to business, however, we must be aware of two tendencies that confuse the issue: one, a woman may handle a particular job differently from the way a man would, and since a male judgment is the one that prevails, she may be thought ineffective when she is merely different; and two, it is sometimes hard for men to admire in women the very qualities they find important in successful men. Although failure to gain the admiration of one's superior may not be the only deterrent to promotion, it is surely a powerful one.

In a deeper context, there is the basic question of how willing men are to have their male world invaded by women, just as in the past, housewives have often protested having their husbands underfoot in the kitchen. Erik Erikson suggests that

no doubt there exists among men an honest sense of wishing to save at whatever cost a sexual polarity, a vital tension and an essential difference which they fear may be lost in too much sameness, equality, and equivalence, or at any rate in too much self-conscious talk.[1]

This fear of sameness may plague women, but, I suspect, not many career-oriented women. Nor is it the case still, as it used to be, that women tend to equate achievement with loss of femininity; hence "in achievement-oriented situations, women will worry not only about failure, but about success."[2] A woman's wish to achieve, one recent study found, conflicts with her wish to avoid success, for "if she fails, she is not living up to her own standards of performance; if she succeeds, she is not living up to societal expectations about the female role."[3] I discount this thesis for the kind of women who aspire to management.

There is also the matter of women's dropping out of their jobs at the childbearing age, a common complaint of businesses which are reluctant to hire female managers or interns, for example. Here, the picture is changing significantly. Observe the pattern of female labor force participation, by age, for the last several decades (figure 1). In 1940, young women left their jobs to have children, and older women, who had done so earlier in their own lives, did not return to the work force. By 1950, however, some of those women who had left to have babies a decade earlier were going back to paying jobs. By 1960, the second peak in the labor force participation of women, by age, was slightly higher than the first; the labor force activity rate was higher for older women than for young. Still, there was a deep valley between the two peak rates. But ob-

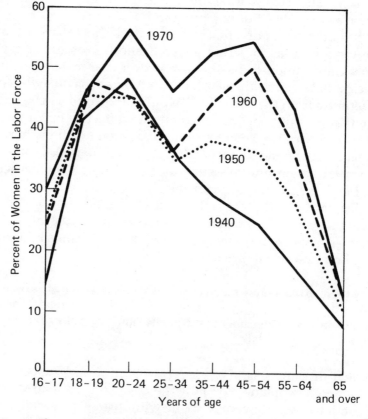

Source: *Monthly Labor Review* 93 (June, 1970), p. 11.

Figure 1.   Labor force participation rates of women by age, 1940–70.

serve, then, the 1970 profile. Not only does it indicate much higher work activity at all ages than in previous years; there is also a much less marked drop in the rate at the age of marriage and childbearing.

An important question occurs. To what extent will the cohort of females now in high school and college leave the labor force during their twenties? If they find it desirable (and possible, with the help of child care arrangements) to stay on the job, industry will not need to discount so heavily their probability of acquiring experience and knowledge, and hence will no longer have this reason to deny these women access to higher level positions. It seems likely that the worklife patterns of this new cohort of women, particularly those who are college educated, will conform much more nearly to the pattern men's worklives have assumed. Such a change would have great significance for industry and the professions.

To what extent is industry's unwillingness to hire women for the better jobs due to the fact that women don't have wives? Has it been true, as often alleged, that the executive's wife was hired, along with her husband, and that she, too, was expected to add her efforts to the company team? If so, has industry not been able to get much more for an executive salary than it first appears, namely, the supportive services, the community activities, and the corporate image building of the man's wife? And while these roles are perfectly acceptable ones for wives, would they not be unacceptable for husbands? In short, does industry not reason, and quite correctly, that it gets more for an executive salary paid to a man whose wife's services also come in the package, than it would gain by hiring a woman?

I think the plight of executive wives has been exaggerated but an interesting, somewhat related question, has to do with high income wives, in general. Why is there an inverse relationship between husbands' incomes and wives' labor force participation (figure 2)? Are the demands of the husband's job, as his income rises, such that the wife has little opportunity to build her own career? Or do these women prefer not to work, once family income is sufficiently high? The puzzle is all the more interesting, since these men are likely to be married to college graduates, and female college graduates' labor force rates are higher than those of high school graduates (figure 3).

What are the signs of improvement? For a bit of history, I refer you to the National Manpower Council's study in 1957 which reveals something of how far we have come, and how far we have yet to go. We note that it was in September, 1957, that a New York City newspaper reporter asked four people at random: "What would happen if all working wives gave up their jobs tomorrow?" A secretary said children would get more attention, resulting in less delinquency; in any event, husbands earned enough to support their families. A singer, also female, said that the ef-

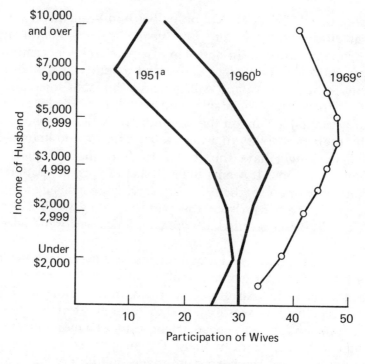

Figure 2.   Labor force participation of wives 1951, 1960, 1969 by income of husband.

fect would be to give better jobs to working girls who really needed them, since "the majority of married women who go to business do so to earn money for luxuries like mink stoles. . . ." A man from Brooklyn thought that in time it would mean higher wages for men. A male post office employee said it would result in a better home life for husband, wife, and family.[4]

At that time, a similar poll in any American city would probably have yielded similar results. The question is whether public endorsement of women's campaigns in the 1970s indicates any significant change in attitude. It is clear that large numbers of women have joined the protest, and it is significant that these are increasingly the young women, many of them still in school. The impact of these younger women on the woman worker a few years from now will surely be an important one. I personally fear that these younger members of the protest movement are somewhat naive in their perception of the opposition they will face from some quarters. Commenting on the attitudes revealed in the earlier inter-

views, Erwin Canham noted the problems ahead: "Look at the misconceptions; look at the jealousy toward married women on the part of the
interviewed females . . . ; the jealousy, possessiveness, and prejudice
on the part of men."[5]

At the family level, the constraints on women's upward movement in
the ranks of both industry and the professions are being eased by
reduced family size. The current societal goal of zero population growth
confirms youth's view that they should have, at most, two children, in
contrast to the grand design of the women of my generation, most of
whom were determined to have six. Fortunately, some of us lost sight of
the goal about halfway there. But certain family constraints remain much
the same. It is still true that the wife has little option as to the location of

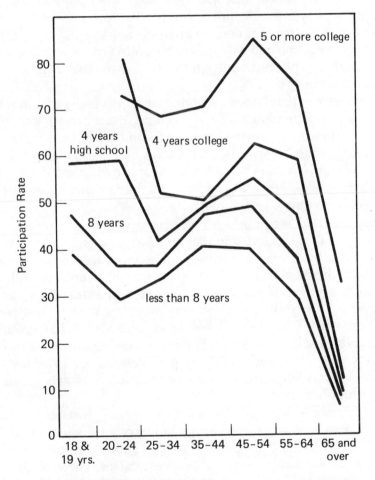

Source: Bureau of Labor Statistics

Figure 3. Labor force participation rates of women, by years of school completed and
age, 1968 (18 years and over).

her job, and this immobility is surely a prime factor in her limited career advancement. Some of the most exciting jobs in industry are those that demand geographical mobility, not just within this country, but to other nations as well. These avenues are simply not options for married women. Or, at least, business assumes that they are not, and rarely asks a woman whether she *can* move.

In time, a wife's job may become sufficiently important to the family to allow that job to take precedence over her husband's. But for now, the wife fits her career into a framework dominated by her husband's work and the needs of her children. These constraints are the fundamental ones on the supply side; they limit the time and attention she can devote to her career, the degree to which she can take advantage of career opportunities, and in the final analysis, her career aspirations. It is not surprising that women do not press harder for entry to the executive suite; would a woman not need to be single to have any realistic hopes of success? If this is true and women are becoming more ambitious, we may see a growth in spinsterhood. And in that case, will men accept single women as "normal?"

Whether or not they are so accepted, it seems likely that in the future more women will remain single, or seek divorces; careers will inevitably absorb the interests of many competent women who no longer need the financial support of husbands, and who are not particularly interested in having children. There is some evidence of growing social acceptance of unmarried females, and contraceptive methods make it unnecessary for these women to forego sexual relationships.

Among married women, who will nevertheless continue to include most women, it seems unlikely that marriage and childrearing will again assume the central role it assumed for women formerly. The working wife and mother is not a new development; on the contrary, nonworking wives are a product of modern technology and affluence. What we are concerned with here is, of course, not whether women will work, but what their work will be—at what level, and with what rewards, demands, and satisfactions. And what we are asking, on the *supply* side, is whether we want to reconsider male-female career priorities and intrafamily responsibilities in such a way as to accommodate greater career flexibility for both sexes.

What we are asking on the labor *demand* side is: What are the pressure points we can lean on, to challenge industry's traditionally antifemale bias with respect to the higher level jobs? It should be noted that in other sectors of the economy the same problem exists. The academic world, too, has "his" and "her" jobs, with females concentrated heavily in the lower ranks in all universities. So, too, has government; both academia and the government ought to be setting standards, not lowering them.

What are the things we ought to do? In directing our thoughts to specifics, I should like to stress two things we ought *not* to do. The first concerns research. We are looking for points of attack not just a basis for complaint—we know things are very bad. If we earn 59 (and not 58) percent of what men earn, we will scarcely notice the difference. My first curb, then, would be on narrowly based statistical inquiries; they are a waste of scarce resources. Phyllis Wallace's references to lifetime earnings is, of course, a different, and very important thrust. In teaching human capital investments, I am unable to compute the returns for women and am forced to talk only of men.

I would also banish from the media those writers who criticize women's seeming lack of professional ambition—criticism which, under close examination, usually emerges as praise. To writers, the preoccupation of the female with love and marriage is fully accepted. It is only when she displays "the old-style careerist's scorching ambition and hostility toward men"[6] that she has to explain herself. It is true, further, that many men and women resist taking women's new career interests seriously. No dinner party is now complete without a few derisive comments on women's ambitions to be stevedores or lumberjacks. I realize that members of both sexes are apprehensive, men perhaps more than women: "Where dominant identities depend on being dominant, it is hard to grant equality to the dominated."[7]

In a positive vein, what can be said? What, in addition to the recommendation that women go into the courts with cases of discrimination?

First, the notion of second careers for men as well as for career women seems quite appealing, since it would open up some good jobs at high levels, and condition us to think of new worklife patterns for both sexes.

Second, it is obvious we have to present some goals to top management: some numbers of women to be hired, or promoted. This will have to be done by personal contact, on a company by company basis, although in the universities we are getting a large assist from HEW.

Third, it is obvious that recruitment—much of it done on our campuses—has got to be rigged in such a way as to promote the selection of women. If I were running a placement office I would not allow inequitable interviewing arrangements, and I would keep very careful records on who hires women and for what jobs.

Fourth, I think we should never underestimate the power of women's threats. If you have ever faced an angry group of women, you know that it makes one very nervous. How can we get groups of women to act in such ways as to make corporations nervous? I should like us to use this method sparingly; but it can be used.

I am optimistic on the long-range future—if we can keep the pressure on—because I see so clearly how many light years ahead my own daughters are, beyond where I was when in college. For the immediate future, I am considerably less optimistic because the state of the economy is so uncertain. We pay a price for slowing down the economy. It is much easier to solve most problems of absorbing new groups into occupations and jobs on the upswing of business activity. And this we don't now have. Universities, under orders (more or less) to hire more women, can do so only if they are hiring somebody—and they are adding very few people.

I asked for no more research. But I would leave, in passing, a couple of questions that are general, framework sorts of questions—those that set the parameters of the problem. One of these has to do with the amount of work each of us is to do—can it be changed so more people work at good jobs, but each for fewer hours?

The other question has to do with the timing of work through the life cycle. It may be that we will make substantial progress in absorbing women into all levels of jobs only when we agree on a retiming of work for both sexes. For example, we now witness retirement as a relatively new life stage. Could we imagine periods of reeducation or sabbaticals, or just plain vacations—thereby spreading one's work differently? This would extend options, not only for new careers, but also for coming in and going out of jobs in accord with individual preferences—and would be infinitely preferable to taking our leisure in the form of unemployment or prevention of women from working.

I am not sure we all agree, quite yet, on how much flexibility and "sameness" we want. But I am sure that relatively few women will reach management's top levels under the constraints imposed by current expectations: those of the society, the family, and the woman herself.

Notes

1. Erik H. Erikson, "Inner and Outer Space: Reflections on Womanhood," *Daedalus*, 93 (Spring 1964): 584.

2. Joy D. Osofsky, "The Socialization and Education of American Women," in Ann F. Scott, *What is Happening to American Women* (Atlanta: Southern Newspaper Publishing Association Foundation, 1970), p. 37.

3. Matina Horner, "Women's Motive to Avoid Success," *Psychology Today*, 62 (November 1969): 36–38.

4. From Esther Lloyd-Jones, "Education for Reentry into the Labor Force," in National Manpower Council, *Work in the Lives of Married Women* (New York: Columbia University Press, 1958), pp. 27–40.

5. "Womanpower in Today's World," in ibid., p. 14.

6. Morton Hunt, *Her Infinite Variety* (New York: Harper & Row, 1962), p. 262.

7. Erikson, "Inner and Outer Space," p. 585. "And finally, where one feels exposed, threatened, or cornered, it is difficult to be judicious."

18
The Workplace Woman

HAROLD H. FRANK and KATHERINE HOOKS

ABSTRACT

Women have made remarkable gains toward that once elusive goal, equal opportunity with men. But although more women are finding that companies are receptive to changes in attitude and commitment, many others are taking legal action to correct patterns of discrimination. This article examines how the opportunities came about, the legal and attitudinal adjustments now in process, and the effects on the workplace of tomorrow.

The Workplace Woman: Who Is She?

In every industry, in every market, women now hold jobs their mothers could not have obtained. In contrast to her predecessor of the 1940s, who was usually young, unmarried, and childless, the present-day female worker is more likely to be a married mother of young children, or one between the ages of thirty-five and sixty-four whose children are grown. The number of working mothers is up nine-fold since 1940, and many are heads of households who must work to support their families. In addition, many women now work by choice, not out of economic necessity.

Since the late 1940s, the number of women in the work force has nearly quadrupled to thirty-four million. The demands of war brought a large number of women into the work force, but although "Rosie the Riveter" did a man's job in the factory and did it well, she went back home when the men returned.

The present high level of female participation in the work force is due to several factors: a rise in the market demand for labor, the advent of

163

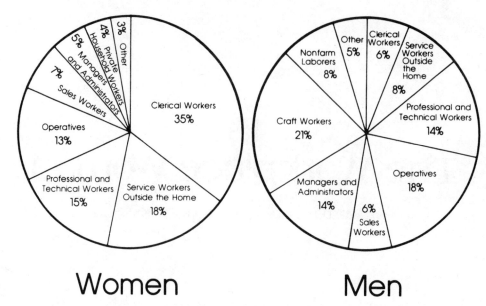

Women   **Men**

Figure 1.   Participation Rates of Men and Women in Basic Occupational Categories.

Source: United States Department of Labor, Employment Standards Administration, Women's Bureau, "Women Workers Today," July 1975, p. 5.

consumerism, the ready availability of labor-saving household devices, smaller families, and changing attitudes towards women with careers.[1]

The Workplace Woman: Where Is She?

While today's female worker is a more mobile—and more accepted—workplace member, she and her thirty-four million counterparts are still concentrated in the same low-paying, low-skilled job brackets women held thirty years ago. As Figure 1 shows, women occupy predominantly clerical and service positions: only 5 percent are managers and administrators compared with 14 percent of employed males.[2] The statistics on the workplace woman are deceptive: most professional females are teachers and nurses, and most female managers belong to the lower echelons.[3]

The wave of change has most deeply affected the movement of women into lower ranks of management and the professions. *Time* estimates that entering medical classes now are 25 percent female, compared to 11 percent in 1971, while law school representation is up from 8.5 to 20 percent. Females in graduate business schools have increased generally from 5 percent of total enrollment to 25 percent since 1971.[4] Possibly as high as 15 percent of those entering management are now female—a massive increase from over ten years ago. As for upper rank management, the once all-male bastions have a few more women, but the walls crumble slowly. Only 1 percent of top management is female; there may be as few as fifteen women (versus twenty-five hundred men) heading major corporations and earning more than $100,000.[5] The Census Bureau reports that women totaled 18.5 percent of all managers and administrators in 1974, up from 15.2 percent in 1958. Since it takes years to find, train, and promote people to executive positions, it is unlikely that these lopsided statistics for top leadership will change as rapidly as the ones for lower and middle management ranks in the coming decade.

The Workplace Woman: How She Got Here

The gains made by working women in mobility and legal rights required major shifts in public sentiment, shifts which began slowly almost 140 years ago. Then most women were legal chattel, with no right to keep their own earnings, control their own property, or make contracts. Beginning in 1839 in Mississippi, a wave of new laws granted married women these rights, but in reality the "emancipation" was illusory. Then came the suffrage movement which culminated in the right to vote for women. Like other movements, however, it was not strong enough to spread its liberating powers to other arenas. The impetus was gone. The Equal Rights Amendment to the Constitution, introduced over fifty years ago in Congress, lay untouched until its revival in the 1970s. A host of "sweatshop" reform laws were enacted in most states over the years, championed as "protective" legislation for women and children. Hindsight tells a clearer story: these laws had the effect of restricting the entry of women into "man's work." Women could not lift "excessive" weights (sometimes defined as more than twenty-five pounds, which most women lifted in household duties), or work "excessive" hours, or perform tasks deemed dangerous—like underground mining. Some of these laws were written or extended as late as the 1950s and '60s.[6]

By the time the 1960s had arrived, though, a new, more permanent shift in public opinion and political support appeared possible, and the latest round of legal improvements in the status of women was ushered in.

Throughout the decade of the 1960s, the myriad of new laws, new watchdog agencies, and favorable court rulings helped raise the upper bounds on careers of women. No longer was the female worker to be protected; her position was to be equalized. Some states repealed their protective legislation; some made efforts to outlaw traditional practices which were discriminatory. For example, Georgia in 1970 prohibited state agencies from denying employment to a woman solely because she was married to a man in the armed forces.[7] If states did not change discriminatory laws creating a discrepancy between state and federal statutes, court decisions and federal rulings overruled the state laws. Where protective legislation was beneficial—such as required rest periods during work—attempts were made to compel extension of those benefits to all employees. It has not always worked without legal prodding. Only in 1974, for example, did the Equal Employment Opportunity Commission require the granting of paternity leave requests for fathers raising children.[8] In 1975, several court decisions established the right of pregnant working women to claim a temporary disability leave.[9]

The new federal laws accorded female employees equal pay and equal access to jobs, seniority, promotion, apprenticeships, fringe benefits, and an unbiased employment testing procedure. These laws, however, have not been uniformly adopted in all states, so that some employees, primarily in small service and retail establishments, may still be unprotected today. The road to normalization of workplace conditions and to equality of opportunity for both sexes has been built piecemeal. The rights of the working woman today are based primarily on three milestones: The Equal Pay Act of 1963, Title VII of the Civil Rights Act of 1964, and Executive Order 11246 of 1965. The difficulties arising from attempts to interpret and apply these laws and the executive order are examined in the next three sections.[10]

The Equal Pay Act

This law's requirement is simple enough: the same pay for men and women doing the same work. A landmark decision by a federal court cleared up one interpretive problem: jobs of men and women do *not* have to be identical for them to be entitled to equal pay, where pay includes wages, overtime pay, and fringe benefits. Wages are *not* required to be equalized if the wage scale differences can be proved to be made "pursuant to (i) a seniority system; (ii) a merit system; (iii) a system which measures earnings by quantity or quality of production; or (iv) a differential based on any factor other than sex. . . ."[11]

Gaps in the coverage of this law have been closed through later measures. For example, although the act says unions shall not "cause or attempt to cause" an employer to violate the act, the Labor Department further declared that labor organizations "must refrain from strikes or picketing activities aimed at inducing an employer to institute or maintain a prohibited wage differential. . . ." Court cases have also overridden union contract provisions calling for lower wages for female employees.[12]

Workers who feel they have a complaint under the Equal Pay Act can write directly to the Wage and Hour Division, Employment Standards Administration, U.S. Department of Labor, Washington, D.C. 20210.

Title VII, Civil Rights Act of 1964

Title VII, as amended by the Equal Employment Opportunity Act of 1972, states that it is an unlawful employment practice for businesses to "fail or refuse to hire or to discharge any individual, or otherwise to discriminate against any individual with respect to his compensation, terms, conditions or privileges of employment because of such individual's race, color, religion, sex, or national origin. . . ." This act has extremely broad coverage and has had tremendous impact on the conduct of American businesses with respect to personnel policies, or the lack of them. Title VII is enforced by the Equal Employment Opportunity Commission (EEOC), 1800 G Street NW., Washington, D.C. 20506. The EEOC's "Guidelines On Discrimination Because of Sex," reprinted elsewhere in this book, provides the agency's clout. While at first the EEOC moved cautiously, it has since tightened up several ambiguities through its guidelines. It is quite difficult now for a firm to prove that a discriminatory employment practice is justifiably based on a "bona fide occupational qualification" if that qualification is gender alone. The commission also decreed that most state protective legislation cannot supersede the Civil Rights Act.

Numerous provisions of Title VII have been challenged through court proceedings. The initial thrust of the act was in race discrimination proceedings. By the 1970s, the United States Supreme Court had signalled its intent to look to the prior discriminatory practices of American businesses. The Court said Congress had mandated "the removal of artificial, arbitrary and unnecessary barriers of employment when the barriers operate invidiously to discriminate on the basis of racial or other impermissible classifications."[13]

Job classifications have often been made different for men and women where in reality the job itself was the same. In late 1973, for example, a U.S. district court found Northwest Airlines guilty of sex discrimination against stewardesses. In a class action suit, eighteen hundred stewardesses charged that while they performed the same job as pursers, they received less pay and were not promoted equally. They also charged they were denied the same quality of lodgings and were subjected to different requirements of appearance.[14]

Arbitrary personnel standards were reviewed by the Supreme Court in 1974, when it ruled in two cases that legislation cannot set a time for pregnant teachers to quit or to return to the classroom.[15] Smoothing out fringe benefit disparities has occupied much court time. In early 1976, Detroit's Wayne State University asked a federal panel to decide whether it should follow an EEOC ruling or a Labor Department edict on equalizing the university's pension benefits. The college was charged with bias against women in 1973 and estimates it would cost well over a million dollars to set up equal pension plans.[16]

Executive Order 11246

Compliance with this presidential order banning discrimination by contractors with federal contracts is assured by the threat of losing the government's business. The Office of Federal Contract Compliance (OFCC) of the U.S. Department of Labor implements the order, which requires contractors to set written goals and timetables for recruiting, hiring, training, and upgrading minorities and women. Complaints under the order can be directed to the Office of Federal Contract Compliance, Employment Standards Administration, U.S. Department of Labor, Washington, D.C. 20210. OFCC sex discrimination guidelines provide employment guards similar to those spelled out under Title VII. Female employees are advised by the Department of Labor (both EEOC and OFCC) that they have a right to complain if:

—an employer's advertisement for employees carries a sex label
—an employer refuses to let you file an application but accepts others
—a union or an employment agency refuses to refer you to job openings
—you are fired or laid off without cause
—you are passed over for promotion for which you are qualified
—you are paid less than others for comparable work
—you are placed in a segregated seniority line
—you are left out of training or apprenticeship programs.[17]

The Workplace Woman: Upward Visions

To the average female factory, clerical, or service worker, the best glimpse of brighter horizons has come from two sources: the "affirmative action" plans and court-ordered back-pay awards to settle former discriminatory practice lawsuits. Such retroactive awards to hundreds of women at a time are proving extraordinarily expensive, and this is making an indelible impression upon American corporations. Even though the laws discussed above gave some female employees greater opportunities, most businesses were not at first committing themselves to wholesale policy changes to advance women workers. But when American Telephone & Telegraph Co. agreed in 1973 to pay an overwhelming $50 million to compensate its female employees for past discrimination, two things happened: the business world took note and hurried to alter its employment practices, and the number of lawsuits alleging sex bias skyrocketed.[18] This trend is not expected to abate, because in June of 1975 the Supreme Court strongly endorsed the use of back-pay awards as a means of erasing the effects of prior job discrimination.[19] In 1970, just thirty-five hundred charges of sex discrimination were filed with the Equal Employment Opportunity Commission; by the first half of 1975, the number was up to twenty-two thousand, and the era of the class action lawsuit had arrived.[20]

The other effective tool has been the affirmative action plans required by the executive order. This has precipitated numerous conflicts over whose "rights" come first: the woman hired under such a plan, or the man whose contract assures him of seniority? Several cases from the early 1970s ensured that unions and management will be held "jointly and severally liable" for discriminatory employment provisions or customs.[21] Seniority rules have had to be adjusted, and some companies have been ordered to advance women through accelerated training programs to their "rightful place."[22]

The Workplace Woman: Where To From Here?

If the workplace woman has more doors open to her today than ever before, she also knows some doors are still shut, especially those carved entrances to the executive suite. Laws can be changed, courts can redress grievances, affirmative action plans can forward the careers of women, but these external processes do not force businesses to realize the possible economic benefits of changing not just policies, but attitudes. Today's workplace woman still lacks the 100 percent approval of the men who control entrance to the job market. Yesterday's female employee was more acutely aware of outright sexual bars to employment; today's working woman faces the subtleties of bias which include built-in notions about female behavior. Today's career woman faces such intangible forms of discrimination in part because of that descriptive adjective, *career* woman. It sets her apart; it means she will be a token for a while longer, subjected to closer scrutiny than her male counterpart for those "womanly" signs of weakness in performance. Even if the standard generalizations about working women are sheer myth, she will often be suspected of greater emotionalism, of more absenteeism, and of putting family above career more often than her male peers. As it now stands, many more women are in the pipeline for better jobs by undergoing training, pursuing the appropriate education (instead of the B.A. in literature their guidance counselors once told them they were suited for), and insisting on recognition for their existing level of experience. More tokenism may be necessary, but that means more women filtering upwards. It also requires a goal of normalization. When the women who are jumping the barriers now are no longer praised for "thinking like a man" but for thinking "like a manager," they can shed the "token" label and win "the right to mediocrity."[23]

Now as in the past, few women occupy line positions, where the skills are intangible and where employment, accomplishment, and recognition come according to less precise rules. Thus it is easier to discriminate according to sex because of old-guard notions of fulfilling the company standards of management. Women do hold a much higher proportion of staff jobs and technical positions, where precise, measurable skills can be demonstrated. Dramatic increases in enrollment by young women are also being seen in trade school programs which give to "blue collar" women the same measurable competence which is more difficult to overlook.[24]

Change comes slowly without prodding. The legal attempts to remove sex discrimination are milestones precisely because of such prodding, to get laws on the books and to enforce them. It is interesting to note that not until major corporations were forced to pay out massive sums to female employees did a major shift in business attitude take place. Companies had to realize that the price of discrimination was money and the loss of government contracts. The prodding came from women more willing to force the issue of discrimination into the courts, because of the encouraging successes of class action lawsuits. Then, as today, one woman alone may be unwilling to risk the loss of future jobs or of future merit promotions by taking her employer to court. Women who did undertake a challenge of the status quo discovered their leverage increased when stockholders lost money and the firm lost goodwill and valuable court time.

The epoch of large awards and out-of-court settlements began during an expansionary period; recessions, however, cause financial strain on corporations, and more than just "pocketbook" leverage by employees is required to maintain such a high payout trend. Political leverage is needed to ensure agency pursuit of such cases. In a recession, the nation turns to more pressing economic issues. Cash-strapped corporations protest the magnitude of settlements, as well as the costly affirmative action procedures. As the nation begins to accept a higher level of structural unemployment, pressures to "favor" female workers will be eased. More women will be anxious to hold onto the positions they have already attained, for "normalcy" in the sexual equality movement means no preferential treatment in an environment of job-rationing.

The profile of the workplace woman will undoubtedly change more as women discover that their "rightful place" can be anywhere they choose. As the occupational distribution of female workers levels out, women and men discover their capacities as working people. Major role shifts are easier: women can prepare themselves for "success," and men can reassess their automatic assumption of the breadwinner role. It requires new choices and commitments, not just for aspiring women, but for men as well. Women are beginning to pay the same price men pay for the opportunity to climb ladders of promotion: long hours, absence from the family, mental stress. But more and more women are discovering, as have men before them, that having an *opportunity* in the workplace does not pay bills or assure success. It only ensures the chance to choose.

Notes

1. The preceeding discussion is based upon two primary sources: "Twenty Facts On Women Workers," Women's Bureau, Employment Standards Administration, U.S. Department of Labor; "News," Bureau of Labor Statistics, U.S. Department of Labor, November 1975. See also Valerie K. Oppenheimer, *The Female Labor Force in the United States*, Population Monograph Series, Number 5 (Berkeley: University of California, 1970).

2. "Women Workers Today," Women's Bureau, Employment Standards Administration, U.S. Department of Labor, July 1975, p. 5. For an analysis of industrial job patterns of women, see Elizabeth Waldman and Beverly J. McEaddy, "Where Women Work—An Analysis By Industry and Occupation," *Monthly Labor Review*, May 1974.

3. "Women of the Year: Great Challenges, New Chances, Tough Choices," *Time* 107 (January 5, 1976): 6–16.

4. Ibid.

5. "Up the Ladder, Finally," chapter 30 in this book.

6. For further information of such "protective" legislation by various states, see Leo Kanowitz, *Women and the Law* (Albuquerque: University of New Mexico Press, 1969); also see Janice Fanning Madden, *The Economics of Sex Discrimination* (Lexington, Mass.: D. C. Heath Co., 1973). A recent reference work is *Women's Rights Almanac*, edited by Nancy Gager, compiled by the Elizabeth Cady Stanton Publishing Co. (New York: Harper & Row, 1975).

7. Other examples: During the 1960s, five states still required formal court approval for a wife to engage in a separate business, four states gave a husband legal control over a wife's earnings, and roughly half of the states allowed women to claim exemptions (not available to men) from jury duty. See "Report of The Committee On Civil And Political Rights," U. S. President's Commission On The Status of Women (Washington: U.S. Government Printing Office, 1963).

8. *Monthly Labor Review*, February 1974.

9. Even though the Equal Employment Opportunity Commission ruled in 1971 that company disability insurance benefit plans must include disability from pregnancy on the same terms as other nonoccupational disabilities, the specific steps had not been settled.

10. The following three sections of this article are abstracted from two sources: "Brief Highlights of Major Federal Laws and Orders on Sex Discrimination," U. S. Department of Labor; and Kanowitz, *Women and the Law*.

11. Kanowitz, *Women and the Law*, p. 135.

12. For a discussion of labor union responsibilities with respect to sex discrimination, see William H. Brown III, former EEOC Chairman, "Can Collective Bargaining Survive Without Protecting the Rights of Minorities and Women?", *Collective Bargaining: Survival of the '70's?*, edited by Richard L. Rowan (Philadelphia: University of Pennsylvania Press, 1972). See also Edna Raphael, "Working Women and Their Membership in Labor Unions," *Monthly Labor Review*, May 1974. For a review of female employment in the skilled trades, see Janice Hedges and Stephen Bemis, "Sex Stereotyping: Its Decline in Skilled Trades," *Monthly Labor Review*, May 1974.

13. "Significant Decisions in Labor Cases," *Monthly Labor Review*, June 1971, p. 80.

14. "Developments in Industrial Relations," *Monthly Labor Review*, January 1974.

15. *Monthly Labor Review*, April 1974.

16. "Pension Puzzle," *Wall Street Journal*, January 20, 1976. The original EEOC ruling came in 1971 and required equal pension benefit treatment for women and men.

17. "A Working Woman's Guide to Her Job Rights," Leaflet 55, revised, U.S. Department of Labor, 1975.

18. The first such back pay award was made by Household Finance in 1972, when the company agreed to hire more women and pay $125,000 to 175 women allegedly denied promotions. ("Developments in Industrial Relations," *Monthly Labor Review*, May 1972.) The concept was expanded in 1973, when a federal court in Pittsburgh approved a proposal by PPG Industries, Inc. to

pay $1.1 million to 371 women to settle a suit filed on behalf of women hired during World War II. The women were laid off in the 1950s, then allegedly passed over in favor of male employees when the company began to rehire. ("Developments in Industrial Relations," *Monthly Labor Review,* August 1973). AT&T's case is not over: during 1975, the corporation agreed to increase its hiring and promoting of women and minorities. (*Wall Street Journal,* May 13, 1975.)

19. *Wall Street Journal,* June 26, 1975.

20. "Up the Ladder, Finally."

21. See Blanton v. Southern Bell Telephone & Telegraph Co., 2 F.E.P. Cases 602, 49 FRD 162 (D.C., Ga., 1970); also, Robinson v. P. Lorillard Corp., 444F. 2d 791 (1971).

22. See Quarles v. Philip Morris, Inc., 279 F. Supp. 505 (E.D. Va. 1968).

23. "Up the Ladder, Finally."

24. Hedges and Bemis, "Sex Stereotyping," p. 20.

19
Equal Opportunity for Women Is Smart Business

M. BARBARA BOYLE

ABSTRACT

Ms. Boyle, president of the New York management consulting firm, Boyle/Kirkman Associates, Inc., established the first affirmative action program for women at International Business Machine. In this reading she enumerates the economic, social, and legal advantages to business of providing equal opportunity for women, and outlines the steps to be taken in establishing a corporate affirmative action program.

Foreword

"In the decades ahead any organization which ignores or underestimates the potential of women—or overlooks any source of talent for that matter—will be making a fatal mistake." So said the chief executive of one of the largest U.S. corporations recently. Discrimination against racial minorities has held the attention of federal civil rights enforcement officals in recent years, but now they are turning the spotlight on the employment situation of another "minority" (51% of the population). This has become particularly important for employers since the issuance a year ago of an order requiring government contractors to initiate affirma-

Reprinted from *Harvard Business Review* 51 (1973): 85-95. Copyright © 1973 by the President and Fellows of Harvard College. All rights reserved.

tive action programs, with goals and timetables, to end sex discrimination. But as the quotation above implies, business has a more important reason than fear of penalties for treating seriously the issue of equal rights for women. In this article a woman who has helped launch affirmative action programs in several large companies shows the steps which organizations must take to foster equal treatment of the sexes. These steps include not only goal setting, job restructuring, and training and development of female employees, but also elimination of discriminatory behavior on the part of managers.

Now a consultant who sets up these programs, Ms. Boyle previously spent 14 years with International Business Machines Corporation. There she developed and coordinated such a program which in its first full year of operation resulted in a significant increase in the number of women managers. She was Marketing Manager and Assistant Branch Manager of one of IBM's largest sales offices when she left to help form the New York City consulting firm, Boyle/Kirkman Associates, Inc., of which she is President.

"This movement is not a fad or an aberration, but a major social force with great and growing impact on business and other social, political, and economic institutions. As such, it must be taken seriously by business managers; its future potential must be foreseen and constructive responses must be designed to meet legitimate demands."

The subject in question is the movement for equality in women's rights, and the statement, from a General Electric publication distributed to all managers in the corporation, is typical of many corporate directives now being issued throughout the country. Even those companies that several years ago were rather hoping that the women's movement *was* a fad—and would go away if ignored—are beginning to recognize its importance. Some are still at the stage of merely mouthing their commitment to the elimination of sex discrimination, but others have begun to follow up their words with clearly defined programs designed to improve the utilization of women in all phases of their business.

The effective development of such affirmative action programs is the subject of this article. But let us look first at the reasons why companies are putting such emphasis on women. In talking with executives of several major corporations, I have found these key motivating factors:

Awareness of social trends—Today, nearly half the women in the United States work; that amounts to more than 33 million women, representing 40% of the work force. Obviously, women's place is no longer necessarily in the home. Furthermore, women work for essentially the same reasons men do; money (60% of the women in the work force are either single, divorced, widowed, or married to a man who earns less than $7,000 a year), self-satisfaction, and fulfillment. So, no matter what a manager's personal view is concerning "women's place," the fact is that women *are* working and must be considered as a resource that needs to be effectively managed, motivated, and utilized—just like men.

Government pressure—The federal government is enforcing equal opportunity for women through the following vehicles:

The Equal Pay Act of 1963. This amendment to the Fair Labor Standards Act prohibits discrimination on the basis of sex in the payment of wages for work requiring equal skills, effort, and responsibility, and performed under similar working conditions. Many women employees with legitimate discrimination complaints are finding how easy it is to file charges against their employers. With sufficient evidence they can cause comprehensive discrimination reviews to be initiated without disclosure of their names to the companies.

In the last two years alone, total settlements from these suits amounted to $30,000,000 with individual amounts ranging from $593,000 (Pacific Telephone & Telegraph) to $901,000 (Wheaton Glass). Recently this act was broadened to include executive, administrative, and professional employees.

Title VII, Civil Rights Act of 1964. This act, extremely broad in scope, prohibits discrimination in all phases of employment. Several large awards have been made under this act, and many of the settlements include full back pay, overtime, travel differentials, and interest from the time the complaint was filed.

Recently the Equal Employment Opportunity Commission (EEOC) and American Telephone & Telegraph reached a landmark settlement, under which AT&T agreed to pay $38 million* in back pay and restitution charges to thousands of employees, most of them women. "Beyond its importance to the employees involved, this agreement could have far-reaching significance to the entire business world," William H. Brown, EEOC chairman, noted. "We expect AT&T to have a considerable ripple effect. The EEOC lawsuits are designed to turn the ripples into waves where necessary."

Executive Order 11246, Revised Order 4 (1972). This makes it imperative for companies that wish to bid on—or keep—federal contracts to establish affirmative action programs that ensure equal promotion and placement opportunities for women in all ranks. Significant contracts have been withheld in cases where it was decided a company's posture has been discriminatory.

The women's equal rights movement—Through demonstrations and court suits, women's organizations have been extremely effective in pushing corporations to action. Moreover, Women's Lib groups are raising the

---

*The correct figure is $50 million (*v.* pp. 168, 273). (ed.)

consciousness of women within company walls. Women employees are starting to ask these questions:

"Why not me?"

"Am I really making use of my college degree by sitting here at this typewriter all day?"

"Why haven't I been given the experience and development necessary to compete for a vice president's position?"

When they fail to get answers to these questions, groups of dissatisfied women are uniting to express their resentment. In many cases they have organized into committees to meet with top management—or the press —to voice their anger.

It is extremely difficult from a credibility standpoint to react effectively to demands from an internal group. Therefore, many companies are taking positive action before they are *forced* to find answers to these questions.

Public image—Because women represents 51% of the population, product-based companies are now seriously considering the implications on their marketplace of internal discrimination. The business manager of a leading women's magazine recently told me, "Let's face it—we sell primarily to women and many of them are becoming increasingly aware of discriminatory behavior. Unless we do something to improve the situation of women here on the magazine from a long-range standpoint, our future is in jeopardy."

A General Mills training program consisting of 65 people, 64 of them white males, was recently the target of a formal charge filed by the National Organization for Women (NOW) and the Urban League. Not only was the publicity damaging, but both groups threatened to launch a nationwide boycott against the company's Betty Crocker products, Wheaties, Cheerios, and Gold Medal flour.

Even companies not dealing directly in the consumer market can suffer from bad publicity; college recruiters report situations involving high-potential graduates who have turned down offers because of a company's poor equal opportunity reputation.

Competition and challenge—Recently, IBM Senior Vice President George S. Beitzel defined industry's biggest problem in the coming years as "a shortage of capable people at all levels of management." If this is true, corporate leaders can no longer ignore half of the population when they are looking for creative and executive talent. It has long been obvious that we are not utilizing the capabilities of the women in our companies. Kept in "women-type" jobs, they have not efficiently used their aptitudes, intelligence, education, and skills. It is a great economic waste. From a dollar standpoint, the female labor force constitutes an important reservoir of talent which is necessary for companies to use to remain competitive in the business world.

Grounds for action

So much for recognizing the issue. The important question is what can be done about it. For fear of backlash or of disrupting the status quo, several companies have tried to soft-pedal the women's issue and, without fanfare or emphasis, have tried to weave it into their ongoing programs for minorities. In most of the companies where I have seen this done, the results have not been favorable. The problems of women and the problems of minorities are too dissimilar at the *initial* stage of awareness to be treated the same.

For example, I once observed a black woman trying to conduct a general awareness session on equal opportunity. Every time she directed the discussion toward the woman problem, the male participants quickly returned to the minority issue. After several years of consciousness raising, they had finally come to feel comfortable discussing minority problems; but the woman issue was newer, more personal, and more threatening to their male security.

A workable solution, which some major corporations have embraced, is the philosophy that there is *one* equal opportunity umbrella, with individual segments of emphasis. Eventually, companies may have just one total program focusing on managing people—all people—as individuals. Then, ideally, there should not be a need for individual emphasis programs.

"But what do I do if there is a black, a woman, and a Mexican-American equally qualified for a certain job?" the executive may ask. "Whom do I promote?" In most cases this is an unrealistic situation. Especially in the white-collar and management areas, seldom are there enough minorities or women at any one level with the same qualifications to compete for exactly the same job. This philosophical issue is frequently debated, however, by the conference set and persons who in many cases want to smoke-screen the issue and do nothing.

The dozen major companies which I have observed closely have experienced a minimum of conflict because the number and characteristics of the resource have been different. For example, many large corporations just do not have enough black employees—or, depending on the locale, Mexican-Americans—so they must establish high recruiting goals. They do have, however, a large percentage of women—all in low level jobs—so development and upgrading objectives are of primary importance and recruiting needs to be done only in specialized areas. One company, which did encounter situations where several minorities, women, and "majority" employees were equally qualified for the same promotion, made their decisions based on the particular mix of the area involved.

Some companies initiate one or two parts of a program, such as a personnel selection procedure stipulating that women candidates be considered first for certain openings, and assume that they have now dealt with the female problem. Others make up elaborately detailed goals, objectives, and timetables and then sit back complacently to wait for things to fall into place. They may wait a long time.

What is needed is a total affirmative action program that involves everything from the identification and development of women to management awareness sessions for men. When a company puts such a program into action, it demonstrates its sincerity and commitment to its managers and employees—especially to the women.

One company that has done this is Norton Simon, Inc. When I visit its office now, I am gratified to hear so many women mention how happy they are that management is paying serious attention to the problem. One woman receptionist I met said, "I never saw a need to go back to school and complete the credits necessary for my degree. But now I'm convinced management is sincere in the commitment to equal opportunity, so I'm really working hard to qualify myself for advancement."

So many of the elements in a "women's emphasis program" are simply good management procedures that it can be viewed as a starting point for implementing personnel systems which benefit all employees.

Before I launch into a description of an effective kind of affirmative action program, let me lay to rest a false assumption many people make about such programs. "Why do you want to make all women into managers when they're happy where they are?" I have been asked. "What's wrong with being a secretary anyway?" An affirmative action program is not an attempt to move *all* women into more responsible positions. The goal is, rather, to encourage women and managers not to accept automatically and blindly the traditional assumptions about who should be doing what jobs, and to give women a chance to think about their interests and potential, so they can investigate other possibilities, make an intelligent choice, and then be considered for promotions or openings on an equal basis with men.

After going through this exercise, many women decide that they are not interested or do not have the ability to move into management positions or new areas of responsibility. They are, however, more productive and happier employees after this decision is reached because they have had a choice.

Action program

A truly comprehensive and viable affirmative action plan should include at least ten basic steps. I shall discuss them in turn.

1. *Establishing Responsibility*

For the clout and support necessary to ensure success, ultimate responsibility for the program should be at the highest practicable level in a company's organization. Attitude and ability, rather than an organization chart, are the most important factors in deciding which top executive should take on the job.

Then who should have responsibility at the coordination, design, and implementation level? There are at least five possibilities:

A male manager. Originally this was the most popular approach, since it was felt that only a man had the requisite knowledge of the company and firmness to carry out the program. However, men placed in this position have often lacked interest and felt they accomplished little self-development applicable to other areas of the business. They also have found it difficult to thoroughly understand the problem, conduct management awareness sessions, and answer questions about women's motivation.

A top-level woman. When companies have an abundance of talented, professional women, this approach is generally used. But it is not advisable when it means taking a valuable woman out of the mainstream or a functional area where she has the opportunity to advance and be an example to other women. For the woman herself, it may also prove detrimental in the long run; she may find it difficult to shed the "Head of Women's Lib" label after her assignment is completed and she wants to move into other management positions.

Consultants. Some companies are now turning to experienced outside consultants. This approach shortens the start-up phase, demonstrates commitment, and minimizes the risk of initiating programs.

A task force. This approach is usually used when women are dissatisfied and begin to meet on their own to try to work out solutions. After management's attention is focused on the issue, it seems natural to let the group continue functioning. But care must be taken so that the group members can implement their ideas, are accountable to the person with top responsibility, and are not overly distracted from their other jobs.

A combination. From what I have observed, this method is now proving to be the most effective. An example of a combination approach is when a woman currently in personnel is given part-time responsibility for program coordination. Consultants are brought in to make high-level management presentations, develop action plans, design management awareness sessions, and work with the coordinator on implementing procedures. If a task force or advisory committee was involved in the beginning stages, it is reassembled on a quarterly basis to review the program and make suggestions.

2. Problem Definition

Once responsibility is established, the next step is to gather statistics and pinpoint the problem areas.[1] It is extremely important to know how women compare in the organization with men in level of jobs, area of employment, educational achievement, tenure, salary, and attrition rate (the latter broken down by position classification and reason for leaving). These data should be supplemented by interviews.

Statistical studies can be enlightening, if sometimes embarrassing. Many corporate executives are confident that the woman problem "can't happen here" because they are such good equal opportunity employers and the women have such good jobs. But even in their organizations, evidence of discrimination can often be found.

An executive of a large women's wear company declared proudly that his company's position was "different" from that of others. "Women have the best jobs in the company," he said. When I cited the facts, he was surprised and chagrined to learn that while women *were* highly visible in the business, accounting for some 65% of employment, the majority of the better-paying and more responsible jobs went to men.

Salary is the area in which it is easiest to identify discriminatory behavior. The average salary of a working woman in this country is less than 60% that of a man—even among professional workers with five years or more of college. If you think things are a lot different in your organization, you may be surprised.

One large, service-oriented company did a study comparing the average salaries of men and women who had the same appraisal ratings and who were in their positions for approximately the same length of time. The results caused the president to exclaim, "I knew most of the women were in lower levels than they deserved to be. But I'm really shocked to see that even within their level, when I know they're the best in that category, their salaries are less than that of the average man."

But many middle managers are not convinced that this is inequitable. Not long ago, a personnel manager (female) asked a department manager to give a raise to one of his women employees, who was the lowest paid of the 12 engineers in his office though she had the highest efficiency, performance, and aptitude ratings. He turned red at the collar. "Let me tell you something," he exclaimed. "That girl drives a red Porsche and I run around in a used Ford. She takes three weeks' vacation in Europe every year, and I take my family to a cottage on Cape Cod that isn't even on the beach. Now why does she need more money?" The personnel manager asked quietly whether one of his male engineers shouldn't be paid more money than he, since the engineer had two more children than the manager.

Discrimination also exists in the kinds of work men and women do.

Women have traditionally been channeled into certain areas and "protected" from the stressful or dirty positions. But this chivalry has worked more against than for them. Not only do these "unfeminine" jobs often pay well; they also can offer more upward mobility. Unless a woman has worked in the "dirty" areas of a plant, for instance, she can never be a plant manager. In many companies, unless she has aggressively knocked on doors as a sales representative, she cannot qualify for the more responsible and rewarding positions.

Finally, there is the question of job development. Many training programs and job assignments in a company are traditionally, and often unconsciously, reserved "for men only." At a recent equal opportunity conference, a woman asked a top executive if he had ever considered naming a woman as his administrative assistant. "You don't understand the nature of that position," he replied. "The idea is to bring a man in for a year or two, to give him the experience of working with a top executive. . . . In short, to give him exposure to the entire company. . . . To let him see. . . . To develop him for increasing responsibility. . . ." He went on for several minutes, employing the words "man," "he," and "him" at least 17 times. Then he stopped and blushed faintly at what he was saying. "I guess maybe some of us here ought to rethink that program," he said.

Some managers rationalize that it is not worth the effort to develop a young woman's potential because "after all, she'll leave after a couple of years to get married." It is generally true that women's attrition rate is higher than men's. But, as in the other areas of discrimination, going beyond the surface statistics reveals interesting facts. Within a given job level there is often no significant difference between the percentages of men and women leaving a company; attrition is higher in low-level jobs, and that is where most women are.

A recent university study indicates that many women rush into marriage simply because they are unhappy and frustrated in their jobs. A large manufacturer recently reviewed its separation statistics and discovered that fewer than half of the women leaving each year resigned for family-related reasons. The company then decided to initiate development programs so that women with potential would see that they could have a future in the company and would weigh that fact when considering other possibilities.

Sufficient analysis can save spending unnecessary dollars. For example, a major pharmaceutical company had established a large recruiting program for college graduates in order to improve its utilization of women. When the company analyzed its work force, however, it discovered that more than 20% of the secretaries had college degrees that were appropriate to the business. So the company placed emphasis on upgrading and development, doing recruiting only in specialized areas.

3. Executive Involvement

Top-management participation is the key to the success of any affirmative action effort. Participation can be conveyed through personal letters to each manager from the president or chairman of the board, or through presentations by the president or chairman at management meetings. Middle echelons have to *know* that top management is serious about the issue and that part of their performance appraisal includes results in the area of women's equality. (This attitude should be communicated repeatedly to the stockholders and the public as well.)

Rawleigh Warner, Jr., the chairman and chief executive officer of Mobil Oil, made a film clip which was shown to all managers in the company. When a divisional director was asked at the end of one session whether he planned to establish a women's program, he remarked, "What do you expect me to say? After hearing Mr. Warner up there telling me that it's a high-priority item, do you think I'd say no? Of course we're going to do it."

General Electric is another good example of commitment beyond the motherhood words on paper. In one division, middle managers constantly complained that it was difficult to promote women and minority members because (a) they could not locate qualified people, and (b) they did not have the funds to pay them. Top management promptly removed these two ancient excuses. It provided the necessary budget and head count and told the personnel department to find the qualified candidates, which it did.

A small manufacturing company, which was unable to augment its head count, established a system whereby no promotion could be made into the white, male-dominated, exempt group until the list of minority and women candidates had been exhausted or approval given by the senior vice president of operations.

Consistency & sincerity: Top-executive commitment and awareness has to be consistent and evident on a day-to-day basis or credibility is lost. One senior executive spent the better part of one day making a videotape concerning the expanding role of women in the business. But he undid himself that evening when he delivered a speech at an employee dinner. At the conclusion of his talk, he launched into a thank-you to "all the women in the audience" for being understanding when their husbands worked long hours and for standing squarely behind the men behind the product. Obviously he did not know that most of the women in the audience were employees (systems analysts and marketing representatives) who were there with their husbands. If he had known, would he have thanked the men behind the women behind the product?

To *demonstrate sincerity, the corporate office also must set an example.* A middle manager of a large travel company, after reading a formal "we must put women in responsible positions" statement from his president, remarked, "I'll believe he means it when I see a woman on one of the executive floors." Appointing capable, qualified women to the highest levels is much more than tokenism; women who have the potential to advance in an organization need role models at the top. So far these role models have been few and far between.

A metropolitan bank realized the fruits of this within a short period of time when it made several women branch managers—a position heretofore held only by men. Several months later bank officers were amazed by the number of younger women in the bank who were establishing personal development plans.

But how does top management acquire this understanding and commitment? This area of personnel management is so new that many top corporate officers do not realize the scope of the problem and know little about it except the radical viewpoints expressed in the media. They honestly believe the equal opportunity words but do not know what to be committed to. However, when they are made aware of business-like approaches to the problem that detail ways in which they can participate, they often get "turned on" and sufficiently involved to ensure success.

4. Identification & Tracking

A formal mechanism is necessary whereby women with potential can be identified, jobs pin-pointed, development plans established, and promotional opportunities reviewed. Under this procedure, many personnel departments have sent out forms to each manager which require this detail on female employees: prior experience, interests, next two possible positions, long-range potential, and personal development plans to ensure progress. All requisitions for personnel have to be first reviewed against this file before other applicants can be considered.

This practice has been quite successful, since it forces the managers to discuss career plans seriously with their women employees. It also provides a mechanism to keep track of women with potential who may get trapped later under a biased manager.

Many organizations already have a procedure to identify high-potential persons and establish replacement lists, but somehow women are often left out because managers fail to recognize their ability. When a utility discovered, for example, that not one woman was included in the high-potential pool of 300 persons, it lowered the level of eligibility and set up a separate procedure for the identification and tracking of talented women.

As part of their resource development system, some organizations are establishing personalized "fast-track" procedures for a few top-notch women who have had a variety of business experiences but who lack necessary exposure in a particular area, such as manufacturing, finance, or sales, to qualify for management positions.

5. *Job Restructuring*

A large chemical company recently addressed the problem of too few female chemical engineers. In examining several positions, the top executives discovered that the real problem was overstatement of qualifications; the jobs could be filled by intelligent nonengineers.

In other areas they found that a portion of the job was nonengineering-oriented, so they combined and restructured certain functions and came up with several meaningful paraprofessional jobs. This made it possible for some women to be far more productive for the company, while they were gaining experience and insights necessary in order to climb professional and managerial ladders.

In the secretarial realm, a new concept called "word processing" is gaining favor in some organizations that want to upgrade women employees and also benefit from improved efficiency. Under this system the typewriter is removed from the woman outside the boss's office and all dictating is telephoned to an in-house word-processing center where it is transcribed and returned in a short time. The former secretary becomes an administrative assistant, performing the nontranscription portion of the traditional job plus taking on additional responsibilities. Job ladders are established in both areas, and the secretaries have the opportunity to choose in which portion of their current functions they prefer to specialize and advance.

This is the kind of job analysis and restructuring which has enabled many employers to discover a wealth of resources in women filling such positions as administrative assistant and manager of the word-processing center. The employees have an opportunity to prove their organizational talents, and this experience will make them candidates for other positions in their organizations which previously were beyond their reach.

6. *Setting objectives*

Three years ago, when I was setting up an affirmative action plan at IBM, I initially opposed the idea of goals. But a veteran manufacturing manager said, "Barbara, I really believe in your program, but you have to understand the climate you're working in. We have all sorts of priorities and unless you give us numbers and dates, nothing will ever get accomplished. It's just easier to fill a job with a male applicant than to go out of your way to look for a woman."

He was right. After nine months of persuasion and "good faith," which resulted in minimal progress, the company established goals that were realistic, measurable, and challenging. These started with input from the first-level managers. During the corporate review, however, they were stretched to meet company objectives. Within another nine months the overall annual goal was nearly reached.

The company also added to its formal planning structure an "equal opportunity" section, in which each division must submit annually a plan stating the objectives for the next two and five years. About that time, a section was added to every manager's appraisal form which deals with objectives and performance in the equal opportunity area. These appraisals are, of course, tied to salary and advancement.

7. Recruiting

"We've advertised for months for a product manager and no woman has ever applied," an executive may say. Or, "I'd be happy to promote a woman if she'd do what the men do: knock on my door and say, 'I want to be a manager.' "

Edward D. Goldstein, president of Glass Containers Corporation, stated a different approach to the situation: "We're not going to wait for women to knock on our doors. I'm serious about solving the problem. We're going out and search for qualified women who have the talent and potential to advance in our company. I know their qualifications won't always be the same as the men's; in sales, for example, just add 'ten years of experience' as an important criterion and you've eliminated most women."

More companies are establishing action programs to recruit women for a broader range of positions. The implementation of these programs, however, sometimes leaves something to be desired. An outstanding MBA student in California described her interview with a representative of a large corporation. The recruiter, evidently unaware of the company's affirmative action program, said, "You'll like this position. It's a good job for a girl, and it pays an excellent salary for a girl." When she asked where she could go in the company, he replied, "Oh, most of the girls stay in this position—they really love it. It offers a lot of challenge and it's a glamorous job." Needless to say, she did not accept the position.

It is also important to make sure your recruiting material portrays the image you want to convey. AT&T has received extremely favorable reaction to its advertisement showing a woman climbing a telephone pole. TRW and General Electric have pioneered in featuring professional women in their ads. One company was successful in attracting women candidates merely by stating in an ad, "We are interested in *both* men and women applicants."

8. Development & Training

Because half the problem lies in the attitudes of the women themselves—their lack of motivation and ambitious career objectives— many companies have developed special awareness and career planning sessions for them. In some cases these seminars have been cited as the turning point to a change in self-image.

The sessions include discussions on stereotypes that women have traditionally accepted and also focus on problems that women face in business. Members of the group share experiences and give each other advice on handling difficult situations, such as how to work with a chauvinistic manager or how to manage a subordinate who refuses to work for a woman. Questions of business style and image arise, such as, "Should a woman act like one of the boys, or be coy and 'feminine'?"

The procedure of investigating traditionally nonfemale job opportunities also gets emphasis; each session begins with reports by group members on various positions within the company. These reports not only increase practical knowledge of the company but also give each person an opportunity to develop her presentation skills.

Women, like men, have to become accustomed to working with women, and here the awareness sessions can help. One engineer who had spent nearly all her business life in strictly male departments remarked that after the sessions she found she enjoyed the association with other women. The sessions had given her a chance to meet intelligent women whom she could respect, use as role models, and with whom she could share experiences.

In addition to specialized seminars, many companies have specified that every regular management training and development program include some qualified minority and women participants. Other companies without internal training opportunities have concentrated on getting women enrolled in outside development courses such as those sponsored by the American Management Association, Katharine Gibbs, or Dale Carnegie.

A discussion leader at one of these conferences commented that he was amazed at the quality of females in attendance—most of them secretaries. One young woman explained the situation succinctly: "It's not surprising that so many secretaries have so much ability; we've learned from working with our bosses. We've had exposure to top-level problem solving and decision making, and in many cases we do most of their work and recommend solutions. The poor management trainees are three floors below and don't get that kind of experience or exposure."

9. *Management Awareness*

Development of awareness on the part of lower-level managers is a crucial aspect of the program, without which the other steps can be fruitless. Discrimination against women is often unconscious behavior resulting from traditional upbringing and the influence of our culture.

In-house awareness seminars give managers a chance to bring out and examine their attitudes and assumptions so that they can change their behavior. The sessions usually start with a discussion of typical remarks such as "women can't travel with our salesmen," "they belong in the home," "they're too emotional," and "they'll leave and get married." Then they proceed to deeper matters, such as societal role changes, fear of competition, and backlash.

An expert discussion leader can bring these things to the surface. (See Appendix to this chapter.) Myths about attrition and absenteeism are vulnerable to demolition by statistics. Stereotypes are handled via case studies. Behavior issues are treated through discussion of management techniques; for example, participants answer the question, "What do you do if a woman cries during her appraisal?" Or "What do you do if a talented woman says she's not interested in advancement?" The last part of the session concentrates on motivation and career counseling of female employees.

There are several industrial programs available to complement internal management awareness procedures. Films and videotape series can be obtained from commercial sources. Not all of them need skilled discussion leaders to make them effective.

10. *Personnel Policies Study*

An organization's personnel practices need to be explored in order to ensure that discrimination does not exist and to create a climate fostering the utilization of women to their full potential. Some of the critical areas are personnel forms, part-time employment, day-care centers, job descriptions, entrance exams, benefits, and policies on overtime, travel, and working conditions.

Sometimes such a study must go beyond policy to interpretation. For example, the employment form of a major oil company included the question, "Can this employee relocate?" On examining the completed forms of 300 women employees, the company officials found the appropriate box marked "no" in every case. On probing further, they discovered that no one had actually asked the women whether they would relocate; it had simply been assumed that they would not.

During personnel reviews, several companies have become aware of *reverse* discrimination practices—such as that of the chivalrous manager who arranged for taxis to drive up at midnight to take the women keypunchers home—and have revised them accordingly. In other cases, policies that affect women have been liberalized; IBM and Polaroid, for example, have followed EEOC guidelines and now treat pregnancy as a temporary disability covered under their regular sickness and accident plans. (This helps reduce costly attrition and attracts feminine talent necessary to the business.)

Reservoir of Skills

The ten steps I have listed here by no means comprise a complete program, and many of these ideas need to be tailored to the particular company environment. However, even some small companies have successfully initiated many of these programs on a limited basis and have experienced a significant increase in the morale and work quality of their women employees.

The establishment of an affirmative action program is not costly—its absence is—and the most important ingredient to its success is commitment. Not only is it the law; it is also smart business. From an economic point of view women are a valuable resource, and it is up to managers to make use of women's creative talent, education, and skills to help meet the challenges of the marketplace.

In the words of George R. Vila, chairman and president of Uniroyal, Inc., "In the decades ahead any organization which ignores or underestimates the potential of women—or overlooks any source of talent for that matter—will be making a fatal mistake."

A study prepared in 1970 for internal consumption at one of the largest U.S. corporations concerned the significant labor force developments anticipated in the United States up to 1979. The study revealed:

"It will be an increasingly female labor force. Women will account for more than half of the 15.5 million growth in the labor force in the decade to 1979. Furthermore, society is not presently making fully effective use of the aptitudes, intelligence, and education of many women in the labor force. The female labor force, therefore, constitutes an important reservoir of skills needed by business. Competitive, political, and social pressures will force greater equality of opportunity for working women and this corporation could gain considerable competitive advantage by prompt and creative moves in this area."

Appendix: When the shoe is on the other foot

Management awareness sessions can sometimes modify behavior, if not change basic attitudes. Here is a tape of a discussion of an issue raised by the discussion leader at one such session.

Leader: Suppose you're the manager of a division of a large organization based in New York. A management opening occurs in your Denver office for which one of your New York women is the best qualified candidate. It would be a very good opportunity for her. However, she is married to a rising young executive in a local company; they have a three-year-old child and a newly purchased home in Chappaqua. Not only that, you play poker with the husband every other week. How many of you would offer her the job? Raise your hands. Hmm, only 2 out of 20. What are your reasons?

Manager A: I wouldn't offer it to her because I wouldn't want to be the cause of a divorce.

Manager B: Right. Anyway, her husband's job is more important than hers. He's the one who's likely to be making the most money for the family in the future as well as now.

Manager C: I know she wouldn't take the job, for all those reasons you mentioned in your question. So why offer it to her? It will only cause conflict.

Manager D: I should probably have been developing her and keeping close enough tabs on her to *know* whether she'd accept it or not.

Manager E: I don't know. How can you be absolutely sure until you actually ask?

Manager F: I might offer her the job—she should be the one to decide, and she could always ask her husband's advice.

Manager G: Well, I wouldn't want to put myself in the position of bringing up a divisive issue. Our job as managers is not to break up families.

Leader: Now let me ask you another question. Suppose that you work for me in this same New York-based company. I know that you moved to New York in the first place because your wife has a serious disease that can be treated only by a certain specialist here. She's now under treatment. An excellent opening comes up in San Francisco for which you'd be ideal. How many of you would like me to offer you that position? Let's see your hands. Now almost all of you would want me to. Why?

Manager G: I must admit that even if I knew I couldn't take it, I'd like you to offer it. Then I'd know you thought a lot of me.

Manager H: Also, even if I couldn't take this particular job at this particular time, my situation might change later. And if you thought I was good enough for this job, I'd be encouraged to think I'd have another good opportunity in the future.

Manager I: How do you really know I wouldn't take it? It's up to me to investigate what kind of medical assistance I can get for my wife in San Francisco.

Manager J: And if you offer the job to me but I can't take it, at least the company gets some mileage out of the offer itself.

Manager F: And who knows? Maybe that person you thought wouldn't take the job will surprise you and accept. Come to think of it, there *is* a woman I've been considering for a great position involving relocation. I think I'll at least give her the opportunity to accept it.

Manager D: I guess the answer is, it's not up to us as managers to make personal decisions for our employees no matter how well we *think* we know them. In the first example you gave us, maybe the woman's husband is dissatisfied with his job and can get a better one in Denver. The position should be offered to the person who's the best qualified. Then it's up to him—uh, her—to make' the decision.

Notes

1. For more on this aspect, see Charles D. Orth, 3rd, and Frederic Jacobs, "Women in Management: Pattern for Change," HBR July-August 1971, p. 139.

20
Statement of Purpose of The National Organization for Women (NOW)

This reading is included as an answer to those students who ask, "What do those women (feminists) really want?" In this statement of purpose, NOW details its commitment "to bring women into full participation in the mainstream of American society now, exercising all the privileges and responsibilities thereof in truly equal partnership with men." This they hope to accomplish "not in pleas for special privilege, nor in enmity toward men, who are also victims of the current, half-equality between the sexes, but in an active, self-respecting partnership."

(Adopted at the organizing conference in Washington, D.C., October 29, 1966)

We, men and women who hereby constitute ourselves as the National Organization for Women, believe that the time has come for a new movement toward true equality for all women in America and toward a fully equal partnership of the sexes, as part of the worldwide revolution of human rights now taking place within and beyond our national borders.

The purpose of NOW is to take action to bring women into full participation in the mainstream of American society now, exercising all the privileges and responsibilities thereof in truly equal partnership with men.

We believe the time has come to move beyond the abstract argument, discussion, and symposia over the status and special nature of women which has raged in America in recent years; the time has come to confront, with concrete action, the conditions that now prevent women from enjoying the equality of opportunity and freedom of choice which is their right, as individual Americans, and as human beings.

NOW is dedicated to the proposition that women, first and foremost, are human beings, who, like all other people in our society, must have the chance to develop their fullest human potential. We believe that women can achieve such equality only by accepting to the full the challenges and responsibilities they share with all other people in our society, as part of the decision-making mainstream of American political, economic, and social life.

We organize to initiate or support action, nationally, or in any part of this nation, by individuals or organizations, to break through the silken curtain of prejudice and discrimination against women in government, industry, the professions, the churches, the political parties, the judiciary, the labor unions, in education, science, medicine, law, religion, and every other field of importance in American society.

Enormous changes taking place in our society make it both possible and urgently necessary to advance the unfinished revolution of women toward true equality, now. With a life span lengthened to nearly seventy-five years it is no longer either necessary or possible for women to devote the greater part of their lives to child-rearing; yet child-bearing and rearing, which continues to be a most important part of most women's lives—still is used to justify barring women from equal professional and economic participation and advance.

Today's technology has reduced most of the productive chores which women once performed in the home and in mass-production industries based upon routine unskilled labor. This same technology has virtually eliminated the quality of muscular strength as a criterion for filling most jobs, while intensifying American industry's need for creative intelligence. In view of this new industrial revolution created by automation in the mid-twentieth century, women can and must participate in old and new fields of society in full equality—or become permanent outsiders.

Despite all the talk about the status of American women in recent years, the actual position of women in the United States has declined, and is declining, to an alarming degree throughout the 1950s and '60s. Although 46.4 percent of all American women between the ages of 18 and 65 now work outside the home, the overwhelming majority—75 percent—are in routine clerical, sales, or factory jobs, or they are household workers, cleaning women, hospital attendants. About two-thirds of Negro women workers are in the lowest-paid service occupations. Working women are becoming increasingly—not less—concentrated on the bottom of the job ladder. As a consequence full-time women workers today earn on the average only 60 percent of what men earn, and that wage gap has been increasing over the past twenty-five years in every major industry group. In 1964, of all women with a yearly income, 89 percent earned under $5,000 a year; half of all full-time year-round women workers earned less than $3,690; only 1.4 percent of full-time year-round women workers had an annual income of $10,000 or more.

Further, with higher education increasingly essential in today's society, too few women are entering and finishing college or going on to graduate or professional school. Today, women earn only one in three of the BA's and MA's granted, and one in ten of the PhD's.

In all the professions considered of importance to society, and in the executive ranks of industry and government, women are losing ground. Where they are present it is only a token handful. Women comprise less than 1 percent of federal judges; less than 4 percent of all lawyers; 7 percent of doctors. Yet women represent 51 percent of the U.S. population. And, increasingly, men are replacing women in the top positions in secondary and elementary schools, in social work, and in libraries—once thought to be women's fields.

Official pronouncements of the advance in the status of women hide not only the reality of this dangerous decline, but the fact that nothing is being done to stop it. The excellent reports of the President's Commission on the Status of Women and of the State Commissions have not been fully implemented. Such commissions have power only to advise. They have no power to enforce their recommendations; nor have they the freedom to organize American women and men to press for action on them. The reports of these commissions have, however, created a basis upon which it is now possible to build.

Discrimination in employment on the basis of sex is now prohibited by federal law, in Title VII of the Civil Rights Act of 1964. But although nearly one-third of the cases brought before the Equal Employment Opportunity Commission during the first year dealt with sex discrimination and the proportion is increasing dramatically, the commission has not made clear its intention to enforce the law with the same seriousness on behalf of women as of other victims of discrimination. Many of these cases were Negro women, who are the victims of the double discrimination of race and sex. Until now, too few women's organizations and official spokesmen have been willing to speak out against these dangers facing women. Too many women have been restrained by the fear of being called "feminist."

There is no civil rights movement to speak for women, as there has been for Negroes and other victims of discrimination. The National Organization for Women must therefore begin to speak.

We believe that the power of American law, and the protection guaranteed by the U.S. Constitution to the civil rights of all individuals, must be effectively applied and enforced to isolate and remove patterns of sex discrimination, to ensure equality of opportunity in employment and education, and equality of civil and political rights and responsibilities on behalf of women, as well as for Negroes and other deprived groups.

We realize that women's problems are linked to many broader questions of social justice; their solution will require concerted action by many groups. Therefore, convinced that human rights for all are indivisible, we expect to give active support to the common cause of equal rights for all those who suffer discrimination and deprivation, and we call upon other organizations committed to such goals to support our efforts toward equality for women.

We do not accept the token appointment of a few women to high-level positions in government and industry as a substitute for a serious continuing effort to recruit and advance women according to their individual abilities. To this end, we urge American government and industry to mobilize the same resources of ingenuity and command with which they have solved problems of far greater difficulty than those now impeding the progress of women.

We believe that this nation has a capacity at least as great as other nations, to innovate new social institutions which will enable women to enjoy true equality of opportunity and responsibility in society, without conflict with their responsibilities as mothers and homemakers. In such innovations, America does not lead the Western world, but lags by decades behind many European countries. We do not accept the traditional assumption that a woman has to choose between marriage and motherhood, on the one hand, and serious participation in industry or the professions on the other. We question the present expectation that all normal women will retire from job or profession for ten or fifteen years, to devote their full time to raising children, only to reenter the job market at a relatively minor level. This, in itself, is a deterrent to the aspirations of women, to their acceptance into management or professional training courses, and to the very possibility of equality of opportunity or real choice, for all but a few women. Above all, we reject the assumption that these problems are the unique responsibility of each individual woman, rather than a basic social dilemma which society must solve. True equality of opportunity and freedom of choice for women requires such practical and possible innovations as a nationwide network of child-care centers, which will make it unnecessary for women to retire completely from society until their children are grown, and national programs to provide retraining for women who have chosen to care for their own children full-time.

We believe that it is as essential for every girl to be educated to her full potential of human ability as it is for every boy—with the knowledge that such education is the key to effective participation in today's economy and that, for a girl as for a boy, education can only be serious where there is expectation that it will be used in society. We believe that American educators are capable of devising means of imparting such expectations to girl students. Moreover, we consider the decline in the proportion of women receiving higher and professional education to be evidence of discrimination. This discrimination may take the form of quotas against the admission of women to colleges and professional schools; lack of encouragement by parents, counselors and educators; denial of loans or fellowships; or the traditional or arbitrary procedures in graduate and professional training geared in terms of men, which inadvertently discriminate against women. We believe that the same serious attention must be given to high school dropouts who are girls as to boys.

We reject the current assumptions that a man must carry the sole burden of supporting himself, his wife, and family, and that a woman is automatically entitled to lifelong support by a man upon her marriage, or that marriage, home, and family are primarily woman's world and responsibility—hers to dominate—his to support. We believe that a true partnership between the sexes demands a different concept of marriage, an equitable sharing of the responsibilities of home and children and of the economic burdens of their support. We believe that proper recognition should be given to the economic and social value of homemaking and child-care. To these ends, we will seek to open a reexamination of laws and mores governing marriage and divorce, for we believe that the current state of "half-equality" between the sexes discriminates against both men and women and is the cause of much unnecessary hostility between the sexes.

We believe that women must now exercise their political rights and responsibilities as American citizens. They must refuse to be segregated on the basis of sex into separate-and-not-equal ladies' auxiliaries in the political parties, and they must demand representation according to their numbers in the regularly constituted party committees—at local, state, and national levels—and in the informal power structure, participating fully in the selection of candidates and political decision-making, and running for office themselves.

In the interests of the human dignity of women, we will protest, and endeavor to change, the false image of women now prevalent in the mass media, and in the texts, ceremonies, laws, and practices of our major social institutions. Such images perpetuate contempt for women by society and by women for themselves. We are similarly opposed to all policies and practices—in church, state, college, factory, or office—which, in the guise of protectiveness, not only deny opportunities but also foster in women self-denigration, dependence, and evasion of responsibility, undermine their confidence in their own abilities, and foster contempt for women.

NOW will hold itself independent of any political party in order to mobilize the political power of all women and men intent on our goals. We will strive to ensure that no party, candidate, president, senator, governor, congressman, or any public official who betrays or ignores the principle of full equality between the sexes is elected or appointed to office. If it is necessary to mobilize the votes of men and women who believe in our cause, in order to win for women the final right to be fully free and equal human beings, we so commit ourselves.

We believe that women will do most to create a new image of women by *acting* now, and by speaking out on behalf of their own equality, freedom, and human dignity—not in pleas for special privilege, nor in enmity toward men, who are also victims of the current, half-equality between the sexes—but in an active, self-respecting partnership with men. By so doing, women will develop confidence in their own ability to determine actively, in partnership with men, the conditions of their life, their choices, their future, and their society.

21
A Review of Sex
Role Research

ARLIE RUSSELL HOCHSCHILD

ABSTRACT

In this selection, Arlie Hochschild presents a guide to the questions and theoretical start-
ing points of four types of research on sex roles. "Most research in the social sciences is on
male subjects," notes Hochschild, and, "as a corrective, most sex role research is on
women." This research, Hochschild observes, reflects four main perspectives: sex dif-
ferences, sex roles and norms, women as a minority group, and the politics of caste
perspective.

This review is offered as a guide to the questions and theoretical starting points of four types of research on sex roles. The range is both
broader and more selective than in most reviews. Most of the articles and
books were written after 1960, but I shall mention a few earlier ones
when theoretical debates cross the decade. Most are within sociology but
some are outside it; a few are about men but most about women; some
have hard data, others soft, and still others none at all. Finally, I shall
suggest what it would do to the rest of sociology were it to assimilate
even a few "token" ideas.

More exhaustive reviews and annotated bibliographies have recently
come out covering various aspects of women's role (Sells, in press;
Suelzle, in press; Steinmann 1971; Spiegal 1969; Cisler 1972; Biggar 1970;
Bruemmer 1970; Whaley 1972; Coelho et al. 1970). There are also specialized bibliographies on women's education (ERIC 1970; Kuvlesky and
Reynolds 1970), on work (U.S., Department of Labor 1969, 1970; Hughes
1970; Frithioff 1969; Spiegel 1970*a*, 1970*b*) and on both education and

work (Radcliffe Institute 1970; Astin, Suniewick, and Dweck 1971; Westervelt and Fixter 1971), on fertility (U.S., Department of Health, Education and Welfare 1970a; Keiffer and Warren 1970), and on marriage (National Council on Family Relations 1970; Laws 1971). In addition, some recent books have good bibliographies (Epstein 1970a; Maccoby 1966; Nye and Hoffman 1963). Theodore has collected 53 articles in her anthology, *The Professional Woman* (1971), and Safilios-Rothschild has collected 31 articles in her recent book, *Toward a Sociology of Women* (1972).

Most research in the social sciences is on male subjects (Holmes and Jorgensen 1971); yet there are significantly different findings on males and females (Carlson and Carlson 1960), which are often ignored. As a corrective, most sex role research is on women. There is little research on men in the family (but see Benson 1968), and less still on men qua men outside it. As measured by sheer volume, most of the traditional research on women has been in the sociology of the family (Bart 1971), and most of that concerns middle-class white women as housewives, college students, and professional workers. We have less on lower-class women (e.g., Rainwater, Coleman, and Handel 1959; Gavron 1966; Komarovsky 1969) or upper-class women (e.g., Domhoff 1970) and almost nothing on single or black women (but see Ladner 1972; Cole 1971).

There seems to be the same mix of methodologies in sex-role research as there is in sociology as a whole; most of it is survey research or secondary analysis of it. There is some content analysis (e.g., Martel 1968; Weitzman et al. 1972), and very little participant observation. In my view, many useful ideas come from nonsociologists. The literary critic Watt (1962), for example, links the step-by-step accounts of courtship in the earliest novels such as *Pamela* (the original female Horatio Alger) to the growing necessity for marriage as single women were pushed out of the parental family to earn a pauper's wage in the textile industry in 18th-century England. Fiedler (1966), in his chapter "Good Good Girls and Good Bad Boys, *Clarissa* as a Juvenile," explores some of the ambiguities of sex roles and social control. Other ideas come from historians (Welter 1966; Bridges 1965; Putnam 1910; Potter 1964) and from journalists. Langer's description of women in the telephone company, for example, is a classic on working women (1970).

In addition, some incidental research is on, but not *about*, sex roles. Some of the work on adolescence, old age, divorce, deviance, crime, small groups, demography, and social movements provides a treasure trove of information and ideas about sex roles. For example, in Neugarten's cross-sectional study based on Thematic Apperception Tests given to 131 men and women in their forties, fifties, and sixties, she found that "women, as they age, seem to become more tolerant of their own aggressive, egocentric impulses; whereas men, as they age, of their own nurturant and affiliative impulses" (Neugarten 1968, p. 71; also see

Cumming and Henry 1961; Kagan and Moss 1962). Again, case studies of the families of 24 unemployed men during the Depression show that men with more leisure in which to do household work and child care in fact did even *less* than when they had worked full time. (Bakke 1940, sec. 2, pp. 109–243).

Some research on such social problems as mental illness, juvenile delinquency, and overpopulation focuses on the problems women cause rather than the ones they have. For example, the schizophrenia research of the 1940s and 1950s deals with the domineering "schizophrenogenic mother" (Kohn and Clausen 1956). Lidz, Fleck, and Cornelison in the 1960s link role reversal between mother and father to schizophrenia in the child (1965; but see Caputo 1963). Again, much research focuses on how a mother's work outside the home affects such things as her child's grades or proneness to delinquency. In some research it has a harmful effect, in some a good effect, and in some no effect (Hoffman 1961; Stolz 1960; Siegel and Haas 1963). Interestingly, the term is "maternal deprivation" for women and "father absence" for men.

Four Types of Research

Apart from incidental research, the sociology of sex roles seems to reflect four main perspectives. The first is concerned with *sex differences*. Many of the studies here are done by psychologists, although they are often cited by sociologists. The second is concerned with *sex roles* and the norms which govern them. This is still the most common perspective in the field. The third is concerned with women as a *minority group*, and the fourth, the *politics of caste* perspective, carries the minority perspective in a different direction. Each perspective permits both macro- and micro-analysis, a stress on both structural and superstructural variables, on both conflict and consensus; but the blend is in each case different. Some of the assumptions shared by all four perspectives are not shared by sociologists outside the field, but among the four there are differences too. They vary and hold constant different variables.

The first type deals with sex differences; the rest, in different ways, deal more with sex equality. I shall first compare them, focusing on the last three, before discussing how they deal with sex inequality—via role strain (type 2), discrimination, prejudice and segregation (type 3), and power differences (type 4). Most assume a plasticity of human nature; Talcott Parsons and Alice Rossi would at least agree on that. But they have different assumptions about the plasticity of the social structure. Whereas those in the first type, and the Parsonians in the second, assume the division of labor between men and women, most of the rest take it as the problem to be explained, and focus on its dysfunctions for the society (e.g., the "brain drain") or for the individual ("role strain").

Beyond that, they use different conceptual vocabularies; type 1 analyzes measures of emotive and cognitive "traits"; type 2 discusses roles, role models, role conflict; type 3, prejudice, assimilation, marginality; and type 4, interest and power. Each puts a different construction on the behavior of the two sexes; what to type 1 is a feminine trait such as passivity is to type 2 a role element, to type 3 is a minority characteristic, and to type 4 is a response to powerlessness. Social change might also look somewhat different according to each perspective; differences disappear, deviance becomes normal, the minority group assimilates, or power is equalized.

Each perspective sees the family differently too. Type 2 sees the family as a social system, or as a role set generating its own conflicts or strains. In the minority perspective, the family is less important, since it is precisely here that the analogy to blacks and other minorities breaks down; and in the final perspective, the family is an important area of latent bargains, of profit and loss.

Each of these perspectives has different intellectual roots. The role perspective draws on George Herbert Mead, Charles Cooley, Ralph Linton, Florian Znaniecki, Talcott Parsons, Robert Merton, and Mirra Komarovsky, who have influenced the work of such modern-day sociologists as P. Bart, H. Lopata, and J. L. Blumen. The minority perspective, on the other hand, draws more from R. Park, L. Wirth, and E. Stonequist. Just as G. Berreman brought caste theory from India to American blacks, so Myrdal brought it in 1944 for modern sociology from blacks to women, to be further elaborated in 1951 by Hacker and more recently by Werner, Wellman, and Weitzman (1971), and others. The politics-of-caste perspective, by contrast, draws more directly on feminist theory from J. S. Mill's *The Subjection of Women* (1869), revived by Rossi (1970), through Gilman's work, *Women and Economics* ([1898] 1966) and Simone de Beauvoir's *The Second Sex* (1951) to Alice Rossi's modern classic, "The Equality of Women: An Immodest Proposal" (1964). In addition, feminist writings from Kate Millet and Shulamith Firestone to Juliet Mitchell have been making their way into sociology through recent generations of female graduate students.

Meanwhile, Marx and Freud have come in from the side to be incorporated into role perspective by Parsons and Bales (1953) and to be refuted (Weisstein 1969) or revised (Firestone 1970; Sampson 1965) or partly incorporated (Collins 1971) by the politics of caste. There is not only the "straight" Freud and the "revised" Freud but the "hip" Freud of Philip Slater, introduced into feminist sociology via Millman (1970), who suggests that society preserves and keeps visible its rejected and denied impulses by depositing them in a special group container which "serves as a kind of safety valve to drain off and confine those impulses which conflict with the conscious dominant values." Thus, man retains his affective neutrality by keeping women's emotional lives in a "psychological zoo" where the animal can be appreciated from a safe distance.

Marx's influence also has a "right" and "left" side, both of which bypass the first two types of research. On the right, Marxist theory supports the notion that class, not sex, is the relevant unit of analysis. On the left, such writers as Juliet Mitchell note that women have their unique relation to the mode of production. Like serfs and peasants, housewives have remained at a preindustrial stage, doing work with "use value" but not "exchange value" (Benston 1969). Via the works of Frederick Engels and Thorstein Veblen, the notion of women as property comes in either as "sexual property" (Gilman 1966; Collins 1971) or as an item of "vicarious conspicuous consumption" (Veblen 1953).

Only in the fourth perspective is the notion of "exploitation" explicit, and there it is ambiguous. As the term passed into sociology with the works of E. A. Ross, Von Wiese, and Howard Becker, its meaning was generalized beyond its original reference to economic exploitation, and it has since fallen into disrepute. Following Gouldner (1960), we might resist dismissing it because of its heuristic overload and use it as in type 4, to mean simply "transactions involving an exchange of things of unequal value."

Underlying the four perspectives are, perhaps, implicit models of equality (Rossi 1969a): a pluralist model which envisages a society which keeps and values race, religious, and sex differences (types 1 and partly 2), an assimilation model which envisages minority groups gradually assimilating to the dominant culture (type 3), and a hybrid model which envisages a change in both the majority and the minority, resulting in a "melting pot" (type 4).

Type 1: Sex Differences

The sexes differ in the way they think (Maccoby 1966), perceive (Bieri et al. 1958), aspire (Horner 1968; Turner 1964), experience anxiety (Sinick 1956), daydream (Singer 1968), and play competitive games (Uesugi and Vinachke 1963). (Men tend to have an exploitative strategy, women an accommodative one, which even wins some games.)

Some studies document these differences; others try to explain them as due to hormones, chromosomes, internal organs, or instinct, on one hand, or upbringing, on the other. In its popular form, it is Sigmund Freud versus the early Margaret Mead, Lionel Tiger versus the feminist anthropologists, and Erik Erikson (1965) versus Naomi Weisstein (1969) and Kate Millet (1970). Actually, in Erikson's own unpublished replication on Indian children of his "inner and outer space" study, the Indian boys did not build towers.

The literature is so vast that I shall cite only a few examples from the work on cognition. Very young girls exceed boys in verbal ability (talking, reading), they do as well in counting and spatial tasks (form boards and block design) and in analytic tasks, and they do better on certain measures of creativity and not on others. But on virtually every measure, boys sooner or later do better (Maccoby 1966; Bradway and Thompson 1952). These abilities are often linked to various traits such as impulse control, fearfulness, anxiety, aggressiveness, competitiveness, degree of aspiration, and need for achievement (Maccoby 1956; Freeman 1970; Suter 1972). These traits are related, in turn, to measures of "masculinity" and "femininity."[1] However, several studies suggest that analytic thinking, creativity, and high general intelligence are linked to cross-sex typing, that is, boys with "feminine" interests and girls with "masculine" ones (Maccoby 1966).

There are two kinds of debate within this genre of research; the first is between biological and sociocultural explanations for sex differences and the second is between various socialization theories. The biological argument usually grounds itself in selected research on animals, neonates, and hormone experiments (Rosenberg and Smith 1972), whereas the sociocultural argument selects other research on animals, questions the general relevance to human behavior, and cites the data on cultural variation (Barry, Bacon, and Child 1957; Mead 1935, 1949; but see Thurnwald 1936; Mead 1937; Weisstein 1969). One interesting study suggests culture's effect, not on sex differences, but on female biology itself; the pain of menstrual cramps was significantly higher for Catholics and Jews than for Protestants (Paige 1969).

The second debate is between various socialization theorists. In Mischel's "social learning" view, children early learn to discriminate between "boy things" and "girl things" and later generalize to new situations. According to Kohlberg, on the other hand, socialization stimulates or retards basic male and female modes of cognition, pretty much regardless of what parents do or say (Maccoby 1966). These cognitive modes are based on how the young child categorizes himself or herself, and sex-linked values "develop out of the need to value things that are consistent with or like the self" (p. 165). But we know that girls as they grow up learn to value boys more and girls less (Smith 1939; Kitay 1940; McKee and Sherriffs 1956; Mendelsohn and Dobie 1970).

Thus, beyond social and biological differences are status differences, as yet dimly recognized in much type 1 research. Moreover, how American middle-class boys and girls do block designs has not yet been systematically compared with the efforts of Arapesh and Mundugumor

---

1. Rosenberg compares the "masculine" and "feminine" typology to the ancient choleric, sanguine, phlegmatic, or melancholic types also based on biology (Rosenberg and Smith 1972, p. 3).

or Arab and Chinese girls and boys. Nor do we have research on the effect of early socialization in the *absence* of later social controls which maintain or accentuate the differences.

Type 2:   The Role Perspective

Role studies usually deal with women in the family and in the economy, and with the "cultural contradictions" of being in both. Many studies of school and college girls try to isolate the cultural ingredients of the career woman and the homebody (Rapoport and Rapoport 1971; Olesen 1961) or to show how such influences as picture books (Weitzman et al. 1972), school counselors, and parents (Aberle and Naegele 1968) socialize girls.

Beyond the few studies of lower-class women and black women mentioned earlier, most of the research discusses white middle-class wives and mothers, and we have a few comparisons between classes (Rainwater, Coleman, and Handel 1959; Gavron 1966). Lopata's study (1971) of 299 housewives in suburban Chicago in the 1950s is a good biography of the "new" traditional role; nearly all had worked at some point. Other works focus on couples' friendships (Babchuk and Bates 1964), on changes through the life cycle (Bart 1970; Neugarten 1961), and on the parenthood of married (Rossi 1968) and unmarried couples (Vincent 1962).

It is always helpful to have a "devil" and some of these studies have tangled with Parsons's functionalist interpretation of the woman in the family. According to Parsons and Bales (1953), in the nuclear family everywhere there is an "instrumental" role (mediating between the family and the outside) and an "expressive" role (concerned with relations within the family). The father usually takes the first, the mother the second, and this is functional for the children, the parents, and the society. Implicitly the career wife is dysfunctional. Attacking Parsons on one flank through psychoanalytic theory, Slater (1964) shows that such a role differentiation can impede a girl's identification with her mother and a boy's with his father. Rossi attacks from the flank of role theory, drawing from type 1 research (Rossi 1968). Other things being equal, the career wife may well put a strain on the family, but it is precisely the "other things" which role theorists are now examining. Both mother and father, according to Parsons, are more powerful than children; but he says virtually nothing about power differences between husband and wife—the source of another debate between Blood and Wolfe (1960) and Gillespie (1971). Komarovsky, also a functionalist, focuses more than Parsons on the dysfunctions (of role differentiation), and she locates the problems in a different place. For example, she argues that women still bound by the apron strings, but married to men who are not, create "in-law" problems (Komarovsky 1950).

The recent research on women at work has yet to filter into the traditional preserve of family theory. About half of employed women are in jobs such as nursing or clerical work where over 70% of the workers are women (Oppenheimer 1968; also see Baker 1969; Smuts 1971). Most research is on the other half of working women, especially those in "male" professions (Epstein 1970*a*; Bernard 1964; Mattfeld and Van Aken 1965; Williams 1964; Fava 1960; White 1967; Simon, Clark, and Galway 1967; Rossi 1969*b*; Astin 1969; Theodore 1971; Hennig 1971).

There is a large body of literature on the "dual roles," much of it, like Myrdal and Klein's *Women's Two Roles: Home and Work* (1956), done in the 1950s, but some, like the Ginzberg studies (Ginzberg and Yohalem 1966), done or published in the 1960s. The "cultural contradictions" of these roles (Komarovsky 1946; Wallin 1950) are explored in Horner's well-known work on women's will to fail (1968), recently replicated by Katz (1972). Only a third of the 1972 sample, compared with two-thirds in the Horner study, showed the motive to avoid success. Another response to the dilemma, of course, is simply not to choose, or to decide to do everything; Rose found that college women, even in the fifties, planned to work full time, to volunteer for church and community work, to entertain, and to raise a large family (1951). This fits with Wilensky's finding that women who work simply add it on to other tasks (1968).

Virtually all the research shows that married career women have—or need—supportive husbands (Rapoport and Rapoport 1971). Bailyn's study (1971) of 200 British women and their husbands shows that men who scale down their career involvement, rather than those who go full steam or those who severely curtail it, have happier marriages. But whatever his career commitment, it seems that a man wants his wife to be more oriented to his than to her work (see Komarovsky in this volume), and this, according to Holmstrom's latest study, even for women Ph.D.s, is how it works out (1971).

Type 3:   Minority Perspective

A minority group, as Louis Wirth defined it, is "a group who because of their physical or cultural characteristics, are singled out from others in the society for differential and unequal treatment, and who therefore regard themselves as objects of collective discrimination" (Hacker 1951, p. 60). The research treats both the objective and subjective sides of minority status. Many studies draw the parallel with blacks, ranging from similarities in discrimination and prejudice to subjective traits such as passivity and helplessness to similarities in such things as the meaning of consumption; in the case of blacks, it's the Cadillac and magenta shirt, and in the case of women, the proverbial expensive new hat (Willis 1970). Both women and blacks have been portrayed as the hero, more courageous and noble than the ordinary, unoppressed mortal, and as the sambo, more childlike and stupid. Warner, Wellman, and Wietzman (1971) suggest a third model, the operator, who uses these images to get his or her way. The female operator, as part of the underdog psychopolitical style, has a heightened awareness of her situation and knows more although she disguises her own feelings. Shuffling, playing dumb, playing up, and dissembling are so many manipulative strategies of rational actors in oppressive circumstances.

Many studies deal with the prevailing prejudice and discrimination to which this is a response. In his landmark study of prejudice, Goldberg gave 140 college women six articles in both "masculine" fields (e.g., law and city planning) and "feminine" fields (e.g., art history, dietetics). There were two identical sets of each article signed by J. T. McKay. Some named the author as John T. McKay, others as Joan T. McKay. The students rated the articles for value, persuasiveness, profundity, writing style, professional competence, professional status, and ability to sway the reader. In both the male and female fields, the students thought John McKay more impressive; out of 54 comparisons, 44 favored John. The experiment illustrates not only the belief that females are inferior and the distorting effect of that belief on judgment, but also the women's *sensitivity* to something as apparently irrelevant as the author's sex (Goldberg 1968).

Using the identical procedure, Pheterson (1969) explored prejudice against women among middle-aged, uneducated women. This time the professional articles were on child discipline, special education, and marriage. The women judged female work to be equal to and even a bit better than male work. In a third study, Pheterson, Kiesler, and Goldberg (1971) reasoned that uneducated women may see an article in print as an achievement in itself, and may overvalue female accomplishment because it is so rare. They then showed eight paintings of 120 female students. Half of the sample thought the artist was a man, half thought it a woman; half thought the painting was just an entry, half thought it a prize-winning painting. Also half thought the artist had faced unusually severe obstacles, and half thought the artist had faced no unusual obstacles. The women judged the female entry less favorably than identical male entries, but judged the female winners equal to identical male winners. Thus, women devalued the work of women in competition until it received recognition, but of course, given the bias against triers, that recognition is hard for a woman to earn.

We can distinguish between paternalistic sex relations in which people "know their place" and in which overt conflict is rare, and competitive sex relations, where people don't know their place and overt conflict is more common (Van den Berge 1966). In the legal system, women, like juveniles, in some ways fit the paternalistic model (Nagel and Weitzman 1971). In the economy, sex relations seem to fit the competitive model, although possibly more in academia or business than in nursing or organized crime, where the paternalistic model may fit better.

In the competitive model, women are more likely to complain of discrimination, and a number of studies examine who does and who does not recognize or experience it. For example, Astin, in her study of women who earned Ph.D.'s in the late fifties, found over a third who siad they had experienced discrimination. This third also published more, had gone to more professional meetings, and earned more (Astin 1969). According to Simon's nationwide study, 15% of married women Ph.D.'s reported running into nepotism rules; and, again, these women had published more than the men or other women in the sample (Simon, Clark and Galway 1967). Another study of 2,500 male and female lawyers found that half the women lawyers said they had been discriminated against (White 1967).

Another approach is to look at those who do the discriminating. Fidell (1970) sent out 10 job applications to 155 college and university graduate psychology departments, and found that male applications received more offers for associate and full professorships, though not more assistant or lower-status offers.

The "marginal woman" is probably more common in the *almost* all-male preserves than in the predominantly female or integrated occupations (Hacker 1951; Stonequist 1961). Like George Simmel's "stranger," and Thorstein Veblen's intellectual Jew, she faces more contradictions than do women who are less, or more, integrated into the male work world. As the position of women improves (and recently it has not), the proportion of marginal women will probably increase. Yet we know little about how marginality affects, say, a woman lawyer's feelings about housewives or office workers, or how she might compare with the assimilated black bourgeois in relation to his "brother" in the ghetto.

Type 4:   The Politics of Caste

Despite overlap between the last perspective and this, the politics of caste is newer and less coherently developed; it has a different center and is going in a different direction. Its stress is on power, the different kinds of power, its distribution, use, and expression, in the parlor and in the marketplace.

As in the minority perspective, the *Realpolitik* view assumes that sex differences are due to socialization, and that differences in socialization are linked to differences in status and power. It sees role strain in power terms, and it takes as assumptions many of the questions in the minority perspective: that women are an inferior caste and experience discrimination and prejudice. It also assumes that what women as a stratum gain in resources, men as a stratum lose; thus its research comes closer to a conflict model than types 1 and 2.

As in the minority perspective, there is a social-psychological analogue to its macroanalysis. The balance of power in society is linked, in complex ways not yet understood, to various characteristics of face-to-face interaction. We have such propositions as the following: The subordinate is more "oriented" toward the superordinate. Just as the student "psychs out" the professor, and the child works his or her way around parental mood, so, too, the woman may be more oriented toward her husband than he is to her. The superordinate initiates more interactions, while the subordinate is typically more passive. The superordinate has the right to exercise certain familiarities (touching, whistling, calling, first-naming) which the subordinate cannot do (Brown 1965). The superordinate also maintains more social distance than does the subordinate. The superordinate is less likely to disclose information about him/herself than vice versa, so that "information about oneself flows opposite to the flow of power" (Henley 1972; Jourard and Lasakow 1958; Jourard and Rubin 1968). This contradicts the observation of Warner et al. that the oppressed "operator" disguises his/her feelings and knows *more* about the superordinate than the superordinate knows about him/her (Warner, Wellman, and Weitzman 1971). These behavioral regularities may vary with factors unrelated to differences in status or power—for example, nationality. Furthermore, there is some counter evidence that needs to be examined. For example, Jourard found that whites had higher self disclosure rates than did blacks, although females had higher rates than males (Jourard and Lasakow 1958, p. 95).

Interaction can be verbal or nonverbal, as, for example, in body movement (kinesics), the use of personal space (proximics), and the non-content aspects of speech (paralanguage). The stress here is not on dominant or submissive personalities but on behaviors, although there is some question about whether these behaviors are related to personality as Maslow (1939) and Sampson (1965) suggest. Erving Goffman has recently applied his grammar of face-to-face interaction to males and females. He has categorized various types of "tie-sign" (the arm lock, hand holding, the back and shoulder embrace, ecological proximity) in body behavior and verbal behavior (e.g., the three-quarter terms such as "honey" and "baby" which men and women can say to each other, and women to women but not men to men). His comparisons with other asymmetrical relations such as parent and child suggest a link to the larger political fabric (Goffman 1972).

Another exploratory study, based on 60 hours of observation of "touch," found that high-status persons (older, white, male) touch lower-status persons (younger, black, female) more than the other way around (Henley 1972). Body position and movement may also have power meanings (e.g., the head tilt and leaning as opposed to a "taut" posture). Self-disclosure, personal space, and touch may be "status reminders" and, as such, forms of informal social control. We do not know to what extent they are indicators or reinforcers of interpersonal control (Spitze 1972). But insofar as they operate in daily life they provide an alternative or supplement to the socialization theory of type 3 (Leffler, Gillespie, and Spitze 1972).

In the macropolitics of caste, Collins's recent article "A Conflict Theory of Sexual Stratification" (1971) stands out. Welding Freud's notion of sexual repression onto a Weberian social-economic history, he outlines a bargaining model of sex stratification (also see Lasch 1967). Theoretically both men and women have the same resources to bargain with—for example, income, sexual attractiveness, or social status. But these resources are not equally available to men and women; men have generally monopolized the wealth, and women, to recoup some power, have made more of a resource of their sexuality by controlling and repressing it, thus making it "cost" something (see Waller 1937). But the pattern varies with history, and with the social control of force. Collins outlines four ideal types of social structure and control of force (for instance, household head or police force), resources available to men and women, sex roles, and ideologies. The old trade of income for sex in the earlier types of social structure changes in the last type, so that women increasingly use income as a resource, and men, increasingly, sexuality. Even in the new distribution and use of resources, however, the market favors men, and the old trade still operates too.

Implications

Despite the diversity, the research in this field yields some questions, data, and ideas (and biases) which can infuse sociology from the ground floor up. It may make sociologists trim their generalizations to size; thus studies of social mobility will have to specify that they concern *male* social mobility, alienation, *man's* alienation. Potter (1964) has done just this specifying of propositions for historical writing. It can also question some key assumptions. For example, most stratification research defines the social class of the family, not the individuals in it; but some estimate that this assumption fails to fit a full two-fifths of American households with consist of females, are headed by females, or are husband-wife families where the husband is retired, unemployed, working part time, or otherwise not in the labor force (Watson and Barth 1964; see also Acker, in this volume).

The sociology of sex roles is not simply adding onto sociology studies about women, though clearly there is a need for this too. Until recently, the research on achievement motivation and birth order was virtually all on male subjects. The sociology of sex roles is research on anyone or anything which reflects, in its assumptions and propositions, one of the perspectives described here, and which takes sex roles in some way to be an important independent variable. This may mean more research on men. Much of the work on dominance gestures is based on a mixed male and female sample. Rossi's (1970) study in the sociology of knowledge focuses on the male biographers of Harriet Taylor Mill.

As a result of some of this work, researchers may even alter their vocabulary. Women have been consistently found to be more "field dependent" (i.e., less able to separate figure from ground); but, as Bart (1972) notes, "it is very useful to be aware of the 'ground' or 'environment.' In any case, not being able to see the forest for the trees [is] not superior to not being able to see the trees for the forest." The term in some research is now "field sensitive."

But most of all this new field means turning former assumptions into new research problems. We don't even know whether, let alone how, women's position has improved with industrialization. According to modernization theorists, as a society develops, the importance of ascription declines, achievement rises, and the position of women improves. As measured by income, education, and occupation, we know women's status (relative to men's) has declined in the last 25 years (Knudsen 1969). But even before that, the picture is unclear. Smith notes a decline from the Puritan era to the 19th century, especially at the end of the 18th century (Smith 1970). And in an excellent economic study of women in the underdeveloped world, Boserup shows that as industrialization rises, the position of women declines (1970; also see Sullerot 1971, p. 35) We also know little about the link between class and caste. The ideology of the companionate marriage to the contrary, is the caste gap greater in the upper classes than in the lower (Goode 1970, p. 21)? Do more rigid class barriers mean less rigid caste barriers, or do these structural rigidities occur in all ways at once? What changes have occurred in the avenues of female mobility? Were witchcraft and spiritualism, for example, early means of female social mobility?

In the study of modern societies or traditional, upper-class or lower-, white or black, now or in the 18th century, the issue of sex roles is the single biggest blind spot in existing sociology. While sociology, like the American government, is gifted at "resistance through incorporation," we may nonetheless move slowly to a sociology of people.

References

Aberle, David F., and Kaspar Naegele. 1968. "Middle-Class Fathers' Occupational Role and Attitudes toward Children." In *The Family*, edited by N. W. and E. F. Vogel. New York: Free Press.

Astin, Helen. 1969. *The Woman Doctorate in America*. New York: Russell Sage Foundation.

Astin, Helen, Nancy Suniewick, and Susan Dweck. 1971. *Women, a Bibliography on Their Education and Careers*. Washington, D.C.: Human Service Press.

Babchuk, N., and A. Bates 1964. "The Primary Relations of Middle Class Couples." *Readings on the Family and Society*, edited by W. J. Goode. Englewood Cliffs, N.J.: Prentice-Hall.

Bailyn, Lotte. 1971. "Career and Family Orientations of Husbands and Wives in Relation to Marital Happiness." In *The Professional Woman*, edited by Athena Theodore. Cambridge, Mass.: Schenkman.

Baker, Elizabeth. 1969. *Technology and Women's Work*. New York: Columbia University Press.

Bakke, E. Wight. 1940. *Citizens without Work*. New Haven, Conn.: Yale University Press.

Barry, Herbert, M. K. Bacon, and Irvin L. Child. 1957. "A Cross Cultural Survey of Some Sex Differences in Socialization." *Journal of Abnormal and Social Psychology* 55 (November): 327–32.

Bart, Pauline. 1970. "Mother Portnoy's Complaints." *Trans-Action* 8 (November–December): 69–74.

———, ed. 1971. Special Issue: "Sexism in Family Studies." *Journal of Marriage and the Family*, vol. 33 (August).

Benson, Leonard. 1968. *Fatherhood: A Sociological Perspective*. New York: Random House.

Benston, Margaret. 1969. "The Political Economy of Women's Liberation." *Monthly Review*, vol. 21 (September).

Bernard, Jessie. 1964. *Academic Women*. University Park: Pennsylvania State University Press.

———, 1966. *Marriage and Family among Negroes*. New York: Prentice-Hall.

Bieri, J., et al. 1958. "Sex Differences in Perceptual Behavior." *Journal of Personality* 26(1): 1–12.

Biggar, Jeanne C. 1970. *Bibliography on the Sociology of Sex Roles*. Charlottesville: Department of Sociology, University of Virginia.

Blood, Robert Jr., and Donald M. Wolfe. 1960. *Husbands and Wives: The Dynamics of Married Living*. New York: Macmillan.

Boserup, Ester. 1970. *Woman's Role in Economic Development*. New York: St. Martin's.

Bradway, Katherine P., and Clare W. Thompson. 1952. "Intelligence at Adulthood: A 25 Year Follow-up." *Journal of Educational Psychology* 53(1): 1–14.

Bridges, W. 1965. "Family Patterns and Social Values in America, 1825–1875." *American Quarterly* 17 (Spring): 3–11.

Brown, R. 1965. *Social Psychology*. Glencoe, Ill.: Free Press.

Bruemmer, Linda. 1970. "The Condition of Women in Society Today: Annotated Bibliography—Part II." *Journal of the National Association of Women Deans and Counselors* 33 (Winter): 89–95.

Caputo, D. 1963. "The Parents of the Schizophrenic." *Family Process* 2(3): 339–56.

Carlson, Earl, and Rae Carlson. 1960. "Male and Female Subjects in Personality Research." *Journal of Abnormal and Social Psychology* 61 (February): 482–83.

Cisler, Lucinda. 1972. "Women: A Bibliography." 102 West 80th Street, New York, N.Y.

Coelho, George, David Hamburg, Rudolph Moos, and Peter Randolph, eds. 1970. *Coping and Adaptation: A Behavioral Sciences Bibliography*. National Institute of Mental

Health; U.S., Department of Health, Education and Welfare; Public Health Service; Health Service and Mental Health Administration. Washington, D.C.: Government Printing Office.

Cole, Johnneta B. 1971. "Black Women in America: An Annotated Bibliography." *Black Scholar* 3 (December): 42–53.

Collins, Randall. 1971. "A Conflict Theory of Sexual Stratification." *Social Problems* 19 (Summer): 3–12.

Cumming, Elaine, and William Henry. 1961. *Growing Old: The Process of Disengagement*. New York; Basic.

Domhoff, G. William. 1970. "The Feminine Half of the Upper Class." In *The Upper Circles*. New York: Random House.

Epstein, Cynthia. 1970*a*. *Woman's Place*. Berkeley: University of California Press.

———, 1970*b*. "Encountering the Male Establishment: Sex Status Limits Careers in the Professions." *American Journal of Sociology* 75(6): 965–82.

ERIC Clearinghouse on Adult Education. 1970. *Continuing Education of Women, Current Information Sources*, vol. 32 (September). Syracuse, N.Y.: ERIC Clearinghouse on Adult Education.

Erikson, Erik. 1965. "Inner and Outer Space: Reflections on Womanhood." In *The Woman in America*, edited by Robert Lifton. Boston. Houghton Mifflin.

Fava, Sylvia. 1960. "The Status of Women in Professional Sociology." *American Sociological Review* 25 (April): 271–76.

Fidell, L. S. 1970. "Empirical Verification of Sex Discrimination in Hiring Practices in Psychology." *American Psychologist* 25(12): 1094–98.

Fiedler, Leslie A. 1966. "Good Good Girls and Good Bad Boys, *Clarissa* as a Juvenile." In *Love and Death in the American Novel*. New York: Stein & Day.

Firestone, Shulamith. 1970. *The Dialectic of Sex*. New York: Morrow.

Freeman, Jo. 1970. "Growing Up Girlish." *Trans-Action* 8 (November-December): 36–43.

Frithioff, Patricia. 1967. *A Selected Annotated Bibliography of Materials Related to Women in Science*. Lund: Research Policy Program.

Gavron, Hannah. 1966. *The Captive Wife: Conflicts of Housebound Mothers*. London: Routledge & Kegan Paul.

Gillespie, Dair. 1971. "Who Has the Power? The Marital Struggle." *Journal of Marriage and the Family* 33 (August): 445–58.

Gilman, Charlotte Perkins. (1898) 1966. *Women and Economics*. New York: Harper & Row.

Ginzberg, Eli, and Alice M. Yohalem. 1966. *Educated American Women: Life Styles and Self Portraits*. New York: Columbia University Press.

Goffman, Erving. 1972. Lecture presented at a meeting of Sociologists for Women in Society, San Francisco.

Goldberg, Philip. 1968. "Are Women Prejudiced against Women?" *Trans-Action* (April), pp. 28–30.

Gouldner, Alvin. 1960. "The Norm of Reciprocity: A Preliminary Statement." *American Sociological Review* 25 (April): 161–78.

Hacker, Helen. 1951. "Women as a Minority Group." *Social Forces* 30 (October): 60–69.

Henley, Nancy. 1972. "Power, Sex and Nonverbal Communication: The Politics of Touch." Psychology Department, University of Maryland, College Park.

Hennig, Margaret. 1971. "Career Development for Women Executives." Ph.D. dissertation, Harvard Graduate School of Business Administration.

Hoffman, L. W. 1961. "Effects of Maternal Employment on the Child." *Child Development* 32 (March): 187–97.

Holmes, Douglas S., and Bruce W. Jorgensen. 1971. "Do Personality and Social Psychologists Study Men More than Women?" *Government Reports Announcements*, December 25.

Holmstrom, Lynda. 1971. "Career Patterns of Married Couples." In *The Professional Woman*, edited by Athena Theodore. Cambridge, Mass.: Schenkman.

Horner, Matina. 1968. "Sex Differences in Achievement Motivation and Performance in Competitive and Non Competitive Situations." Ph.D. dissertation, University of Michigan.

Hughes, Marija Matich. 1970. "The Sexual Barrier: Legal and Economic Aspects of Employment." 2422 Fox Plaza, San Francisco, Calif.

Jourard, S. M., and P. Lasakow. 1958. "Some Factors in Self-Disclosure." *Journal of Abnormal and Social Psychology* 56(1): 91–98.

Jourard, S. M., and J. E. Rubin. 1968. "Self-Disclosure and Touching: A Study of Two Modes of Interpersonal Encounter and Their Interreaction." *Journal of Humanistic Psychology* 8(1): 38–48.

Kagan, Jerome, and Howard A. Moss. 1692. *Birth to Maturity: A Study in Psychological Development*. New York: Wiley.

Katz, Marlaine L. 1972. "Female Motive to Avoid Success: A Psychological Barrier or a Response to Deviance?" Manuscript. School of Education, Stanford University.

Keiffer, Miriam, and Patricia Warren. 1970. *Population Limitation and Women's Status: A Bibliography*. Princeton, N.J.: Educational Testing Service.

Kitay, P. M. 1940. "A Comparison of the Sexes in Their Attitudes and Beliefs about Women." *Sociometry* 34(4): 399–407.

Knudsen, Dean. 1969. "The Declining Status of Women: Popular Myths and the Failure of Functionalist Thought." *Social Forces* 48 (December): 183–93.

Kohn, Melvin, and John Clausen. 1956. "Parental Authority Behavior and Schizophrenia." *American Journal of Orthopsychiatry* 26 (April): 297–313.

Komarovsky, Mirra. 1946. "Cultural Contradictions and Sex Roles." *American Journal of Sociology* 52 (November): 185–89.

———, 1950. "Functional Analysis of Sex Roles." *American Sociological Review* 15 (August): 508–16.

———, 1969. *Blue Collar Marriage*. New York: Random.

Kuvlesky, William and David Reynolds. 1970. *Educational Aspirations and Expectations of Youth: A Bibliography of Research Literature II*. College Station: Department of Agricultural Economics and Rural Sociology, Texas A & M University.

Ladner, Joyce A. 1972. *Tomorrow's Tomorrow*. New York: Doubleday.

Langer, Elinor. 1970. "The Women of the Telephone Company." *New York Review of Books*, March 26.

Lasch, Christopher. 1967. "Mable Dodge Luhan: Sex as Politics." In *The New Radicalism in America*. New York: Vintage.

Laws, Judith Long. 1971. "A Feminist Review of Marital Adjustment Literature: The Rape of the Locke." *Journal of Marriage and the Family* 33 (August): 483–516.

Leffler, Ann, Dair Gillespie, and Glenna Spitze. 1972. Presentation in graduate seminar, "Sociology of Sex Roles." Sociology Department, University of California, Berkeley.

Lidz, R., S. Fleck, and A. Cornelison. 1965. *Schizophrenia and the Family*. New York: International Universities Press.

Lopata, Helena Zananiecki. 1971. *Occupation: Housewife*. London: Oxford University Press.

Maccoby, Eleanor, ed. 1966. *The Development of Sex Differences*. Palo Alto, Calif.: University of Stanford Press.

McKee, J., and A. Sheriffs. 1956. "The Differential Evaluation of Males and Females." *Journal of Personality* 25 (2): 357–71.

Martel, Martin. 1968. "Age-Sex Roles in American Magazine Fiction 1890–1955." In *Middle Age and Aging*, edited by B. Neugarten. Chicago: University of Chicago Press.

Maslow, A. H. 1939. "Dominance, Personality and Social Behavior in Women." *Journal of Social Psychology* 10 (1): 3–39.

Mattfeld, Jacqueline, and Carol Van Aken. 1965. *Women and the Scientific Professions.* Cambridge, Mass.: M.I.T. Press.

Mead, Margaret. 1935. *Sex and Temperament in Three Primitive Societies.* New York: Dell.

———, 1937, "A Reply to a Review of Sex and Temperament in Three Primitive Societies." *American Anthropologist* 39 (3): 558–61.

———, 1949. *Male and Female.* New York: Mentor.

Mendelsohn, Robert, and Shirley Dobie. 1970. "Women's Self Conception: A Block to Career Development." Manuscript. La Fayette Clinic, Department of Mental Health, Detroit, Michigan.

Millet, Kate. 1970. *Sexual Politics.* New York: Doubleday.

Millman, Marcia. 1970. "Some Remarks on Sex Role Research." Paper delivered at the meeting of the American Sociological Association, Washington, D.C., August 31–September 3.

Myrdal, Alva, and Viola Klein. 1956. *Women's Two Roles: Home and Work.* London: Routledge & Kegan Paul.

Nagel, Stuart, and Lenore Weitzman. 1971. "Women as Litigants." *Hastings Law Journal* 23 (November): 171–98.

National Council on Family Relations. 1970. *Annotated Bibliography, Family Life: Literature and Films.* Minneapolis: Minnesota Council on Family Relations.

Neugarten, Bernice L. 1961. "Women's Changing Roles through the Life Cycle." *Journal of the National Association of Women Deans and Counselors* 24 (June): 163–70.

———, ed. 1968. "Age, Sex Roles, and Personality in Middle Age: A Thematic Apperception Study." In *Middle Age and Aging.* Chicago: University of Chicago Press.

Nye, F. Ivan, and Lois Wladis Hoffman, eds. 1963. *The Employed Mother in America.* Chicago: Rand McNally.

Olesen, Virginia L. 1961. "Sex Role Definitions among College Undergraduates: A Study of Stanford Freshmen." Ph.D. dissertation, Stanford University.

Oppenheimer, Valerie. 1968. "Sex Labelling of Jobs." *Industrial Relations,* vol. 7 (May).

Paige, Karen. 1969. "The Effects of Oral Contraceptives on Affective Fluctuations Associated with the Menstrual Cycle." Ph.D. dissertation, University of Michigan.

Parsons, Talcott, and R. F. Bales. 1953. *Family, Socialization and Interaction Process.* Glencoe, Ill.: Free Press.

Pheterson, Gail I. 1969. "Female Prejudice against Men." Connecticut College, New London.

Pheterson, Gail I., Sara B. Kiesler, and Philip Goldberg. 1971. "Evaluation of the Performance of Women as a Function of Their Sex, Achievement and Personal History." *Journal of Personality and Social Psychology* 19 (1): 144–48.

Potter, David M. 1964. "American Women and the American Character." In *American Character and Culture,* edited by J. Hogue. De Land, Fla.: Everett.

Putnam, Emily J. 1910. *The Lady.* New York: Putnam.

Radcliffe Institute. 1970. "Womanpower, Selected Bibliography on Educated Women and the Labor Force." 3 James Street, Cambridge Mass. 02138.

Rainwater, Lee, Richard Coleman, and Gerald Handel. 1959. *Workingman's Wife: Her Personality, World and Life Style.* New York: Oceana.

Rapoport, Rhona, and Robert Rapoport. 1971. "Early and Later Experiences as Determinants of Adult Behavior: Married Women's Family and Career Patterns." *British Journal of Sociology* 22 (March): 16–30.

Rose, Arnold. 1951. "The Adequacy of Women's Expectations for Adult Roles." *Social Forces* 30 (April): 69–77.

Rosenberg, B. G., and Brian Sutton Smith. 1972. *Sex and Identity.* New York: Holt, Rinehart & Winston.

Rossi, Alice. 1964. "The Equality of Women: An Immodest Proposal." *Daedalus* 93 (Spring): 607–52.

———, 1968. "Transition to Parenthood." *Journal of Marriage and the Family* 30 (1): 26–39.

————, 1969a. "Sex Equality: The Beginnings of Ideology." *Humanist* (September-October).

————, 1969b. "The Status of Women in Sociology." *American Sociologist* (Fall).

Rossi, Alice, ed. 1970. *Essays on Sex Equality*. Chicago: University of Chicago Press.

Safilios-Rothschild, Constantina. 1972. *Toward a Sociology of Women*. Lexington, Mass.: Xerox.

Sampson, Ronald V. 1965. *The Psychology of Power*. New York: Pantheon.

Sells, Lucy. In press. *Current Research on Sex Roles*. Published by author. Available from Sociology Department, University of California, Berkeley.

Siegel, A. E., and M. B. Haas. 1963. "The Working Mother: A Review of Research." *Child Development* 34 (September): 513–42.

Simon, Rita J., Shirley Merritt Clark, and Kathleen Galway. 1967. "The Woman Ph.D.: A Recent Profile." *Social Problems* 15 (Fall): 221–36.

Singer, Jerome. 1968. "The Importance of Daydreaming." *Psychology Today* 1 (April): 18–27.

Sinick, D. 1956. "Two Anxiety Scales Correlated and Examined for Sex Differences." *Journal of Clinical Psychology* 12 (4): 394–95.

Slater, Philip. 1964. "Parental Role Differentiation." In *The Family, Its Structure and Functions*, edited by Rose Coser. New York: St. Martins.

Smith, Page. 1970. *Daughters of the Promised Land*. Boston: Little, Brown.

Smith, S. 1939. "Age and Sex Differences in Children's Opinions concerning Sex Differences." *Journal of Genetic Psychology* 54 (1): 17–25.

Smuts, Robert W. 1971. *Women and Work in America*. New York: Schocken.

Spiegel, Jeanne. 1969. *A Selected Annotated Bibliography: Sex Role Concepts*. Washington, D.C.: Business and Professional Women's Foundation.

————, 1970a. *A Selected Annotated Bibliography: Working Mothers*. Washington, D.C.: Business and Professional Women's Foundation.

————, 1970b. *A Selected Annoted Bibliography: Women Executives*. Washington, D.C.: Business and Professional Women's Foundation.

Spitze, Glena. 1972. "Non-Verbal Behavior and Interpersonal Control: An Exploration of Casual Relations." Sociology Department, University of California, Berkeley.

Steinmann, Ann. 1971. *Bibliography on Male-Female Role Research*. New York: Maferr Foundation.

Stolz, Lois Meek. 1960. "Effects of Maternal Employment on Children: Evidence from Research." *Child Development* 31 (4): 749–82.

Stonequist, Everett V. 1961. *The Marginal Man: A Study in Personality and Culture Conflict*. New York: Russell & Russell.

Suelzle, Marijean. In press. *The Female Sex Role*. Urbana: University of Illinois Press.

Sullerot, Evelyn. 1971. *Women, Society and Change*. New York: McGraw-Hill.

Suter, Barbara A. 1972. "Masculinity-Feminity in Creative Women." Ph.D. dissertation, Fordham University.

Theodore, Athena. 1971. *The Professional Woman*. Cambridge, Mass.: Schenkman.

Thurnwald, R. 1936. "Review of *Sex and Temperament in Three Primitive Societies*, by Margaret Mead." *American Anthropologist* 38 (4): 663–667.

Turner, Ralph. 1964. "Some Aspects of Women's Ambition." *American Journal of Sociology* 70 (November): 271–85.

Uesugi, T. K., and W. E. Vinachke. 1963. "Strategy in a Feminine Game." *Sociometry* 26 (1): 75–88.

U.S., Department of Health, Education and Welfare. 1970a. *The Federal Program in Population Research: Inventory of Population Research Supported by Federal Agencies during Fiscal Year 1970*. Washington, D.C.: Government Printing Office.

————, Office of Education, International Organizations. 1970b. *The United States of*

America—Equality of Access of Women and Girls to Education, 1959–1969. Prepared for the *International Bureau of Education Bulletin*.

U.S., Department of Labor. 1970. *Women—Their Social and Economic Status*. No. 903.590. Washington, D.C.: Government Printing Office.

———. Wage and Labor Standards Administration, Women's Bureau. 1969. *Handbook on Women Workers*. Women's Bureau Bulletin no. 294. Washington, D.C.: Government Printing Office.

Van den Berge, Pierre. 1966. "Paternalistic versus Competitive Race Relations: An Ideal-Type Approach." In *Racial and Ethnic Relations: Selected Readings*, edited by Bernard E. Segal. New York: Crowell.

Veblen, Thorstein. 1953. *The Theory of the Leisure Class*. New York: Mentor.

Vincent, Clark E. 1962. *Unmarried Mothers*. New York: Free Press.

Waller, Willard, 1937. "The Rating and Dating Complex." *American Sociological Review* 2 (August): 727–34.

Wallin, Paul. 1950. "Cultural Contraditions and Sex Roles: A Repeat Study." *American Sociological Review* 15 (2): 288–93.

Warner, Steve, David Wellman, and Lenore Weitzman. 1971. "The Hero, the Sambo and the Operator: Reflections on Characterizations of the Oppressed." Paper presented at the American Sociological Association Convention.

Watson, Walter, and Ernest Barth. 1964. "Questionable Assumptions in the Theory of Social Stratification." *Pacific Sociological Review* 7 (Spring): 10–16.

Watt, Ian. 1962. *The Rise of the Novel: Studies in Defoe, Richardson and Fielding*. Berkeley: University of California Press.

Weisstein, Naomi. 1969. "Kinder, Küche, Kirche as Scientific Law: Psychology Constructs the Female." *Motive* (March-April).

Weitzman, Lenore, Deborah Eifler, Elizabeth Hokada, and Catherine Ross, 1972. "Sex Role Socialization in Picture Books for Pre-School Children." *American Journal of Sociology* 77 (May): 1125–50.

Welter, Barbara. 1966. "The Cult of True Womanhood: 1820–1860." *American Quarterly* 18 (Summer): 151–74.

Westervelt, Esther, and Deborah A. Fixter. 1971. *Women's Higher and Continuing Education with Selected References on Related Aspects of Women's Lives*. New York: College Entrance Examination Board.

Whaley, Sara Stauffer, 1972. *Women Studies Abstracts*, vol. 1, no. 1. P.O. Box 1, Rush, New York 14543.

White, James. 1967. "Women in the Law." *Michigan Law Review* 65 (April): 1051–1122.

Wilensky, Harold, 1968. *Women's Work: Economic Growth, Ideology and Structure*. Institute of Industrial Relations, Reprint Series, no. 7. Berkeley: Institute of Industrial Relations, University of California.

Williams, Josephine. 1964. "Patients and Prejudice: Lay Attitudes toward Women Physicians." *American Journal of Sociology* 51 (January): 283–87.

Willis, Ellen, 1970. "Women and the Myth of Consumerism." *Ramparts* (June).

22

A Bright Woman is Caught in a Double Bind

MATINA HORNER

A woman who is guided by the head and not the heart is a
social pestilence: she has all the defects of a passionate and
affectionate woman, with none of her compensations: she
is without pity, without love, without virtue, without sex.

—HONORÉ DE BALZAC

ABSTRACT

*Women have traditionally received little more than a footnote in major works on achieve-
ment and motivation. In this short reading, for which she has drawn considerable ac-
claim, Matina Horner summarizes her findings on women and success. "A bright
woman", writes Ms. Horner, "is caught in a double bind. In testing and other achievement-oriented situations she worries not only about failure, but also about success. If she
fails, she is not living up to her own standards of performance; if she succeeds, she is not
living up to societal expectations about the female role." This internal conflict, asserts
Ms. Horner, can lead to an inhibition of a woman's achievement motivation.*

Consider Phil, a bright young college sophomore. He has always done
well in school, he is in the honors program, he has wanted to be a doctor
as long as he can remember. We ask him to tell us a story based on one
clue: *"After first-term finals, John finds himself at the top of his medical-school
class.* Phil writes:

John is a conscientious young man who worked hard. He is pleased with himself. John has always wanted to go into medicine and is very dedicated . . . John continues working hard and eventually graduates at the top of his class.

Now consider Monica, another honors student. She too has always done well and she too has visions of a flourishing career. We give her the same clue, but with "Anne" as the successful student—*after first-term finals, Anne finds herself at the top of her medical-school class.* Instead of identifying with Anne's triumph, Monica tells a bizarre tale:

Anne starts proclaiming her surprise and joy. Her fellow classmates are so disgusted with her behavior that they jump on her in a body and beat her. She is maimed for life.

Next we ask Monica and Phil to work on a series of achievement tests by themselves. Monica scores higher than Phil. Finally we get them together, competing against each other on the same kind of tests. Phil performs magnificently, but Monica dissolves into a bundle of nerves.

The glaring contrast between the two stories and the dramatic changes in performance in competitive situations illustrate important differences between men and women in reacting to achievement.

In 1953, David McClelland, John Atkinson and colleagues published the first major work on the "achievement motive." Through the use of the Thematic Apperception Test (TAT), they were able to isolate the psychological characteristic of a *need to achieve*. This seemed to be an internalized standard of excellence, motivating the individual to do well in any achievement-oriented situation involving intelligence and leadership ability. Subsequent investigators studied innumerable facets of achievement motivation: How it is instilled in children, how it is expressed, how it relates to social class, even how it is connected to the rise and fall of civilizations. The result of all this research is an impressive and a theoretically consistent body of data about the achievement motive—in men.

Women, however, are conspicuously absent from almost all of the studies. In the few cases where the ladies were included, the results were contradictory or confusing. So women were eventually left out altogether. The predominantly male researchers apparently decided, as Freud had before them, that the only way to understand woman was to turn to the poets. Atkinson's 1958 book, *Motives in Fantasy, Action and Society*, is an 800-page compilation of all of the theories and facts on achievement motivation in men. Women got a footnote, reflecting the state of the science.

To help remedy this lopsided state of affairs, I undertook to explore the basis for sex differences in achievement motivation. But where to begin?

My first clue came from the one consistent finding on the women: they get higher test-anxiety scores than do the men. Eleanor Maccoby has suggested that the girl who is motivated to achieve is defying conventions of what girls "should" do. As a result, the intellectual woman pays a price in anxiety. Margaret Mead concurs, noting that intense intellectual striving can be viewed as "competitively aggressive behavior." And of course Freud thought that the whole essence of femininity lay in repressing aggressiveness (and hence intellectuality).

Thus consciously or unconsciously the girl equates intellectual achievement with loss of femininity. A bright woman is caught in a double bind. In testing and other achievement-oriented situations she worries not only about failure, but also about success. If she fails, she is not living up to her own standards of performance; if she succeeds she is not living up to societal expectations about the female role. Men in our society do not experience this kind of ambivalence, because they are not only permitted but actively encouraged to do well.

For women, then, the desire to achieve is often contaminated by what I call the *motive to avoid success*. I define it as the fear that success in competitive achievement situations will lead to negative consequences, such as unpopularity and loss of femininity. This motive, like the achievement motive itself, is a stable disposition within the person, acquired early in life along with other sex-role standards. When fear of success conflicts with a desire to be successful, the result is an inhibition of achievement motivation.

I began my study with several hypotheses about the motive to avoid success:

1) Of course, it would be far more characteristic of women than of men.

2) It would be more characteristic of women who are capable of success and who are career-oriented than of women not so motivated. Women who are not seeking success should not, after all, be threatened by it.

3) I anticipated that the anxiety over success would be greater in competitive situations (when one's intellectual performance is evaluated against someone else's) than in noncompetitive ones (when one works alone). The aggressive, masculine aspects of achievement striving are certainly more pronounced in competitive settings, particularly when the opponent is male. Women's anxiety should therefore be greatest when they compete with men.

I administered the standard TAT achievement motivation measures to a sample of 90 girls and 88 boys, all undergraduates at the University of Michigan. In addition, I asked each to tell a story based on the clue described before: *After first-term finals, John (Anne) finds himself (herself) at the top of his (her) medical-school class.* The girls wrote about Anne, the boys about John.

Their stories were scored for "motive to avoid success" if they expressed any negative imagery that reflected concern about doing well. Generally, such imagery fell into three categories:

1) The most frequent Anne story reflected strong fears of social rejection as a result of success. The girls in this group showed anxiety about becoming unpopular, unmarriageable and lonely.

Anne is an acne-faced bookworm. She runs to the bulletin board and finds she's at the top. As usual she smarts off. A chorus of groans is the rest of the class's reply . . . She studies 12 hours a day, and lives at home to save money. "Well it certainly paid off. All the Friday and Saturday nights without dates, fun—I'll be the best woman doctor alive." And yet a twinge of sadness comes thru—she wonders what she really has . . . ."

Although Anne is happy with her success she fears what will happen to her social life. The male med. students don't seem to think very highly of a female who has beaten them in their field . . . She will be a proud and successful but also a very *lonely* doctor.

Anne doesn't want to be number one in her class . . . she feels she shouldn't rank so high because of social reasons. She drops down to ninth in the class and then marries the boy who graduates number one.

Anne is pretty darn proud of herself, but everyone hates and envies her. *previous page*

2) Girls in the second category were less concerned with issues of social approval or disapproval; they were more worried about definitions of womanhood. Their stories expressed guilt and despair over success, and doubts about their femininity or normality.

Unfortunately Anne no longer feels so certain that she really wants to be a doctor. She is worried about herself and wonders if perhaps she isn't normal . . . Anne decides not to continue with her medical work but to take courses that have a deeper personal meaning for her.

Anne feels guilty . . . She will finally have a nervous breakdown and quit medical school and marry a successful young doctor.

Anne is pleased. She had worked extraordinarily hard and her grades showed it. "It is not enough," Anne thinks. "I am not happy." She didn't even want to be a doctor. She is not sure what she wants. Anne says to hell with the whole business and goes into social work—not hardly as glamorous, prestigious or lucrative; but she is happy.

3) The third group of stories did not even try to confront the ambivalence about doing well. Girls in this category simply denied the possibility that any mere woman could be so successful. Some of them completely changed the content of the clue, or distorted it, or refused to believe it, or absolved Anne of responsibility for her success. These stories were remarkable for their psychological ingenuity:

Anne is a *code name* for a nonexistent person created by a group of med. students. They take turns writing exams for Anne . . . .

Anne is really happy she's on top, though *Tom is higher than she*—though that's as it should be . . . Anne doesn't mind Tom winning.

Anne is talking to her counselor. Counselor says she will make a fine *nurse*.

It was *luck* that Anne came out on top because she didn't want to go to medical school anyway.

Fifty-nine girls—over 65 per cent—told stories that fell into one or another of the above categories. But only eight boys, fewer than 10 per cent, showed evidence of the motive to avoid success. (These differences are significant at better than the .0005 level.) In fact, sometimes I think that most of the young men in the sample were incipient Horatio Algers. They expressed unequivocal delight at John's success (clearly John had worked hard for it), and projected a grand and glorious future for him. There was none of the hostility, bitterness and ambivalence that the girls felt for Anne. In short, the differences between male and female stories based on essentially the same clue were enormous.

Two of the stories are particularly revealing examples of this male-female contrast. The girls insisted that Anne give up her career for marriage:

Anne has a boyfriend, Carl, in the same class and they are quite serious . . . She wants him to be scholastically higher than she is. Anne will deliberately lower her academic standing the next term, while she does all she subtly can to help Carl. His grades come up and Anne soon drops out of medical school. They marry and he goes on in school while she raises their family.

But of course the boys would ask John to do no such thing:

John has worked very hard and his long hours of study have paid off . . . He is thinking about his girl, Cheri, whom he will marry at the end of med. school. He realizes he can give her all the things she desires after he becomes established. He will go on in med. school and be successful in the long run.

Success inhibits social life for the girls; it enhances social life for the boys.

Earlier I suggested that the motive to avoid success is especially aroused in competitive situations. In the second part of this study I wanted to see whether the aggressive overtones of competition against men scared the girls away. Would competition raise their anxiety about success and thus lower their performance?

First I put all of the students together in a large competitive group, and gave them a series of achievement tests (verbal and arithmetic). I then assigned them randomly to one of three other experimental conditions. One-third worked on a similar set of tests, each in competition with a member of the same sex. One-third competed against a member of the opposite sex. The last third worked by themselves, a non-competitive condition.

Ability is an important factor in achievement motivation research. If you want to compare two persons on the strength of their *motivation* to succeed, how do you know that any differences in performance are not due to initial differences in *ability* to succeed? One way of avoiding this problem is to use each subject as his own control; that is, the performance of an individual working alone can be compared with his score in competition. Ability thus remains constant; any change in score must be due to motivational factors. This control over ability was, of course, possible only for the last third of my subjects: the 30 girls and 30 boys who had worked alone *and* in the large group competition. I decided to look at their scores first.

Performance changed dramatically over the two situations. A large number of the men did far better when they were in competition than when they worked alone. For the women the reverse was true. Fewer than one-third of the women, but more than two-thirds of the men, got significantly higher scores in competition.

When we looked at just the girls in terms of the motive to avoid success, the comparisons were even more striking. As predicted, the students who felt ambivalent or anxious about doing well turned in their best scores when they worked by themselves. Seventy-seven per cent of the girls who feared success did better alone than in competition. Women who were low on the motive, however, behaved more like the men: 93 per cent of them got higher scores in competition. (Results significant at the .005.)

Female Fear of Success & Performance

	perform better working alone	*perform better in competition*
high fear of success	13	4
low fear of success	1	12

As a final test of motivational differences, I asked the students to indicate on a scale from 1 to 100 "How important was it for you to do well in this situation?" The high-fear-of-success girls said that it was much more important for them to do well when they worked alone than when they worked in either kind of competition. For the low-fear girls, such differences were not statistically significant. Their test scores were higher in competition, as we saw, and they thought that it was important to succeed no matter what the setting. And in all experimental conditions—working alone, or in competition against males or females—high-fear women consistently lagged behind their fearless comrades on the importance of doing well.

These findings suggest that most women will fully explore their intellectual potential only when they do not need to compete—and least of all when they are competing with men. This was most true of women with a strong anxiety about success. Unfortunately, these are often the same women who could be very successful if they were free from that anxiety. The girls in my sample who feared success also tended to have high intellectual ability and histories of academic success. (It is interesting to note that all but two of these girls were majoring in the humanities and in spite of very high grade points aspired to traditional female careers: housewife, mother, nurse, schoolteacher. Girls who did not fear success, however, were aspiring to graduate degrees, and careers in such scientific areas as math, physics and chemistry.)

We can see from this small study that achievement motivation in women is much more complex than the same drive in men. Most men do not find many inhibiting forces in their path if they are able and motivated to succeed. As a result, they are not threatened by competition; in fact, surpassing an opponent is a source of pride and enhanced masculinity.

If a woman sets out to do well, however, she bumps into a number of obstacles. She learns that it really isn't ladylike to be too intellectual. She is warned that men will treat her with distrustful tolerance at best, and outright prejudice at worst, if she pursues a career. She learns the truth of Samuel Johnson's comment, "A man is in general better pleased when he has a good dinner upon his table, than when his wife talks Greek." So she doesn't learn Greek, and the motive to avoid success is born.

In recent years many legal and educational barriers to female achievement have been removed; but it is clear that a psychological barrier remains. The motive to avoid success has an all-too-important influence on the intellectual and professional lives of women in our society. But perhaps there is cause for optimism. Monica may have seen Anne maimed for life, but a few of the girls forecast a happier future for our medical student. Said one:

Anne is quite a lady—not only is she tops academically, but she is liked and admired by her fellow students—quite a trick in a man-dominated field. She is brilliant—but she is also a woman. She will continue to be at or near the top. And . . . always a lady.

23
Fear of Success: Popular, but Unproven

DAVID TRESEMER

ABSTRACT

People everywhere seized upon research that traced many of women's problems to a "fear of success." The only trouble is that the public rushed in before the results were final. Until we get more careful data, the jury must remain out.

MOST WOMEN FEAR SUCCESS, DOCTOR CLAIMS," ran the head-line of *The National Enquirer*. "Fear of success: is it curable?" discussed the experts. "Psychologists found women's data indicated a hopeless will to fail," explained *Ms.* magazine.

In 1968 Matina Horner finished her doctoral research, based on 178 University of Michigan undergraduates. To explain why women hadn't acted like men in two decades of achievement-motivation studies, Horner argued that women had a "motive to avoid success in intellectual competence or leadership potential." Because women view femininity and achievement as "two desirable but mutually exclusive ends," Horner explained, they are more likely than men to develop this motive.

Horner's conclusions, and the dramatic methods she used, captured both the popular and professional imagination. The media have re-counted her findings widely, usually oversimplifying them in the process. Psychologists too have been guilty of misconceptions. Some have used her data to explain why the lone woman in an otherwise male professional group drops out or isolates herself. Others have confused the "motive to avoid success," supposedly more characteristic of women

than men, with what psychiatrists call a "success neurosis (or phobia),"
traditionally a male complaint. And almost everyone has tended to
generalize from Horner's undergraduates to all women. The popularity
of this ground-breaking study has led, unfortunately, to misconceptions.

Scores of psychologists and students have by now been involved in
some variation of Horner's basic study. Researchers have even collected
data in Yugoslavia, Italy, Norway, Jamaica, and the British West Indies.
The intuitive appeal of the "fear-of-success" concept, however, has
resulted in an unfortunate tendency to regard the concept as proven and
to overlook its many complexities. The "motive to avoid success" may
not be a motive and may have little to do with avoiding success. And it is
by no means unique to women.

The Original FOS Work

Let me briefly recapitulate Horner's work [See chapter 22, "A Bright
Woman is Caught in a Double Bind."] First she asked 178 students to
write four-minute stories to this cue: *At the end of first-term finals, Anne
finds herself at the top of her medical school class.* Females wrote about Anne,
males about John in this situation. (This thematic cue should not be
confused with the TAT, Thematic Apperception Test, a proven clinical
test that Henry Murray developed in 1943.)

Horner examined the wide variety of stories that emerged, and
identified three themes that she thought would theoretically indicate
"fear of success": 1) social rejection, fear of losing friends as a result of
success (*Everyone hates and envies Anne*); 2) fears and negative feelings because of success (*Anne feels guilty, unhappy, unfeminine,* etc.); 3) bizarre or
hostile responses, or denial of the cue altogether (*Anne is a code name for a
group of medical students*). Many of the stories were entertaining and unexpected, which contributed to the popularity of this study.

	males	*females*
FOS imagery present	8	59
FOS imagery absent	80	31
	N = 88	N = 90

Using this threefold classification scheme, Horner found that many
more young women than men showed fear of success imagery (FOS),
65.5 percent to 9 percent. This little table set the precedent for the
percentages of women expected to show FOS imagery, and for the obvious difference between men and women.

To find out how this imagery related to achievement behavior, Horner
put all her subjects in a "mixed-sex competition" condition. She gave
them an anagram test, in which they had to make as many words as

possible in ten minutes from the word *generation*. In a second session, one third of the students worked by themselves on a similar problem, the "noncompetitive" condition. (Horner did not include the other two thirds in this analysis.) She found that two thirds of the men did better in competition than alone, while half of the women did so.

(women only)	*Perform Better Working Alone*	*Perform Better in Competition*
FOS imagery present	13	4
FOS imagery absent	1	12

Horner thus concluded that women who show FOS imagery do worse in competition, and thereby related FOS to achievement behavior, suggesting that it acted like a "motive."

I reviewed a wide variety of studies, many unpublished, since Horner's original work. They cover both sexes and a diverse age and geographical range. First I wondered whether it was really the case that more women show "fear of success" than men. In 61 studies, the proportion of women who wrote FOS themes varied from 11 percent to 88 percent, the median being 47 percent. Thirty-six of these studies included men, and the percentages of men with FOS themes ranged from 14 percent to 86 percent, the median being 43 percent—not much lower than the level for women. Indeed, in 17 of the 36 samples, males had *higher* levels of FOS imagery. (Medians are crude statistics, and should be taken only as illustrations that men show FOS too. To interpret a median as a norm for men or women is tempting, but bad science.)

For instance, Lois Hoffman meticulously recreated Horner's study in 1972. She used a similar male experimenter, an introductory psychology class at the same university, the same room, the same time of year. Hoffman used four different forms of the medical-school cue, such as . . . *Anne finds that she is the top child-psychology graduate student* (success that is supposedly "nonmasculine"). She found that percentage levels of FOS imagery were nearly identical on the four stories, but that males consistently showed more fear of success than females, 77 percent to 65 percent. Among women who wrote FOS imagery, the most common theme was social rejection because of success (42 percent); among men with FOS, the most common theme was a denigration of the goal or questioning of the values of success in the first place (30 percent). Other studies have found a similar sex difference. The claim, then, that women "fear success" more than men do is wrong. Some have pointed to the women's liberation movement to explain why women fear success less, and to the counterculture ethic to explain why men fear success more than they used to. But the data do not show such a shift in attitudes, at least in recent years. I arranged the studies in chronological order, and found no trends in the five years since Horner's research was reported.

The huge fluctuation in levels of FOS across these studies made me curious. One reason is that the arousal of FOS has been dramatically different in each of the situations tested. Another reason might be that researchers have different ideas about what fear-of-success imagery *is*. When I went back to Horner's study, I was struck with the fact that there is no extensive scoring manual with sample stories for making sure that coders will rate alike, standard procedure in testing all motivation constructs.

As a result, there has been a large degree of subjectivity involved in the scoring of FOS, along with predictable confusion. Lillian and Edwin Robbins, psychologists at Rutgers, asked five women and four men to code a set of stories for FOS; the women found more such imagery than the men did. The psychologists concluded that perhaps Horner, being a woman, exaggerated the extent of FOS themes in her original data. They could be right only if all coders had used the same scoring criteria, which has not been the case.

Scoring the Motive

A common coding mistake has been to label all negative comments in a story as part of "fear of success." Aside from the fact that there is often no justification for doing so, this ignores the theoretical basis of a motive to avoid success: the anxiety that success will have negative *consequences*. Properly, only consequences should be counted as FOS imagery. But some researchers have scored many unrelated negative elements as FOS: references to illness, murder, drugs, accidents, robberies, physical handicaps, and so on. If these themes appear in a story, but are not a consequence of success, they are not fear-of-success images. They may reflect the subject's fear of something, to be sure, or general anxiety; they are not FOS.

For example, a young woman wrote: . . . *Judy has been working in a hospital with children who have speech difficulties. Judy's goal . . . was to help these children get over their problem and speak like everyone else . . . Judy had gotten what she worked for.* The researcher might score the reference to physical handicap as FOS imagery, but this would be incorrect.

Nor can we consider negative *antecedents* of success in the FOS category. The following story was a response to a cue that I gave a group of 221 high-school students (*After much work, Joe has finally gotten what he wanted*):

Joe Smith seems happy because he has just gotten his report card. All year long his parents have been haunting him about his grades but Joe was more interested in sports. But in his senior year Joe found out from his football coach that he could not play football on a good college team unless his grades improved immensely. Joe sacrificed many things in order to be better in school . . . it paid off.

The negative aspects of this story occur *before* Joe's success, and should not be scored as FOS.

In order to learn Horner's system, I rescored her original stories, comparing her results with mine as I went along. Among my high-school students, 23 percent of the 110 males and 22 percent of the 111 females wrote pure FOS imagery. An additional 28 percent of the boys and 36 percent of the girls included negative antecedents in their stories, and 21 percent and 15 percent respectively mentioned negative events that were unrelated to success. A large proportion of these two categories overlap with Horner's criteria for fear of success; if I had included the other scores with pure FOS imagery, I would have been able to classify half of my subjects as harboring "fear of success."

Another way to increase the proportion of FOS scores in a sample is to add the themes from different stories. There is a very low correspondence of FOS imagery across stories; that is, finding FOS in one story is unrelated to the chance of finding it in another. But by adding or subtracting negative elements across stories, I can (and other researchers have) inflate or deflate my sample's fear-of-success rate. If I had counted up all the negative imagery from responses to the two cues I gave my high-school students, I would have concluded that 76 percent of the boys and 73 percent of the girls had fear of success. This is a far cry from my original figures of 23 percent and 22 percent.

Some psychologists have experimented with the story-writing cue. Vary the story, and you vary the likelihood of getting fear of success. M. L. Katz wanted to see, for example, whether it made a difference if Anne was the only woman in her medical class. She introduced the original cue—Anne being first in her class—with *All Anne's classmates are men* or with *Half of Anne's classmates are women.* Fear-of-success imagery decreased in the second case, suggesting that the female respondents were more concerned about Anne's being deviant than about her being successful.

A few researchers were curious as to how males would respond to a story about female success, and vice versa. There have been two consistant findings. Males write more FOS stores about Anne in medical school than they write about John; and males write more FOS stories about Anne than females write about Anne *or* John. The researchers have generally interpreted these findings as evidence that men have a deep-seated prejudice against a woman's success. However, motivation theory would say that the male's FOS stories are projections of his own motives, somewhat altered because the cue stimulus is female rather than male. The point is that these interpretations are not compatible. We cannot use Horner's medical-school story, and similar cues, to measure both a woman's "*motive* to avoid success" and a man's *reaction* to female success.

The Muddled Meaning of Success

Such work reflects another fundamental problem with fear-of-success research: scant agreement on just what success *is*. In 1904 Bessie Stanley wrote that, "He has achieved success who has lived well, laughed often, and loved much." Does this definition include the ability to solve anagrams or to be first in medical school? Although Kurt Lewin's early work on success and failure emphasized that it was the person's *subjective* feeling of success that mattered, our society tends to view success in what Oliver Wendell Holmes called "its vulgar sense—the gaining of money and position." Many philosophers, notably Erich Fromm and Herbert Marcuse, have questioned the assumption that this kind of success is intrinsically good and that we should encourage its development. Recent work in achievement motivation has tried to separate the power and status connotations from the word, but much confusion remains.

In talking about the "motive to avoid success," then, we must specify what we mean by success, and also what we mean by fear of success. We must determine whether such fear is the same thing as Freud's success neurosis, which he described as an inhibitor of the full use of one's resources. If we mean only fear of vocational success, we must say so. Or fear of failure. Or plain old anxiety.

A number of experiments that have followed Horner's lead have sought to test imaginative hypotheses about the correlates of FOS. R. I. Watson Jr. studied the relationship between FOS and drugs (including marijuana, speed, and LSD), and discovered that heavy drug users were far more likely to write FOS imagery. A. E. Berens thought that fear of success might be learned from parents, and indeed found that fifth-grade children who show FOS tend to have mothers with high FOS. And two independent studies compared race differences, finding that FOS levels are higher for black men (and white women) than for black women, since this culture gives black women more opportunities and encouragements to achieve.

Other work has explored the connection between fear of success and traditional femininity. Molly Schwenn found that among college students FOS was linked with changes in career hopes; that is, women with high FOS eventually decided to work for a politician instead of being one, to become a teacher instead of a lawyer. (She argued that their decision was related to their boyfriends' attitudes. However, Joe Pleck showed that males who are threatened by female competence write FOS stories themselves, but their girlfriends do not.) Vivian Makosky found that high-FOS girls consider having a family to be more important, and having a career less important, than others girls do. However, high-FOS girls consider themselves to be less feminine than low-FOS girls.

These experiments have produced ideas to explore, not results that are fully confirmed. But they illustrate the wide range of possibilities that the concept of "fear of success" has provoked.

Horner's theory has generated much research, but she has not yet demonstrated that fear of success is a *motive*, within the tradition of motivation research that she purports to extend.

Validating the Motive

David McClelland at Harvard and John Atkinson at the University of Michigan formulated the "Expectancy × Value" theory of motivation. They defined motives as stable predispositions to action that we learn early in life. An adult's *motives*, e.g. to eat, interact with the *incentives* of a particular goal, e.g. the juiciness of a thick steak, to give the goal a *value*. The *expectancies* of reaching that goal (very good if the steak is on your plate, very bad if it's at the next table) in turn interact with the value, resulting in a *tendency to act* to get the goal.

Achievement motivation is a function of the strength of a motive to approach success (or, popularly put, the need for achievement) minus the strength of the negative motive to avoid failure, a worry about performing poorly that produces debilitating anxiety in a testing situation. (Success refers to one's personal standards of excellence.) The incentives and expectancies of success and failure meditate each motive. To these two motives, Horner added the motive to avoid success: when a person anticipates negative consequences of success, he or she feels anxious, which in turn inhibits performance. This is not the same as a motive to approach failure, which applies to people who are gratified by doing poorly.

But Horner never used the traditional, well-established method to show that the motive exists. To validate a motive, one group of subjects writes imaginative stories to ambiguous pictures under conditions that arouse the motive. If you want to prove that there is a motive to eat, for example, you deprive subjects of food for 16 hours, and then compare the stories that these ravenous subjects write with those from subjects who are not hungry. The themes from the hungry (aroused) group are the basis for a scoring system that can show the strength of that motive.

But that is not all. Next, an entirely new group of subjects, each presumably with a different level of the motive in question, writes stories to similar pictures. The new scoring system records each subject's relative motive strength. Finally, we put everyone in a situation where they can act on the supposed motive; in this case, we offer them food. If those who score high on the motive then *act* on it—if they eat more than low scorers—then our measure has been crossvalidated. You must be able to predict behavior to show that your measure is useful.

Horner left out the first step in this process: she never compared the story themes of an aroused and a nonaroused group. Thus she cannot really say whether the themes she found truly reflect a "motive to avoid success" or some other sort of anxiety. She is now doing research on this crucial step, but we cannot yet call fear-of-success *imagery* a motive. It is not a proven personality trait. Further, few of the follow-up studies on this topic have sought to relate FOS to actual behavior.

FOS in Competition

Indeed, Horner's own interpretation of the relationship between FOS and behavior is open to debate. She concentrated on the 13 women in her study who showed FOS and who did better on the anagram task by themselves. (Horner did not explain why 92 percent of the low-FOS women did much better in competition, when only two-thirds of the men did so.) She concluded that high-FOS women become inhibited when they compete with men. But an alternate interpretation is that the women *boosted* their performance when they worked alone, a situation in which they could work against their own standards of excellence—an opportunity that appeals to the high achiever. "Inhibited with men" and "enhanced by themselves" are two sides of the same coin. Perhaps we can look at FOS as an indicator of those who do their best work by themselves as well as an indicator of those who finch under competition.

Some studies have been able to replicate Horner's finding, but others have not. Part of the problem rests on another sort of misinterpretation of Horner's data, namely that competition with *men* causes high-FOS women to perform worse.

But Horner herself found that the sex of one's competitor made no difference in a woman's ability to perform on the test (though she never analyzed how this related to FOS). And subsequent studies have not been able to clear up the matter. Vivian Makosky found that women who showed FOS imagery performed more poorly when they competed with men, but not when they competed with other women. But a study by a group of psychologists in Canada concluded that women who show FOS do *better* in competition with men.

One reason for these contradictions is that the actual effect of FOS on performance, while it may be "statistically significant," is typically very small. For example, subjects who show FOS imagery might make 35 anagrams, on the average, in competition; while subjects who don't show FOS might come up with an average of 38 anagrams. This small difference is unlikely to have occurred by chance. But how important is a three-word difference on an anagram test? A person's initial ability to do a task is stable from situation to situation, as many studies have confirmed. "Fear of success" causes only minor fluctuations in performance, under special circumstances. Horner found that FOS imagery was more prominent among honors than among nonhonors students. If the people who show FOS imagery are the ones who get good grades, just how deeply debilitating is it?

The point is that the relationship between FOS imagery and behavior is still unclear. Researchers and the media must be careful when they generalize from small samples of high-school or college students to the whole society. The temptation to do so is great, and the resulting popularization of Horner's work has itself influenced this research. Consider this college student's answer to the medical-school cue:

Anne is being congratulated by the male and female members of her class. The males are somewhat chagrined, as is Anne. However, Anne has read Psychology Today *and knows that studies such as this indicate that this is an expected reaction. Anne will try to continue to do well—because she wants a career—but not necessarily number one.*

This story has fear-of-success imagery, all right, but obviously we could not count it in the results. At least this student made her awareness of the research explicit in the story. What about all the people who don't? Such bias may now be widespread and contribute to a systematic error in the results.

A New Direction for FOS

In response to the theoretical and methodological problems of Horner's original system, my colleagues and I at Harvard are developing a more comprehensive scoring system. It is not limited to the outdated medical-school cue but will apply to ambiguous cues of all sorts, and it provides a detailed scoring manual. (In addition, Marice Pappo has created a questionnaire that successfully measures fear of success in academic settings.)

Our approach also gets around the problem of the specificity of Horner's cue. That is, Horner forced subjects to react to a narrow, focused concrete situation: a person is *number one* in a male-dominated field. We have reinstated the traditional ambiguity of projective tests, using such cues as "After much work, Joe [Judy] has finally gotten what he [she] wanted." This way we do not impose our assumptions of success and goal on the respondents. We are thus able to tap their dispositions about personal success and their views of their own ability to reach goals. And we lessen the influence of situations that have special meaning in our culture.

Another line of research we are pursuing is to vary the nature of success in the cue, and see how males and females react. For example, we want to know how women respond to success in a *traditional* setting (e.g. *At the end of first-term finals, Jane finds she is doing well in her nursing-school class*), and how men respond to success in a *nontraditional* setting (e.g. *At graduation from his school of social work, Jack is being commended for his ability to listen to and support his clients*). If women show less FOS imagery to the nursing-school cue than to the medical-school cue, it may be that Horner did not find "fear of success" but "fear of sex-role inappropriateness." If men show increased FOS to their social-work cue, we might label their problem a "fear of emotional competence."

Horner's work is unquestionably a powerful first step in an important area of human motivation. All of us, male and female, share many fears, along with many ambitions, about many sorts of success. Today, however, many researchers are finding that "the motive to avoid success" is only one explanation of how and why some people inhibit their potential for growth and action.

References

Alper, Thelma G. "The Relationship Between Role-Orientation and Achievement Motivation in College Women" in *Journal of Personality*, Vol. 41, pp. 9–31, 1973.

Atkinson, John W., ed. *Motives in Fantasy, Action and Society*. Van Nostrand, 1958.

Atkinson, John W. and Norman T. Feather, eds. *A Theory of Achievement Motivation*. Wiley, 1966.

Entwisle, Doris R. "To Dispel Fantasies About Fantasy-Based Measures of Achievement Motivation" in *Psychological Bulletin*, Vol. 77, pp. 337–391, 1972.

Hoffman, Lois. "Fear of Success in Males and Females: 1965 and 1972" in *Journal of Consulting and Clinical Psychology*, in press.

Horner, Matina Souretis. "The Psychological Significance of Success in Competitive Achievement Situations: A Threat As Well As a Promise" in *Intrinsic Motivation: A New Direction in Education*, H.I. Day, D.E. Berlyne and D.E. Hunt, eds. Holt (Canada), 1971, paper.

Horner, Matina Souretis. "Sex Differences in Achievement Motivation and Performance in Competitive and Non-Competitive Situations." Unpublished doctoral dissertation, University of Michigan, 1968. Available from University Microfilms, Ann Arbor, Michigan, #69–12, 135.

Morgan, Sherry Ward and Bernard Mausner. "Behavioral and Fantasied Indicators of Avoidance of Success in Men and Women" in *Journal of Personality*, in press.

Pappo, Marice. "Fear of Success: A Theoretical Analysis and the Construction and Validation of a Measuring Instrument." Unpublished doctoral dissertation, Columbia University, 1972. Available from University Microfilms, Ann Arbor, Michigan, #282–161.

Schuster, Daniel B. "On the Fear of Success" in *Psychiatric Quarterly*, Vol. 29, pp. 412–420, 1955.

Tresemer, David and Joseph Pleck. "Sex-Role Boundaries and Resistance to Sex-Role Change" in *Women's Studies*, in press.

24
Woman as Nigger

NAOMI WEISSTEIN

ABSTRACT

In this selection psychologist Naomi Weisstein argues persuasively against the uncritical acceptance of traditional theories of feminine personality, particularly those derived from clinical observation. Ms. Weisstein cites several studies which show that the outcome of an experiment can be greatly influenced by the expectations of the experimenter. We all have hypotheses or prejudices as to what men and women are and should be, and hence, Ms. Weisstein reasons, the validity of our observations is questionable. Further, widely publicized experiments conducted by Stanley Milgram and others, have shown that people behave in accordance with others' expectations of them.

Psychology has nothing to say about what women are really like, what they need and what they want, for the simple reason that psychology does not know. Yet psychologists will hold forth endlessly on the true nature of woman, with dismaying enthusiasm and disquieting certitude.

Bruno Bettelheim, of the University of Chicago, tells us:

We must start with the realization that, as much as women want to be good scientists or engineers, they want first and foremost to be womanly companions of men and to be mothers.

Eric Erikson, of Harvard University, explains:

Much of a young woman's identity is already defined in her kind of attractiveness and in the selectivity of her search for the man (or men) by whom she wishes to be sought.

Some psychiatrists even see in woman's acceptance of woman's role the solution to problems that rend our society. Joseph Rheingold, a psychiatrist at Harvard Medical School, writes:

. . . when women grow up without dread of their biological functions and without subversion by feminist doctrine and . . . enter upon motherhood with a sense of fulfillment and altruistic sentiment, we shall attain the goal of a good life and a secure world in which to live it.

These views reflect a fairly general consensus among psychologists, and the psychologists' idea of woman's nature fits the common prejudice. But it is wrong. There isn't the tiniest shred of evidence that these fantasies of childish dependence and servitude have anything to do with woman's true nature, or her true potential. Our present psychology is less than worthless in contributing to a vision that could truly liberate women.

And this failure is not limited to women. The kind of psychology that is concerned with how people act and who they are has failed in general to understand why people act the way they do and what might make them act differently. This kind of psychology divides into two professional areas: academic personality research, and clinical psychology and psychiatry. The basic reason for the failure is the same in both these areas: the central assumption for most psychologists of human personality has been that human behavior rests primarily on an individual and inner dynamic. This assumption is rapidly losing ground, however, as personality psychologists fail again and again to get consistency in the assumed personalities of their subjects, and as the evidence collects that what a person does and who he believes himself to be will be a function of what people around him expect him to be, and what the overall situation in which he is acting implies that he is.

Academic personality psychologists are looking, at least, at the counter evidence and changing their theories; no such corrective is occurring in clinical psychology and psychiatry. Freudians and neo-Freudians, Adlerians and neo-Adlerians, classicists and swingers, clinicians and psychiatrists, simply refuse to look at the evidence against their theory and practice. And they support their theory and their practice with stuff so transparently biased as to have absolutely no standing as empirical evidence.

If we inspect the literature of personality theory that has been written by clinicians and psychiatrists, it is immediately obvious that the major support for theory is "years of intensive clinical experience." Now a person is free to make up theories with any inspiration that works: divine revelation, intensive clinical practice, a random numbers table. He is not free to claim any validity for this theory until it has been tested. But in ordinary clinical practice, theories are treated in no such tentative way.

Consider Freud. What he accepted as evidence violated the most minimal conditions of scientific rigor. In *The Sexual Enlightenment of Children*, the classic document that is supposed to demonstrate the existence of a castration complex and its connection to a phobia, Freud based his analysis on reports from the little boy's father, himself in therapy and a devotee of Freud. Comment on contamination in this kind of evidence is unnecessary.

It is remarkable that only recently has Freud's classic theory on female sexuality—the notion of the double orgasm—been tested physiologically and found just plain wrong. Now those who claim that fifty years of psychoanalytic experience constitute evidence of the essential truth of Freud's theory should ponder the robust health of the double orgasm. Before Masters and Johnson did women believe they were having two different kinds of orgasm? Did their psychiatrists coax them into reporting something that was not true? If so, were other things they reported also not true? Did psychiatrists ever learn anything that conflicted with their theories? If clinical experience means anything, surely we should have been done with the double-orgasm myth long before Masters and Johnson.

But, you may object, intensive clinical experience is the only reliable measure in a discipline that rests its findings on insight, sensitivity and intuition. The problem with insight, sensitivity and intuition is that they tend to confirm our biases. At one time people were convinced of their ablility to identify witches. All it required was sensitivity to the workings of the devil.

Clinical experience is not the same thing as empirical evidence. The first thing an experimenter learns is the concept of the double blind. The term comes from medical experiments, in which one group takes a drug that is supposed to change behavior in a certain way, and a control group takes a placebo. If the observers or subjects know which group took which drug, the result invariably confirms the new drug's effectiveness. Only when no one knows which subject took which pill is validity approximated.

When we are judging human behavior, we must test the reliability of our judgments again and again. Will judges, in blind experiment, agree in their observations? Can they repeat their judgments later? In practice, we find that judges cannot judge reliably *or* consistently.

Evelyn Hooker of U.C.L.A. presented to a group of judges, chosen for their clinical expertise, the results of three widely used clincial projective tests—the Rorschach, the Thematic Apperception Test (TAT) and the Make-A-Picture Story Test (MAPS)—that had been given to homosexuals and a control group of heterosexuals. The ability of these judges to distinguish male heterosexuals from male homosexuals was no better than chance. Any remotely Freudian-like theory assumes that sexuality is of fundamental importance in the deep dynamic of personality. If gross sexual deviance cannot be detected, then what do psychologists mean when they claim that "latent homosexual panic" is at the basis of paranoid psychosis? They can't identify homosexual *anything*, let alone "latent homosexual panic."

More astonishing, the diagnoses of expert clinicians are not consistent. In the Kenneth Little and Edwin S. Shneidman study, on the basis of both tests and interviews, judges described a number of normals as psychotic, assigning them to such categories as "schizophrenic with homosexual tendencies," or "schizoid character with depressive trends." When the same judges were asked to rejudge the same test results several weeks later, their diagnoses of the same subjects differed markedly from their initial judgments. It is obvious that even simple descriptive conventions in clinical psychology cannot be applied consistently. These descriptive conventions, therefore, have no explanatory significance.

I was a member of a Harvard graduate seminar to which two piles of TAT tests were presented. We were asked to identify which pile had been written by males and which pile by females. Although the class had spent one and a half months intensively studying the psychological literature on the differences between the sexes, only 4 students out of 20 identified the piles correctly. Since this result is far below chance, we may conclude that there is a consistency here. Within the context of psychological teaching, the students judged knowledgeably; the teachings themselves are erroneous.

Some might argue that while clinical theory may be scientifically unsound, it at least cures people. There is no evidence that it does. In 1952, Hans Eysenck of the University of London reported the results of an "outcome-of-therapy" study of neurotics that showed that 44 percent of the patients who received psychoanalysis improved; 64 percent of the patients who received psychotherapy improved; and 72 percent of the patients who received no treatment at all improved. These findings have never been refuted, and later studies have confirmed their negative results, no matter what type of therapy was used. In Arnold Goldstein and Sanford Dean's recent book, *The Investigation of Psychotherapy*, five different outcome-of-therapy studies with negative results are reported.

How, in all good conscience, can clinicians and psychiatrists continue to practice? Largely by ignoring these results and taking care not to do outcome-of-therapy studies.

Since clinical experience and tools are shown to be worse than useless when they are tested for consistency, efficacy and reliability, we can safely conclude that clinical theories about women are also worse than useless.

But even academic personality research that conforms to a rigorous methodology has only limited usefulness. As stated above, most psychologists of human personality have assumed that human behavior rests on an individual and inner dynamic, perphaps fixed in infancy, perhaps fixed by genitalia, perhaps simply arranged in a rigid cognitive network. But they have failed repeatedly to find consistency in the assumed personalities of their subjects. A rigid authoritarian on one test will be unauthoritarian on another. The reason for this inconsistency seems to depend more on the social situation in which a person finds himself than on the person himself.

In a series of experiments, Robert Rosenthal and his coworkers at Harvard showed that if experimenters have one hypothesis about what they expect to find and another group of experimenters has the opposite hypothesis, each group will obtain results that are in accord with its hypothesis. Experimenters who were told that their rats had been bred for brightness found that their rats learned to run mazes better than did the rats of experimenters who believed their animals had been bred for dullness. These results would have happened by chance one out of one hundred times.

In a recent study, Robert Rosenthal and Lenore Jacobson extended their analysis to the classroom. They found that when teachers expected randomly selected students to "show great promise," the I.Q.s of these students increased significantly.

Thus, even in carefully controlled experiments, our hypotheses will influence the behavior of both animals and people. These studies are extremely important when we assess psychological studies of women. Since it is fairly safe to say that most of us start with hypotheses as to the nature of men and women, the validity of a number of observations on sex differences is questionable, even when these observations have been made under carefully controlled situations. In important ways, people are what you expect them to be, or at least they behave as you expect them to behave. If, as Bruno Bettelheim has it, women want first and foremost to be good wives and mothers, it is likely that this is what Bettelheim wants them to be.

The obedience experiments of Stanley Milgram point to the inescapable effect of social context. A subject is told that he is administering a learning experiment, and that he is to deal out shocks each time the other "subject" (a confederate of the experimenter) answers incorrectly. The equipment appears to provide graduated shocks ranging from 15 to 450 volts; for each four consecutive voltages there are verbal descriptions such as "mild shock," "danger", "severe shock," and finally, for the 435- and 450-volt switches, simply a red XXX marked over the switches. Each time the stooge answers incorrectly, the subject is supposed to increase the voltage. As the voltage increases, the stooge cries in pain; he demands that the experiment stop; finally, he refuses to answer at all.

When he stops responding, the experimenter instructs the subject to continue increasing the voltage; for each shock administered, the stooge shrieks in agony. Under these conditions, about 62.5 percent of the subjects administered shocks that they believed to be lethal.

No tested individual differences predicted which subjects would continue to obey and which would break off the experiment. When 40 psychiatrists predicted how many of a group of 100 subjects would go on to give the lethal shock, their predictions were far below the actual percentage; most expected only one tenth of one percent of the subjects to obey to the end.

Even though psychiatrists have no idea how people will behave in this situation, and even though individual differences do not predict which subjects will obey and which will not, it is easy to predict when subjects will be obedient and when they will be defiant. All the experimenter has to do is change the social situation. In a variant of Milgram's experiment, two stooges were present in addition to the "victim"; these worked with the subject in administering electric shocks. When the stooges refused to go on with the experiment, only 10 percent of the subjects continued to the maximum voltage. This is critical for personality theory. It says that the lawful behavior is the behavior that can be predicted from the social situation, not from the individual history.

Finally, Stanley Schachter and J. E. Singer gave a group injections of adrenalin, which produces a state of physiological arousal almost identical to a state of extreme fear. When they were in a room with a stooge who acted euphoric, they became euphoric; when they were placed in a room with a stooge who acted angry, they became extremely angry.

It is obvious that a study of human behavior requires a study of the social contexts in which people move, the expectations as to how they will behave, and the authority that tells them who they are and what they are supposed to do.

We can now dispose of two biological theories of the nature of women. The first theory argues that females in primate groups are submissive and passive. Until we change the social organization of these groups and watch their subsequent behavior, we must conclude that—since primates are at present too stupid to change their own social conditions—the innateness and fixedness of these sexual differences in behavior are simply not known. Applied to humans, the primate argument becomes patently irrelevant, for the salient feature of human social organization is its variety, and there are a number of cultures in which there is at least a rough equality between men and women.

The second theory argues that since females and males differ in their sex hormones, and since sex hormones enter the brain, there must be innate differences in *psychological nature*. But this argument tells us only that there are differences in *physiological state*. From the adrenalin experiment we know that a particular physiological state can lead to varied emotional states and outward behavior, depending on the social situation.

Our culture and our psychology characterize women as inconsistent, emotionally unstable, lacking in a strong superego, weaker, nurturant rather than productive, intuitive rather than intelligent, and—if they are at all normal—suited to the home and family. In short, the list adds up to a typical minority-group stereotype—woman as nigger—if she knows her place (the home), she is really a quite lovable, loving creature, happy and childlike. In a review of the intellectual differences between little boys and little girls, Eleanor Maccoby has shown that no difference exists until high shool, or, if there is a difference, girls are slightly ahead of boys. In high school, girls begin to do worse on a few intellectual tasks, and beyond high school the productivity and accomplishment of women drops off even more rapidly.

In light of the social expectations about women, it is not surprising that women end up where society expects them to; the surprise is that little girls don't get the message that they are supposed to be stupid until they get into high school. It is no use to talk about women being different-but-equal; all the sex-difference tests I can think of have a "good" outcome and a "bad" outcome. Women usually end up with the bad outcome.

Except for their genitals, I don't know what immutable differences exist between men and women. Perhaps there are some other unchangeable differences; probably there are a number of irrelevant differences. But it is clear that until social expectation for men and women are equal, until we provide equal respect for both sexes, answers to this question will simply reflect our prejudices.

25
Assertiveness Training

HAROLD H. FRANK

ABSTRACT

Assertiveness training is a helpful tool in teaching women to compete with men on an equal basis. This article discuses what assertiveness training is and how it works.

Learning To Be Assertive

Assertiveness training is an increasingly popular method for women, socialized for thousands of years into subservient roles, to effect changes in both their behavior and attitudes. It is a specialized extension of Behavior Modification, which is used to change behavior patterns without necessarily uncovering or treating deep-seated psychological causes for such patterns. The theory underlying assertiveness training is that the submissive, unassertive behavior patterns associated with the traditionally subordinate status of women are largely learned and can therefore be unlearned with the proper training and reinforcement. If women are to assume equal status with men in society, it is imperative that the habit of submission to men be broken.

The Submissive Person

Although a well-balanced personality engages in both submissive and aggressive behavior at various times, characteristically submissive persons live in a constant state of intimidation and often become anxious when a situation calls for some kind of assertive action. Unfortunately,

241

this applies to many women under many circumstances. Psychotherapist Herbert Fensterheim describes extreme cases as subject to a "neurotic spiral" and gives the following example:

From the fear of losing your job you acquire a whole new set of doubts: What is wrong with me? . . . I am no good . . . I never succeed. . . . These thoughts in turn lead to inadequate behaviors which in turn strengthen the fears and doubts which lead to still more inadequate behavior.[1]

Other situations which elicit this kind of response from submissive individuals range from conversations, especially with strangers, to coping with high-pressure sales talk, and include complaining about defective merchandise, inadequate service or others' obnoxious habits, and the expression of personal opinions, especially if they are contrary to those of superiors.

In general, then, submissive, nonassertive persons deny themselves and are denied by others their rights, because they are inhibited from expressing their feelings. Dr. Joseph Wolpe, one of the foremost authorities on behavior modification, uses role-playing to teach these individuals to "express feelings other than anxiety," thereby setting the stage for them to practice assertiveness.[2] He describes assertive behavior as including the proper expression of any emotion other than anxiety in dealing with others.

Other Roles Of Training

Assertiveness, however, should not be confused with aggression. The former means claiming one's legitimate rights, whereas the latter means claiming those rights, and more, without regard for the rights of others and often in a hostile manner. Although assertiveness training can be modified to moderate the overly aggressive behavior often found in men, it has been used more extensively to correct overly submissive behavior in women. It is a popular technique, Catherine Calvert explains, because:

Realizing all healthy people have needs that are important is especially difficult for many women, (since) nurturing others' needs is implicit in their training from their first drink 'n wet doll.[3]

In Search Of Positive Reinforcement

Assertiveness training enforces the concept "that no one has a right to take advantage of another simply on a human-to-human level."[4] It shows people in need of it step-by-step how to handle specific situations which cause them anxiety with the concomitant inability to respond in an adequate manner. For example, if the office manager's repeated tardiness causes a subordinate unnecessary work, and the latter feels unable to protest, a scenario is created in which the person tells the manager, played by another participant, the effects of such lateness. With repeated run-throughs of this simulated confrontation, an individual learns the most positive and effective way of asserting him/herself.

The assertive person, Dr. Fensterheim believes, possesses four salient characteristics: the freedom of self-revelation through words, the ability to communicate with people on all levels, an active orientation toward life, and the ability to act with a dignity and a knowledge of his/her limitations.

Group Participation

Although it is possible to engage in assertiveness training on an individual basis with the use of specially written program guides, participation in an assertiveness training group led by a trained leader is likely to produce better results much more quickly because of the immediate feedback and reinforcement a group is able to give. The participants watch each other practice assertion, which allows them to learn from each others' strengths and weaknesses. Leaders have found that this interaction gives reluctant and timid participants the encouragement they need to change behavior patterns. Role-playing, the most important aspect of a group program, is naturally possible only in groups, unless the individual has an extraordinarily vivid imagination. It allows the actor to experiment with different behaviors harmlessly, with immediate feedback from the group.

Learning The Skills of Interaction

The principal skills an assertiveness training group teaches are verbal skills (both speaking and listening) and "body language" skills. Learning the implications of body language is essential, for most people are unaware of the great amount of information they communicate about themselves by the way they stand, sit, gesture, and look at others (see Alberti and Emmons). The participant finds that others react positively to a body stance or gesture that suggests self-assurance. Good "eye contact" during conversation induces others to pay more attention. These changes in relations with others may pave the way for more difficult behavior modification.

Dr. Manuel Smith employs the following terms for some of the verbal skills that are taught:[5]

Self-disclosure: the skill of disclosing personal information, such as one's thoughts and feelings with regard to another person's actions, words, and attitudes.

Negative assertion: the ability to accept assertively and with equanimity negative things about oneself, which allows one to cope with criticism more effectively.

Broken record: the ability to be persistent, learned by practicing the repetition of the same assertion without becoming irritated, angry, or loud.

Fogging: the skill of agreeing in principle, but still saying "no." For example, "I'm sure you are right that the cameras are lost, but I'll have to check on it myself."

Free information: a listening skill. While engaging in conversation the individual practices listening to all the "free" information other participants give about themselves. If s/he is also disclosing valuable personal clues, s/he is able to keep communication flowing.

The group leaders or facilitators properly emphasize the importance of starting small and working up. Initial attempts at behavior change for a submissive individual might involve asking someone not to talk loudly in a theatre, joining a group of strangers engaged in conversation, or returning a defective item to a store. The situations presenting the most anxiety should be worked out with the facilitator. Setbacks can be expected, but as an individual's confidence is built up by the success of minor behavior changes, s/he may eventually accomplish major permanent changes.

A Word of Caution

Assertiveness training, however, is not a panacea, and the results can generate problems. Not everyone on the receiving end of a newly assertive person's change in behavior will be a willingly receptive target. Negative reactions may include hostility and even revenge, temper tantrums, or psychosomatic illness.[6] Catherine Calvert cites instances of divorce as a direct result of a wife's newly assertive behavior. Larouche and Russianoff, who lead career workshops for women, conceded that some men cannot deal with assertive females. But, they point out, other men leave their submissive wives for more interesting women. "And a woman who is assertive is usually much more interesting."[7]

Another objection voiced to assertiveness training is that it presents only a superficial solution because it fails to explore or treat the causes of submissive, nonassertive behavior patterns. But proponents counter that assertiveness training is not designed to do that: it works on the assumption that attitude change is preceded and initiated by behavior change, which is admittedly the reverse of traditional theory. But whatever the theoretical argument, assertiveness training is often successful in what it is supposed to do: change submissive behavior to assertive behavior. It halts the vicious cycle that produces negative self-esteem; it replaces insecurity with confidence by enabling an individual to reinforce his/her efforts at behavior change through practicing and doing. Though the change may initially be superficial, negative attitudes are eventually changed, as well as inadequate behavior.

Notes

1. Herbert Fensterheim and Jean Baer, *Don't Say Yes When You Want To Say No* (New York: Dell Publishing Co., 1975).

2. Ibid., p. 23.

3. Catherine Calvert, "Assertiveness," *Mademoiselle* (March 1975), p. 224.

4. Robert E. Alberti and Michael L. Emmons, *Your Perfect Right: A Guide to Assertive Behavior*, 2nd ed. (California: Impact Press, 1974), p. 27.

5. Manuel J. Smith, *When I Say No I Feel Guilty* (New York: Bantam Books, 1975).

6. Alberti and Emmons, *Your Perfect Right*, pp. 48–49.

7. Marsha Dubrow, "Female Assertiveness," *New York Magazine* (July 28, 1975), p. 44.

26

The Solo Woman
in a Professional
Peer Group

CAROL WOLMAN and HAROLD H. FRANK

ABSTRACT

In this reading students are introduced to original research on the group dynamics of a lone or solo woman in an otherwise all-male group, a not uncommon situation in the business and professional world. Wolman and Frank studied six small groups, each containing a solo woman. All the women became deviants, isolates, or low status regular members of their groups, leading in many cases to anxiety or depression. The women, Wolman and Frank concluded, were the victims of that special all-male peer group dynamic, found in neighborhood bars and playing fields as well as in work situations. Implications of and alternate means of coping with the solo woman's dilemma are discussed.

More and more women are joining the professions these days. Nevertheless, most fields will continue to be dominated by men for some time to come, and a woman may often find herself the only female in her working group, both as she goes through school, and as she takes on a job. In psychiatry, for instance, a residency or a hospital staff may include only one woman. This paper will analyze six peer groups of graduate students or psychiatric residents, each containing one woman. We will examine overall group dynamics, the woman's role in the group and how it was determined, and the woman's feelings; ways of altering these dynamics will be suggested.

Originally published in the *American Journal of Orthopsychiatry* 45 (1) (January 1975). Copyright © 1975 by the *American Journal of Orthopsychiatry*.

Method

We took our model for conceptualizing group behavior from Athos and Coffey.[1] Their system, derived from the interactionist tradition of Pareto and Henderson,[8] and best described by Homans,[9] treats social behavior as an exchange of scarce resources, such as alliances, support, emotions, information or sexual recognition. In an ideal exchange, each party feels he has acquired something of greater value than he has given. By many such exchanges, an informal or emergent group assigns roles to each member and evolves group norms, which tend to govern the group's behavior.

An emergent group, such as the T-groups and resident peer groups that we studied, is a subsystem defined by a larger organization, such as a graduate school offering the T-group course, or a residency training program. Observed group behavior emerges from the summation of responses of individuals to formal or required expectations of the larger system, which prescribes the group's activities, but does not wholly determine them. For example, the training program expected members of the first-year residency groups we studied to work smoothly together in delivering patient care, and also to learn about psychotherapy by exploring themselves and their patients. In addition, the residents created an emotional support system, which was not specified as a group task by the required system.

The larger, formal system is in turn influenced by background factors, such as geography, culture, and its own resources. Every group member finds himself in a role, assigned through a process of interacting and negotiating. There are four basic roles available, all operationally defined. 1) *Group leader:* each other member initiates toward him more often than he initiates toward that member; overall, he upholds group norms, but also can change them. 2) *Regular member:* he gives and receives interactions about equally, tends to uphold the group norms. 3)*Deviant:* initiates toward others more often than he receives, tends to break the group norms. By ignoring him, the group punishes his deviant behavior and thereby tends to extinguish it. For a while, members may pressure him to conform to group norms, temporarily initiating toward him. A member may be intermittently or permanently deviant. 4) *Isolate:* he participates little in group interactions. A *norm* is defined as what a good group member is expected to do. An *interaction* is doing something with somebody.

The regular members tend to establish a dominance hierarchy or pecking order, headed by the leader. Members negotiate for roles and positions in the hierarchy by making allies who will support them, by arguing and other power maneuvers, and by exerting personal influence, charisma, or sexiness. Once the leader has emerged, his support and protection become very important.

We led or observed six groups of peers, each including a lone woman. Three were T-groups (*i.e.*, unstructured discussion groups) of the sort described by Bennis and Shepard,[3] with the stated goal for members of learning about group function by participating in and observing themselves in the group. Each met for a total of 30 hours. The authors received written reports from all members of these groups, which corroborated our observations. The other three were work groups of first-year psychiatric residents, each with one woman and four or five men. Each group worked on an inpatient unit for six months. The authors observed these groups in work-related interactions, and interviewed both male and female members.

Two of the three T-groups were fully tape recorded. In the third, an observer was present at all meetings and took verbatim transcriptions of most conversations and summaries of others. Members were encouraged to keep diaries of their impressions duirng the course of the group discussions and to use them as the basis for a paper analyzing the group's dynamics and their own behavior. Prior to and following training two of the groups filled out questionnaires from the Bales[2] group space system. The Johnson/Frank Quick Score Method for Analyzing Bales Ratings[11] was used to create a composite display of member perceptions of each other. Using methods descirbed by Dalton,[4] members of the small work teams were observed and interviewed periodically.

Data obtained under the variety of procedures described above do not readily lend themselves to statistical manipulation or integration. The Bales data provide an analysis of member behavior based on the dimensions of friendliness, dominance, and task orientation in orthogonal relationship to one another. When displayed graphically, it is possible to differentiate regular group members from those who are in a deviant, isolate, or leadership position. As the women in the groups occupied most of these roles, the data do not differentiate men from women. That is, they do not explain if gender alone is sufficient to foster deviant or isolate status. Analysis of the tape recordings and notes does provide information to explain why women were defined by one role or another. For example, attempts to influence the group made by a woman were ignored while similar attempts made subsequently by a man were heeded and credited to him. Women who persisted in trying to influence the group after having been ignored received coordinated reaction, or no reaction, typical of the way groups react to deviants and isolates respectively.

Observation of the work groups revealed similar patterns but showed the variety of options women might employ to cope with the treatment they received. Those who sought to avoid contact with male peers were able to do so by merely keeping busy. An excessive orientation toward work served to reduce the significance of social isolation or peripheral group status. Since these data do not lend themsleves to quantitative integration, we have presented our findings in the form of case studies.*

T-Groups

Alice,** who was married, entered as a peer, and at once competed actively for leadership, waving the banner of openness and sharing of feelings. She received little support for her efforts and the one male who allied with her, although he early emerged as a leader, soon found himself treated as a deviant and was forced to withhold active support from her. Alice was seen as oversensitive, and was ignored. She reacted with depression and anger; her expressions of these feelings were interpreted as phony power plays which men would disdain to use. At one point she considered dropping out, but instead tried to become a regular member, and supported the group norms and the leader. She seldom flirted, but her sexuality was joked about as a commodity by regular members. The men persisted for some time in ignoring her and treating her as an "isolate." She remained depressed for the life of the group, but stopped fighting actively. Her passivity was rewarded with an occasional solicitation of her opinion or mention of her name, indicating she was not being completely ignored and had earned a deviant membership role.

Betty, engaged, presented herself as young and naive, but then fought for regular membership by rationally pointing out that she didn't fit the "little sister" stereotype the group had imposed on her. This earned her a "women's lib" label. She also announced that she had sexual feelings, just as men did; the men then asked who in the group attracted her. When she named one man, the rest were relieved that she had rejected them *en masse*, rather than individually. She was treated as a deviant for the duration of the group, and felt frustrated and unhappy. The chosen male moved from "regular" membership status to self-imposed, but group-supported, near-"isolate" status.

Cora, who was single, had her right to participate questioned at the onset of the group, although the graduate school defined her as eligible. She presented herself as assertive, rational, and self-assured. The men provoked her into becoming emotional, and then defined her as deviant

*See Frank, H. and Katcher, A. 1977. The qualities of leadership: how male medical students evaluate their female peers. *Human Relations* (in press), for a more rigorous test of the solo woman hypothesis based on a study of twenty-four, six-person gross anatomy dissection groups. Twelve groups contained one woman; eight, two women; and four, three women. The findings corroborate those reported here.

** Names are fictitious and listed alphabetically as a mnemonic aid.

for being naive, bitchy, and overemotional. She felt that at times they ignored her, and at times they competed to control her as a way of establishing and maintaining their "pecking order." Her sexuality was ignored by all, and she never escaped the deviant role, despite her continued efforts.

Resident Groups

Debby, single, entered residency with a history of depression, and presented herself as less able to cope than the other residents, taking several brief leaves of absence during a six-month period. Nevertheless, she frequently expressed her wish to be treated as a "regular" group member. The men early evolved a norm of taking care of Debby, despite her objections and rebuffs. Later, they tended to ignore her. She was seen as nonsexual, although both she and the men worried about their wives' jealousy of her. The men formed many close ties among themselves, but none got individually close to Debby, although they met as a group at her house several times. Eventually she dropped out of the residency.

Eva, married, presented herself as a peer who wanted to avoid personal ties with the men in her group, and they accepted this readily. They dealt with her only as needed in working together; her sexuality was ignored. Conflicts occasionally arose when she felt that extra work was being shifted to her, and objected after doing the work. The men listened politely to her objections, but ignored them. The whole group, including Eva, seemed content with her role as an isolate.

Fran, married, presented herself as naive, less competent than the other residents, and frightened. Although she occasionally expressed feelings of depression, other residents talked more about their feelings than she did. The men accepted her almost at once as a low-status "regular" member, and several of them formed a subgroup with her. They perceived her as "up tight about sex" and did not flirt with her. In time, she proved extremely competent, and her status rose. She was always seen as an individual, rather than a representative of a female stereotype.

Results

In four of the six peer groups, the solo woman occupied a deviant role that made her unhappy; in one she was an isolate by choice, and in one a low status regular member. It is obvious why a woman would be perceived as deviant when the group first assembled; in Cora's case, the men immediately attempted to exclude her. When the members started to interact, the woman was not allowed to compete freely for status. The men labeled her assertiveness as bitchiness or manipulation, and appeared more threatened by competition with her than with each other. Often, they simply ignored assertive behavior from a woman.

Although the required systems (*i.e.*, T-group course, residency program) placed high value on the expression of feelings, most of the men talked intellectually. When a woman showed feeling, or advocated its expression as Alice did (*i.e.*, tried to establish it as normative), emotionality became identified as feminine behavior, and the men avoided it more, reinforcing the norm of intellectualizing by using the behavior to emphasize their masculinity. Sometimes the women (*e.g.* Debby) carried the emotional load for the group, fulfilling the stereotype upon which her deviancy was based.

Men avoided pairing or allying with the lone woman, fearing to share her deviant role. If she seemed needy or depressed, no one man wanted the job of taking care of her. Debby's group defined solacing her as a group project. In all the groups but Fran's, the men all remained equidistant from the woman, although the distance varied from very close in Debby's case, to very far in Eva's. This served to prevent sexual rivalry and preserve the all-male nature of the group. Her sexuality was a scarce resource that could easily disrupt cohesiveness, and in these six groups it was all but ignored. Alice's was joked about as a commodity; Debby's was denied yet recognized as threatening. When Betty proclaimed that the resource belonged to her to bestow as she chose, the men felt threatened and decreased their interactions with her to defuse the threat.

The four female deviants disliked this role and tried to escape. They became anxious and sometimes quite depressed. In order to earn regular member status, the woman tended to increase the number of interactions she initiated toward others, which by definition increased her deviance. A vicious circle ensued. Many coping mechanisms carry sex-role labels in our culture. If she acted friendly she was thought to be flirting. If she acted weak, the men tried to infantilize her, treating her as a "little sister" rather than a peer. If she apologized for alienating the group, she was seen as a submissive woman knowing her place. If she asked for help, she earned a "needy female" label. If she became angry, or tried to point out rationally what the group process was doing to her, she was seen as competitive, in a bitchy unfeminine way. "Feminine" coping mechanisms increased her perceived differences; "masculine" ones threatened the men so that they isolated her more. Any internal ambivalence about her sexual role was rekindled by these labels, and increased her anxiety, which increased her coping behavior, which further increased her deviance!

Discussion

We found it helpful, in understanding these groups, to look at how an all-male peer group works, because men have traditionally claimed the professions as their territory. Tiger[12] suggests that all-male groups, whether in neighborhood bars, playing fields, or at work, descend from primitive hunting groups, and that most men want regular membership in such a group. Ethologists study patterns of behavior in such groups with this view in mind, considering male groups as basic to human society almost in the way that families are basic. We realize this model is a controversial one, but found it useful in helping us understand the dynamics of the groups studied.

Men ally in male groups on the basis of imitation and identification; male-male bonds are strong but forbidden to be overtly sexual. The dominance hierarchy is worked out by overt aggression, usually verbal, and members tend to relieve their anxiety by acting out (*e.g.,* joking, arguing) rather than through asking for help or revealing fear. Independence, aggressiveness, and toughness have high value; passivity and emotional displays lower status. All-male groups usually talk about women as objects to be conquered, prizes to be awarded, or proofs of the masculinity of the members; possession of women is sometimes a way for a man to gain status and prestige from his peers.

Obviously, the presence of a woman in the groups we have studied interferes with many of these mechanisms, and is resented by the men. They lose their "hunting-group" atmosphere, and must mourn its loss, or else maintain this atmosphere by ignoring the woman. They must deal with their hostility toward her somehow; to express it overtly would be taboo, both because of cultural prohibitions, and because the woman enters defined as a peer by the larger required system, so that the group is formally required to accept her. They fear that she will act weak and demand that they take care of her, violating the norm of independence and toughness. They fear that she will compete successfully with them, violating the norm that women are seen as objects, and threatening their masculinity. It is as if any man below her in the pecking order has been castrated. And they fear that she will stir up sexual rivalry among them, disrupting their friendships and violating the norm that sexual feelings are taboo. Any man who affiliates with her risks being identified with her and sharing her differentness; this both stirs up any internal doubts about his masculinity and threatens his position in the male peer group.

The lone woman entering a small group of male professionals usually does not realize that she is felt to be trespassing, or resents and rejects this notion. She wishes to be accepted with full membership, with the right to express herself freely, and compete actively for status according to her professional merits. Often, however, she has not resolved internal conflicts about her sex role. Feminine socialization, described at length by many writers,[5,6,7] trains her to value passivity, helplessness, and show of feelings. In dealing with men, a traditionally feminine woman is supposed to get taken care of, avoid competition, and emphasize her sexuality. Horner[10] showed that most women are afraid of success, especially that achieved in competition with men. To succeed professionally, a woman must reevaluate the "feminine" traits she has been taught, and become independent, assertive, and competent.

We feel that the women in four of the six groups we have described were stereotyped, and pushed into a deviant role that they disliked and resisted. Their gender served as the salient cue determining their deviant role. Usually, the men found a way to minimize their impact and ignore their efforts to become regular members so that they could almost have an all-male group. The woman tended to give up her efforts after a while, becoming depressed instead. Alice and Betty considered themselves group casualties, in Yalom's[3] sense.

Even though the required systems behind our six groups placed high value on the expression of feelings and awareness of group process, they all failed to recognize overtly and to deal constructively with the "solo woman" group dynamic. We would guess that the same dynamics take place in other professional peer groups containing only one woman. They might also apply to groups containing other sorts of solo deviants, such as one black. We feel, though, that gender is probably a more powerful cue determining people's expectations of each others' behavior than any other. Also, no other external feature carries the same potential for arousing group dynamics around the issue of sex and pairing.

Suggestions

We want to emphasize that our conclusions are drawn from a small number of groups, and so must be tentative. Also, in all these groups, the women were peers. We doubt that the same dynamics occur when the required system defines a female as clearly of higher or lower status than the men; the competition for status is then removed.

How can the solo woman's dilemma be avoided or resolved? A woman finding herself alone in a peer group can choose the role of deviant or isolate, as Eva did, and obviate conflict. Or she can accept low status and minimize competition, as Fran did, letting people get to know her as a person while she occupies the bottom spot in the pecking order. In any case, she should realize that the men see her as an unwanted interloper and will feel hostile for a while. She is advised to minimize sexual cues and flirting behavior, if she wants to avoid becoming a competed-for sex object. Alternately, she could pair sexually with the male leader if he wished and take her place as "his woman," but none of the professional women we observed chose to do this.

If she finds herself in a deviant role and unhappy about it, she should realize that very powerful group forces will operate to keep her there, and avoid self-blame. She can leave the group, or introduce another woman if group norms allow new members, or speak privately with the male leader about her plight and try to persuade him to see what is happening. If he will state that the group has stereotyped the woman and should discuss this, it might help. To escape deviance unilaterally, she should decrease all behavior drastically for a long time, since her appearance alone will continue to evoke the realization that she is female. Alternately, she could share her feelings about being the lone female, and try gently to raise group consciousness. This takes much patience, strength, and emotional stability. If she remains silent, the men may eventually notice that their view of her is no longer being reinforced to her and give her another chance to join the regular members. If the men can accept the loss of their hostility toward the woman who caused it, then they can see the hostility as a group phenomenon rather than something that she as an individual deserves. Then, they may release her from her deviant role.

Conclusion

A professional peer group containing a solo woman faces difficult problems. Its overall productivity may be lowered by conflict over the woman's role, and the woman stands a fair chance of becoming a group casualty. Administrators setting up T-groups or working groups would be wise to avoid lone women members, making sure that two or three women are included if any are.

If such a group is formed, the leader should be aware that powerful group forces will tend to isolate the woman and keep the group in conflict with her. He should take responsibility for pointing this out to the group, and helping the men to accept her on her merits. If a woman finds herself in a group where the leader does not do this, she should realize that she is in a stressful situation with little leverage for changing it. She should mobilize emotional support from outside the group if she needs it, decrease her behavior in the group, accept the role of deviant or isolate without becoming depressed by it, and function as well as she can from this position. She also can give feedback to the larger system about the outcome of the group for her, as we are doing in this paper.

References

1. Athos, A. and Coffey, R. 1968. Behavior in Organizations: A Multidimensional View. Prentice-Hall, Englwood Cliffs, N.J.

2. Bales, R. 1970. Personality and Interpersonal Behavior. Holt, Rinehart and Winston, New York.

3. Bennis, W. and Shepard, A. 1956. A theory of group development. Human Relations 4.

4. Dalton, M. 1959. Men Who Manage, John Wiley, New York.

5. De Beauvoir, S. 1970. The Second Sex. Bantam Books, New York.

6. Friedan, B. 1964. The Feminine Mystique. Dell, New York.

7. Greer, G. 1972. The Female Eunuch. Bantam Books, New York.

8. Henderson, L. 1935. Pareto's Sociology. Harvard University Press, Cambridge, Mass.

9. Homans, G. 1961. Social Behavior: Its Elementary Forms. Harcourt, Brace and World, New York.

10. Horner, M. 1969. Fail: bright woman. Psychol. Today (Nov.).

11. Johnson, M. and Frank, H. 1973. Johnson/Frank quick score method for analyzing Bales group space ratings. Working Paper #139, Management Department, The Wharton School. University of Pennsylvania, Philadelphia.

12. Tiger, L. 1972. Men in Groups. Random House, New York.

13. Yalom, I. 1970. Report of the American Psychiatric Associations's task force on recent developments in the use of small groups. Amer. J. Psychiat. (April).

27
Strategies of Women Academics

KAREN FOLGER JACOBS and CAROL S. WOLMAN

In the pyramidal hierarchy of the academic world, advancement is dependent upon the strategies of the players, according to the authors of this reading. For women academics, however, the strategies used can and often do backfire, because the rules of the game give them such a handicapped starting point and because their efforts to use strategies successful with males are thwarted by their gender. Jacobs and Wolman succinctly delineate these "game plans" in the world of academics and show why female participants face a hard struggle upward.

There are two major groups of people who inhabit the territory of Academe—Academics and Supporters. Academics include undergraduates, graduate students, and faculty of all ranks. "People" hereinafter refers to Academics. Supporters include spouses and other emotional and financial sustainers of Academics—secretaries, typists, assistants, lab technicians, and all other workers whose services keep Academe lubricated. They are nonpersons in Academe.

Academics are tightly organized into a pyramidal hierarchy which calls itself a meritocracy. According to the professed rules of Academe, one must show more merit than one's peers to rise in the hierarchy. After the undergraduate years, the pyramid narrows rapidly, so an Academic must show himself to be better than his peers and thus worthy of promotion, or stop being an Academic.[1] Excellence is judged and promotions are controlled by those at the top of the hierarchy. The majority of Academics are white males, and the percentage of white males increases dramatically as one glances up the hierarchy.

Supporters are not so rigidly organized. Some serve the Academics en

Paper read at the Eighth World Congress of Sociology, Toronto, Canada, August 20, 1974. Reprinted by permission of the authors.

masse, e.g., librarians, cafeteria workers, switchboard operators. Others are at the service of individual Academics; in fact, one sign of an Academic's status is the number of Supporters he commands. Supporters tend to be female, low-status, poorly paid or not paid at all (wives). Often they are pressed to serve in ways not written in their formal job descriptions—running errands and providing sexual solace.

Academics pour their life-energy into their work. They race against each other and against time. Since the rule is "up or out," older people are expected to be at higher echelons or out. Thus, the young Academic must subordinate his private life to the exigencies of his work. Needs of spouse, children, aging parents, and friends are all secondary to competing in the race for survival.

An Academic who is female starts with multiple handicaps; her deviant biology grounds her in marginality. She constantly struggles to distance herself from Supporters, by presenting herself either less sexually or more flamboyantly to compensate or overcompensate for her deviance from the male model, or by refusing to run errands and play secretary or hostess.

Alternatively, she can attempt camouflage by behaving like a Supporter in certain ways, and accept the nonpersonhood and low status intrinsic to Supporters.

People in her private sphere expect her to not subordinate their needs regardless of Academe's demands. And she has been socialized from birth to do so. Thus she can either reconcile herself to having a smaller proportion of time and energy available for work than her male competitors, or she can burn her energies fighting her own emotional conditioning toward nurturing and self-sacrifice. If she chooses the latter course, she frustrates the expectations of those close to her and runs the risk of converting her support system into enemies. Society provides men with Supporters to do their laundry, care for their children, type their term papers, prepare their meals, tend their illnesses, and fulfill their sexual needs. Women are expected to be Supporters, not to have Supporters. If the women academic tries to resolve her dilemma by slowing down and taking time to do everything, she loses the race against time and also encounters the American prejudice against older women, an obsolescence structured to occur decades earlier than in males despite women's demonstrated longer life expectancy.

Nevertheless, some intrepid women become Academics and try to rise in the meritocracy. Usually they ape strategies for survival and upward mobility exhibited by their male peers. Each strategy involves a set of psychodynamics and group dynamics which changes markedly with the gender of the strategist, often in ways that the woman Academic fails to anticipate or recognize as operant. Women have also invented some new strategies.

We will first delineate five archetypal strategies for viability in Academe and then show how they are altered when employed by female Academics. Most people, of course, use more than one strategy, depending on their psychological makeup, the political and social situation at their university, and their career stage/life-stage. Underlying our models lies our assumption that universities are hardly meritocracies, and that advancement is secured in a multiplicity of ways.

The Devotee of Excellence Strategy

This Academic seeks redemption and acceptance to more exclusive circles by sheer exhibition of competence. He may publish more respectable papers, turn out more acceptable research, and devote more energy to teaching, or concentrate on very high-quality work. This sort of behavior derives from a real belief in the rhetoric of the meritocracy, and faith in its scales of justice. Or, the person may have a strong set of internal standards and believe in doing quality work without caring about recognition and job security. Such a person may not be viable for long in the political maelstrom of Academe.

Women Academics who adopt this strategy are at greater risk than are men: work with a female byline is rated by experts as of lower quality than identical pieces of work with a male byline.[2] Resumes of academics are differentially rated by people who serve on hiring committees according to the gender of the name on the resume.[3] Thus, a women has to generate more excellence than her male competitor in order to demonstrate equivalent excellence. Even when women do obtain positions on the hierarchy, they are paid less and have lower status than equivalent males.[4]

If a woman pours her energies on the quest for excellence, she may become labelled unfeminine. If she elects to not marry and become a mother she may be labelled an unfulfilled "old maid" or a lesbian. Such labels may work against academic advancement. To counter this, some women adopt the uniquely female Superwoman strategy, a combination of the Excellence model with an attempt to be a perfect Supporter. Since this takes more energy than most human beings possess very few women do manage it. Most who attempt to be Superwomen end up damaged, physically, emotionally, or both.

The Father-Son Strategy

This is the modal strategy in the authoritarian, patriarchal system of Academe. In this mode the junior Academic seeks adoption by a higher and more powerful Academic (more certainly a male the higher up one goes), in the hopes of gaining teaching, protection, and advancement from this father figure by contagion. In time, the properly-behaved son, the intellectual offspring of the father, will grow into manhood after a suitable adolescence/indenture. Indenture means that the father has total access to the son's academic energies, time, and talent. He can direct the junior Academic's research, and be named first author on junior's papers. He is not, however, supposed to treat the son as a Supporter and demand clerical assistance or sexual access.

Fathers take pride in the growing assertiveness and competence of their sons. Young males are expected to be exploratory and inventive, and competitive with their fathers.[5] Though a man may be ambivalent about being equalled or surpassed by his son (generating castration anxiety in young men), he expects that the son will eventually replace him.

When the junior Academic is female, the model becomes, de facto, a father-daughter one. Daughterhood carries significantly different implications than sonhood. Father-son incest is almost unheard of in our society, whereas father-daughter incest is not uncommon, especially when the taboo afforded by blood-relationship is absent.

In her role as daughter, the young female Academic conjures up images of pink bows, deference, and uncreative passivity. Her increasing competence threatens the father's hegemony not just with visions of his feeble age supplanted by her vigorous youth, but also with emasculation, domination by a mere female, a biological misfit for his position. So the father, as fathers do, tends to limit his daughter's success more strongly than his son's. Thus, besides the fear of female success described by Matina Horner, the woman has to contend with exaggerated standard castration anxiety experienced by her junior and senior men.[6]

Women struggling for intellectual independence cannot evolve into manhood; at best they can divorce Daddy—or, be "given away" by him (to another man). An upwardly mobile Academic woman employing the daughter strategy may well try to unite with a higher-status, older male who is in an ideal position to sexploit her. She may slip, irreversibly, into a Supporter role (concubine or wife) before she realizes what strategy she's transferred to.

The Warrior Strategy

This strategy concentrates on the need to compete with peers. It employs specific styles and posturings. The Academic using it tends to bully and exploit subordinates and minimize the energies he directs toward fulfilling responsibilities to them—e.g., in teaching and advising. He is arrogant to his peers, and to Supporters, seeking to dominate them and perhaps commandeer their services. He's mobilized so as to exhibit superiority to his superiors. Toward authority he may be likewise arrogant, or more likely, exceedingly deferential. The Warrior uses ritualistic jousting and garnering of power to push his way upward. He makes many enemies, of course, and must counter these with allies who, smelling power, join his camp. His way is dangerous, but potentially victorious.

A female warrior is called an Amazon. She generates great fear and hatred in men, and quickly receives such denigrating epithets as "castrating bitch" or aggressive bitch.[7] Little of her strength or belief in her power will accrue to her; enemies will be many and allies very rare indeed. Male warriors generally command a retinue of Supporters and even some younger female Academics who perform Supporter functions for them—often such warriors command a small cottage industry. Amazons are unlikely to encounter such succor even with financial payment.

Women are subtly and strongly judged on how competitive and assertive they *appear* to be. There are documented cases of women being dropped from school because they weren't "competitive" enough, whereas others have been denied admission as students or denied jobs because they were "too aggressive."

The Class President Strategy

This strategy involves becoming a leader of the peer group and in this way gaining prominence and recognition from higherups, as well as lateral alliances and support. The class president is a Good Guy to all—his students, his peers, and his superiors. By granting people favors, he aggregates indebtedness. He works for group cohesiveness, thus satisfying the affiliative needs of those around him. When a threat confronts the group, this Academic has seen it coming and mobilizes the group into coherent action to meet the crisis. When the crisis comes from above, the class president leads his peers in negotiations with authority. This wins him high visibility, and if he is adept, he becomes a mediator and earns the gratitude of both sides. In short, this is the strategy of the politician, and the young Academic who employs it may be destined for a high administrative job in the university.

The success of this strategy depends on the perception by other Academics that the Class President is unusually helpful. When a woman tries this strategy, a Good Gal, her services are willingly accepted, but she is unlikely to be given leadership recognition for them (Solo Women).[8] She may be seen as a Supporter (masquerading as an Academic) and actually lose status in the group because of her leadership capabilities. Her efforts may be seen as an expression of her female affiliative needs and her intrinsic field-dependence. She may be labeled "weak," "seductive," "hysterical," or "manipulative." Women are supposed to exude nurturing and sustaining; her use of them with benefits to her Academic colleagues underlies their belief that "she's only a woman."

Change of gender in the model again changes the dynamics of the situation drastically. Can a woman lead men? Will men follow any woman for any reason other than why the Trojans followed Helen?

The Drop Out Strategy

Some Academics cope with the struggle for viability by electing nonviability. They select themselves out of the race.

This remains the only model which is looked upon as healthy for women and unhealthy for men. It is viewed as particularly healthy if a woman drops out by transferring, a lateral and irreversible transfer for a woman, into a Supporter of a male peer or superior.[9] Also women are regarded as engaging in wholesome behavior if they drop out to have a baby or another baby. Thus, women can retreat into Mom and focus on excellence in the female sphere. By doing so, by sacrificing their status as an Academic person to assume Supporter nonpersonhood, they enrich the Academic valence of whatever Academic man they chose to support. What better accessory for an Academic man—as Thorstein Veblen so well described it in *Theory of the Leisure Class* half a century ago. Correspondingly, men cannot retreat from Academe by becoming a husband or father and get gold stars for doing so. Men who drop out are out.

There are also two new strategies a few women adopt. Both of these are almost exclusively adopted by women, and both are but marginally (or less) viable in the groves of Academe.

The "Women's Lib Freak" is a label thrust upon women who teach about women or who raise the issues of women too frequently. This may mean raising the issue once.

Another style which women may adopt is a style of cooperation in a nonhierarchical manner. One tenet of much feminist ideology is that people are equal. This would include Academics and Supporters which Academe divides into Persons and Nonpersons. Another tenet is that women should support and help each other. Such tenets are in direct conflict with the climate of Academe. It is a model which, as the Chinese model, believes in helping all people improve regardless of where they are. It's a model of growth as opposed to the model of Anglo-chauvinism whose goal is to separate the Academic men from the boys.

Women who act in this "feminist" style, which seeks to include all persons rather than screen out most, are seen as unprofessional, incompetent, or slumming.

The authors of this paper have both chosen the Drop Out Strategy—to leave Academe. Karen Jacobs, Ph.D.,[10] is an author. Carol S. Wolman, M.D., a practicing feminist psychiatrist, is organizing women therapists in the San Francisco area.

Notes

1. We use the word him advisedly. The more one rises in the hierarchy the more accurate the gender-specific pronoun becomes.
2. Goldberg, Philip "Are Women Prejudiced Against Women?" *Transaction*, Vol. 5, No. 5, 1968.
3. Fidell, Linda A. "Empirical Verification of Sex Discrimination in Hiring Practices in Psychology," *American Psychologist*, December 1970, Vol. 25, No. 12.
4. Kashket, Eva Roth; Robbins, Mary Louise; Leive, Loretta and Huang, Alice S. "Status of Woman Microbiologists based on objective and subjective criteria is presented," *Science*, February 8, 1974, Vol. 183, pp. 488–494. This excellent article starts its conclusion:

The general picture that emerges from this study is that the woman microbiologist, upon entering the professional job market, faces (i) slow advancement, (ii) restricted extramural recognition; and (iii) fewer positions of a supervisory or administrative nature, when compared to men. Most striking is the salary differential, which increases with increasing educational level, with increasing rank, and with increasing seniority.

Rossi, Alice "Status of Women in Graduate Departments of Sociology, 1968–1969," *American Sociologist*, 1970, Vol. 5, pp. 1–12. Rossi found that after 20 years in academe, 90% of males became full professors whereas less than half the women became so appointed.

Carnegie Commission on Higher Education, *Opportunities for Women in Higher Education* (New York: McGraw-Hill, 1973).

There appears to be two components underlying the differences between male and female salaries: (1) a general shift of the entire distribution of male salary residuals, amounting to $2000 (so that a man of specified qualification tends to earn about $2000 more than a woman of the same qualifications) and (2) an excess of men with exceptionally high salary deviations.

5. *Dick and Jane as Victims: Sex Stereotyping in Children's Readers*, Women on Words and Images, P.O. Box 216, Princeton, New Jersey, 1972, (mimeo).
6. Horner, Matina, "Women's Will to Fail," *Psychology Today*, November 1969, Vol. 2, No. 6, pp. 36–41.
7. Fascinating how the valence of adjective is dependent upon the gender of the noun it modifies! Aggression, in academe and elsewhere, is generally regarded as normal and desirable in male persons and abnormal and undesirable in female persons.
8. Wolman, Carol S. & Frank, Hal, "The Solo Woman in a Professional Peer Group," chapter 26 in this book.
9. Perhaps the classic example of this phenomenon is Betty Friedan herself. She dropped out of graduate school at Berkeley to marry a peer and bear children as her husband finished a Ph.D. She dedicated her book *The Feminine Mystique* to him and their three children; subsequently he divorced her and married a younger woman.
10. Karen Folger Jacobs, Ph.D. is the author of *Ward 81* a book about her experiences as a resident of a locked ward in a state hospital, coauthored with photographer Mary Ellen Mark, to be published by DeCapo Publishing Co., 1977, and *Girl Power* to be published by Bantam Book, 1977.

28
"A House Is Not a Home": Women in Publishing

LAURA FURMAN

A friend of mine who works for a New York publishing house explained to me that publishing is the gentlemanly profession. She meant by this that publishing has been traditionally for gentlemen and ladies, a very right occupation for members of the educated middle and upper classes. For young lady graduates of Eastern women's colleges, a job in a New York publishing house seems like a logical and easy extension of the academic life, a pleasant and respectable career.

I like making books, and I enjoy the work itself. What I found not only unsatisfactory but enraging was the attitude which I saw and felt existed toward women, an attitude that has been confirmed by numerous other women in publishing whose specific experiences were different from mine. Recently I heard of a white woman who was hired by a house as an editor. Her previous position with another house had been a good one, she was a talented and professional woman, and the second firm was apparently pleased to hire her. When the discussion of salary began she told the man who was hiring her that she didn't necessarily want a raise immediately, but that she wouldn't take a cut in pay. Unashamedly, her future employer said, "But women simply don't make that much money." She replied, "If I were a black man, you wouldn't dare say that."

I had dropped out of college for a year, and for nine months of that year had worked at a publishing house as a production editor in the college text department. When I finally graduated from college, I went to New York and got a job as assistant to the senior editor of a small publishing house. She had worked there for many years and I recognized in

263

her numerous other women I had met in publishing. She was intelligent, sophisticated, well educated, conscientious—and she was a martyr. She was a martyr not because she worked hard, but because she worked hard in a vacuum. She had gone as far as she would go in the house, and she was resigned to it, if more conscious of it than other women in the same position might have been. She was very good at her job, but the work was without pleasure or satisfaction, save the brief moment when the bound books arrived—and then the books were quickly scrutinized for possible slip-ups, mistakes, or negligence.

It is not maliciousness or obsessiveness that at least initially limits pride in one's work. In publishing, women are kept "in the home." They work at a craft and learn the best way to make a manuscript into a book. There are many women like the woman I described who have worked in publishing for years, and who act and work as martyrs. They give the impression that without them the house would cease to function, and their attachment to the house and to the books becomes something more than attachment to a job. To the women who make books, books are something more than a better brand of corn flakes, packaged brightly and attractively, to be sold for the profit of the owner of the house. There is, as yet, no union of women in the publishing industry, and the fight for better salary, a full chance to advance and work as one is best able to is kept on a personal, "family" basis.

Women are allowed to craft the books, and even to promote them, but the really public life of the book is left to the male salesmen, who take the perfected product into the outside world. Once the book is a book, it is no longer any part of the job or concern of those who have made it—it is a better brand of corn flakes, something for the menfolk to tend to and profit from while the little women remain in the house to care for the next book.[1]

The reasons women hold such positions are many, not the least of which is the desire on the part of women to prove themselves as good as men, never to complain, never to refuse to do anything. Another reason is the attitude of the men in publishing. I can easily see that it would be gratifying for a normal, ambitious, American man who is pressured by the demands of his chosen job—to keep sales high, to know which books to publish when, which can be pushed and which will be quiet but steady sellers, and in some way how to scoop the competition and get the best-seller or the latest controversial issue before the rival houses do, for such is the show-biz quality of modern American publishing—for such a man to have someone there, female, obedient, preferably pretty, well educated, and kindly, to make dentist appointments, come along to lunch with a difficult author, do his correspondence, make his phone calls, see to reservations for authors at hotels, restaurants, and airlines, locate a hard-to-find book for his wife, remember everything, and to just be there and willing to do anything. The position of such men is not a totally enviable one, and they receive not only sympathy from their female helpers but loyalty. Not only would the house fall down if such a saintly lady left, but so would her favorite male in the place. But where is the satisfaction for the *woman*, whether the woman be a demi-executive or a filing clerk? She certainly isn't receiving the salary the man is, or the power (however shared) to make decisions that will affect the publishing program of the house. If she is very useful where she is, that is usually where she will stay, lapping up second-hand sunbeams. That the woman's possibilities are much more severely limited than she deserves for her intelligence, hard work, and professional experience, does not occur to most men in publishing or any industry; and if one woman is rebellious and "demanding" she leaves that house and is replaced by another willing, professional woman.

With women and other minority groups tending the home fires, and men hustling the books along to their fates and profiting from them, publishing continues to function, if a bit hysterically. It will probably continue to do so as a profession until people come to resent being treated so automatically as separate functionaries, until women begin to protest the ease with which they themselves accept from first to last positions of lesser power and lesser salary, but equal pressure. One day at work I looked up at my desk lamp and saw that a fellow worker had put up a little sign that said: Change or Die. Some of us are trying to change, for the alternative is indeed a kind of death—accepting the daily overlooking, the distance between the quality of the work we have put into the book and the quality of the treatment we receive for such work. I changed. I quit.

Notes

1. A family chart of most houses would place white males at the highest levels at least of decision-making, because men are the owners, the managers, and the top editors. Women and other oppressed groups begin appearing further down—down also in salary and power—as head copy editors, copy editors, production managers, production assistants, secretaries, to the point in one avant garde house where the mailroom is run by one Puerto Rican, one black, and one Irish Catholic.

29
On Being Black
and Female
and an Accountant

JACQUELINE THOMPSON

ABSTRACT

In this reading, Jacqueline Thompson asserts that black women enter the accounting profession with a different viewpoint from white women. Discussing the experiences of black female accountants, she says black women operating under a double "handicap" take a more cynical outlook than white women who have "bought the equal opportunity pitch." She observes that some black women found sex to be a bigger handicap, but others found race to be a more decisive factor in career advancement.

Today's young white professional woman expects to be treated fairly in the business world. When she isn't, she becomes indignant, then angry, and eventually completely disillusioned with the equal opportunity pitch she bought at her Seven Sisters college or high-powered MBA program.

Black professional women see discriminatory barriers from a markedly different vantage point. They enter business with a view that encompasses the history of their race in white America—a cynicism about what the establishment is going to do for them, first and foremost as blacks, second as women. Burdened with two "handicaps," they tend to view the white businessman's efforts on their behalf with a sardonic aloofness, as if to say, "Show me. I dare you to treat me decently!"

This is not to say that black women are unwilling to give the corporate world a chance. While to some, "affirmative action" is just another phrase in the overall rhetoric of discrimination, to others it is a hopeful opening in the barriers to minority and female careers in white-male-dominated corporations, banks, and service firms. It's just that for black women, the barriers appear to be higher so skepticism runs stronger.

And nowhere would the barriers seem to be higher than in the large public accounting firms. Bastions of white Anglo-Saxon conservatism, the large accounting firms have nevertheless greatly improved their record of hiring minority group accountants (female employment has never been surveyed). According to a survey of the American Institute of Certified Public Accountants, the 43 largest firms have almost tripled their hiring of minorities since 1969.

Drawing encouragement from this sort of growth, black women are entering accounting firms in greater and greater numbers, and their observations and reactions to working in this conservative environment can be enlightening and instructive.

Sheila Clark, a senior auditor in the Houston office of Peat, Marwick, Mitchell & Co., the world's largest public accounting firm, typifies the growing vanguard of black women accountants who are willing to give "equal employment opportunity" a try. Eminently qualified for her job, she joined PMM&Co. in 1972 with a B.S. in accounting and a master's degree in business administration from North Texas State, graduating in the top 10 percent of her class as the school's first black woman MBA.

Surprisingly, Clark has observed that her sex far outranks her race as a drawback in public accounting. "When you're a black woman in business, you're got both white and black men looking at you as if you don't quite belong there. You are a woman and, by nature, not as smart, you see."

She concedes there are advantages accruing to women in business, although these are largely based on a chivalric code that women's liberationists would consider outmoded, if not downright insulting. But she has found such solicitous treatment a help on occasion. "I think a lot of courtesies are bestowed upon you because you are a woman," says Clark. "For instance, a client once told one of our black auditors straight out that he didn't want to go to lunch with him. I may be black, but because I'm a woman I don't think that would ever happen to me. The client might not go to lunch with me, but I doubt he'd be so outspoken about the reason. Men, especially older men, feel that all women require more delicate treatment."

The emergence of both black and women professionals has put accounting firms in an awkward position with their clients. While accounting firms may welcome blacks and women, they are not sure clients will. Public accounting firms in some sections of the country try to second-guess client attitudes—"Will they object if we send a minority-group auditor over to their offices?"—or else simply ask the client if he would object to working with a nonwhite.

Gray C. Wakefield, PMM&Co.—Houston's managing partner, explains that accounting firms have had to gradually educate many of their clients. "Since affirmative action became a crucial issue a few years ago, I'd say our clients have gone through an evolution in their thinking about blacks. In Sheila Clark's case, she's so bright that you could paint her any color you wanted, or any sex, and you'd still have an outstanding accountant. Her superiors request her for job assignments, she's so good. Once in a while we have to do a little selling job to a client before we can send over someone like Sheila. But once they work with a client, they usually sell themselves." As an aside, he adds, "Personally, I think that in general young women are more mature than their male counterparts and have more common sense."

J. Curt Mingle, the personnel director of Clifton, Gunderson & Co., located in Peoria, Illinois, candidly admits that his firm considers how a client will react—"not just to black women, but to any women. In scheduling engagements, we always consider client reaction to a particular staff person. It is quite possible we are overreacting, since personality conflicts between our people and clients are extremely rare."

For the past couple of years, public accounting firms have been frantically engaged in outreach programs designed to infuse minority high school and college students with zeal for the profession. They have helped upgrade the accounting faculties at predominantly black colleges and offered promising minority candidates scholarships and jobs. A number of latterday EEO statutes, particularly Revised Order No. 4, have spurred accounting firms into action. Revised Order No. 4, an executive branch fiat, set April 1972 as the date when all companies with 50 or more employees (in March 1973 the number was lowered to 25) and at least a $50,000 government contract had to file personnel statistics with Washington and publicize to their employees an affirmative action program outlining equal hiring, training, and promotion goals and timetables for women and minorities.

Ask public accountants what special problems they've had in recruiting blacks and women and the answer will invariably be: "a lack of qualified applicants." But embedded in that comment is the fear that blacks and women will somehow compromise the accountant's professional image. That carefully cultivated image calls for a white male, progressive-looking in his Brooks Brothers suit, with the right hobbies (golf and, more recently, tennis), a wife and children nestled in the white upper-middle-class suburbs, and a smattering of knowledge on subjects that might come up over a business luncheon or at a country club social. That image has helped inspire clients with confidence and push accountants to stage center with the more established professionals in medicine and the law.

From a black woman accountant's point of view, the problem is not so much one of fitting into a prescribed mold as how to relate to male colleagues on an informal, social level. In both public accounting and private industry, the ability to fraternize with both peers and superiors is important for advancement. Many entry-level black women, recognizing that they will never be part of the prevailing social order, are understandably pessimistic about advancement in public accounting firms.

Is private industry the answer? Sheila Clark worked in the accounting department of a large oil company for a year and has a decided preference for public accounting: "I disliked industrial accounting immensely. The work was generally repetitive and boring, there was a lot of back stabbing to get ahead, and the climate was unprofessional. I was tossed in with people with high school educations who felt no qualms about expressing their prejudice. I haven't found any pronounced examples of discrimination since I've been in public accounting. CPAs are constantly concerned with maintaining their professional image, which, among other things, means being careful not to offend anyone."

Catherine Cullars, who spent two years at a large pharmaceutical firm, also has objections to corporation accounting. She recalls the moments of overt discrimination, such as the time a superior told her that women don't need as much money as men because they aren't heads of households. Or the time a superior told her he was convinced that an education at a predominantly black college wasn't worth much, based on his previous experience with black accountants. Cullars is divorced, has one child, and graduated from predominantly black Southern University in Baton Rouge.

Cullars feels that affirmative action has helped break through these barriers but also that the battle for good jobs has just begun. "When it comes to women escaping from the proverbial feminine occupations in business, men are still putting up a fight," she says.

She learned a lesson from her job with the pharmaceutical firm: in large companies, even college-educated accountants tend to get stuck in glorified clerk positions for far too long unless one goads, prods, pressures, and finally threatens to leave. Cullars, in fact, did leave to join a small black personnel firm as its financial manager. While there, she decided she wanted "all the tools for promotion" and went for an MBA at Columbia Business School.

Another alternative for the black woman accountant is government. Governmental agencies have long had to conform to equal opportunity regulations, and their appointments follow civil service criteria and GS pay scales. Here, blacks and women are guaranteed objective treatment.

The governmental equivalent to a public accounting firm is the General

Accounting Office. As of October 31, 1974, the GAO employed in its headquarters and 15 regional offices 319 women professionals (some of whom are lawyers). Of those, there are 59 black women auditors; four have made it as far as GS 13, paying between $20,677 and $26,878.

Joyce Stevens, a GS 11 auditor who chose to go with GAO, concedes she probably started at a lower salary initially than her peers in industry and public accounting. She points out, however, that she has advanced regularly.

Catherine Farrow, another black accountant, also has gravitated to government work. She had been with a Big Eight accounting firm, but felt she was continually being given jobs without responsibility, possibly because the firm was trying to second-guess its clients' attitudes about her race and sex. She is now a revenue agent at the Internal Revenue Service, where she has progressed from a GS 7 to a GS 13.

Eileen Dottin, who recently moved from a Big Eight firm to a job as a tax accountant for a major bank, faults the accounting firm for stereotyping her as unaggressive. Throughout her career evaluation sessions there, the pat criticism of all the women on the staff was that they weren't aggressive enough, she says.

"When it comes to getting information out of clients," says Dottin, "I think many of the guys are less effective because they are too aggressive. Also, I think there is a rivalry between men that can lessen a male auditor's effectiveness with a male client. Women auditors get answers by being politely determined. The mere fact that you are a woman sometimes disarms the client, and you can play on that—and I'm not talking about feminine wiles. Clients often think their comments are going over your pretty little head, especially if you don't interrupt them with a barrage of questions immediately. Then when you do start asking questions, they are so surprised that you got their point that they end up spilling more beans than they originally intended."

Sheila Clark says that clients are often taken aback when she, as a black woman, doesn't buy their initial evasive response. Catherine Farrow contends that women have their own way of handling clients and still getting results. "I think women are more subtle," she says.

Joyce Stevens has had no problems as the only professional woman on an auditing team. "You're different, so you get more attention paid to you. Of course, then the burden is on you to be just a little better than the average man."

Whether they are actually better or only just as good, black women in business are tired of having to prove their professional worth. "The problem with proving yourself continually," says Eileen Dottin, "is that it takes so much time and energy. Women could spend the rest of their business lives trying to convince men that they were as good or better professionally. Frankly, I don't know whether men will ever believe it."

30

Up the Ladder, Finally

ABSTRACT

The corporate woman in the executive suite is still rare, but a legion of businesswomen are poised in the wings for top-brass posts in American business. This article traces five developments which Business Week *magazine highlights as the turning points in the corporate world's treatment of female employees. It profiles successful women executives and how they reached the top of the corporate ladder.*

It took a decade of federal legislation, relentless agitation from the women's movement, and seismic shifts in public opinion, but women—at last—are moving boldly into the mainstream of corporate management. The battle for equality in blue-collar and clerical jobs moved faster because bias was easier to prove. The far more complex struggle for equal status up the corporate ladder has taken longer and is far from over. But the big news is that women are making headway—slowly in the executive suite, faster at the lower rungs of middle management.

"So you're looking for top-level women executives," says one who has arrived at the prestigious top. "Have you got a microscope?" It is true that General Electric Vice-President Marion S. Kellogg has only 15 or so counterparts among the 2,500 presidents, key vice-presidents, and chairpersons who direct the country's major corporations. This excludes entrepreneurs and inheritors, who never competed for their corporate jobs.

Yet even when one allows for the glacial change at the very top, the startling fact is that more women than ever before are within striking distance of the top spot. Boston executives, for instance, predict that Kay Knight Mazuy, 36, senior corporate vice-president at Shawmut Assn. Inc., will become president of a major Boston company in a matter of years. If their predictions hold true for Shawmut, an eight-bank holding company, Mazuy could become the country's second woman to head a major bank with which she has no family ties, following Catherine Cleary, 59, at First Wisconsin Trust Co. And though often opposed by older men and welcomed with mixed feelings by younger ones, thousands of women are joining males in the corporate management competition. The huge numbers of women at university business schools attest to their new ambitions.

Most women executives still wind up in personnel, consumer relations, and similar corporate niches—slightly outside the mainstream. But some are beginning to fill management slots formerly sacred to men: brand manager, industrial marketing manager, even plant manager. This comes through clearly in *Business Week's* survey of women at the top. Retailing, advertising, banking, and other service areas are also traditional favorites. But new industries—including some in male-dominated manufacturing—are opening up. In Portland, Ore., Christine Hodgson, the first saleswoman employed by Georgia-Pacific Corp., sells building materials for the forest products company so effectively that her superiors think she could become GP's frst woman distribution center manager.

As the numbers of Marion Kelloggs increase substantially by the 1980s, the corporate world can expect conflict, tension, and ultimately better use of executive resources. The women face problems, among them: What does a woman executive do if her superior automatically bypasses women? They also generate problems, such as: What does a male executive do if one of his staff will not work for a woman?

The solutions are often individual—and fraught with sociological and psychological complications. Because of the difficulties of adjustment, the movement of women into management has created a whole new industry that—as one executive puts it—"is recruiting women managers, training them, promoting them, sensitizing them, and preparing us men for their arrival."

No hard facts are available regarding how many women have arrived. The Census Bureau reports that women totaled 15.2% of all managers and administrators in 1958, 15.9% in 1968, and 18.5% last year. This reveals how recently the percentages have risen, but tells little about the actual numbers who hold executive posts. To the Census Bureau, Marion Kellogg and an office chief who supervises secretaries are equally managers. And the latest earnings figures, from the 1970 census, describe a vanished era, before five developments changed the corporate world for women:

1) American Telephone & Telegraph Co.—encompassing 20 Bell systems employing 800,000 people, 51% of them women—signed the January, 1973, consent decree that pledged sweeping reforms in female hiring and promotion policies and agreed to pay $50 million to compensate victims of past bias. In the view of most qualified observers, this remains the single strongest influence on corporate employment policies regarding women.

2) The U. S. Labor Dept. issued its April, 1972, Revised Order 4. This put teeth in an earlier Executive Order mandating the hiring and promotion of women by government contractors, a category that includes almost every major corporation in the U. S.

3) Sex bias complaints filed with the Equal Employment Opportunities Commission under the 1964 Civil Rights Act suddenly increased. Previously swamped by minority bias complaints, the number tripled from 3,497 in 1970 to 10,436 in 1972—a precursor of the 22,110 filed with the EEOC during the first half of this year. Many led to legal suits, interminable negotiation and litigation, fines, government-directed promotion programs, and a widespread corporate resolve to avoid similar trouble.

4) Radical changes in social attitudes, long developing beneath the surface, rose inexorably into view. This exposed the corporate executive to new phenomena ranging from media coverage of the women's movement to breakfast conversations with a daughter unexpectedly bound for law school.

5) Companies responded to all these events. Queried by the American Society for Personnel Administration regarding how promotion practices have changed to put more women into management, ASPA directors gave answers ranging from "general consciousness of need" through "early developmental programs" and "earmarking specific jobs" to a bitter "reverse discrimination and lowering of standards." But no one answered that nothing had changed.

Today, a hundred light-years after the 1970 census, executive recruiters and others in the know estimate that women total 15% of entry management (a huge jump over 10 years ago), 5% of middle management (a sizable rise), and 1% of top management (a slight rise).

Interviews with members of that topmost 1% and the testimony of their colleagues indicate that these women are very special people. They work, they achieve, they fight for their judgements, they let no one push them around, and they sacrifice more in time, private life, and emotional energy than the most enthusiastic woman MBA student can possibly imagine.

Says Kellogg, 55, who has helped solve managerial problems from Seattle to Swaziland: "A vacation for me is to lock the door and stay home. There is nothing so heavenly as to clean out the closets, wash your hair, and make sure the house wasn't broken into while you were away."

The house, a Stratford (Conn.) condominium bought recently near GE's new Fairfield headquarters, would disappoint any housebreaker. As a $100,000-plus vice-president for corporate consulting services (which advice GE's engineering, manufacturing, and marketing divisions and any noncompetitive outsider willing to pay the fee), Kellogg has been too busy to furnish more than the bedroom of her new home. She spends whatever weekends she can in her New York City apartment. But she is not complaining. "I'm a workaholic," she says.

Says Diane Duerr Levine, 37, staff vice-president for advertising and promotion at Continental Air Lines in Los Angeles: "Management style? If I have any style, it's to work my tail off."

Twelve years ago no one would even interview her when she graduated from Columbia University B-School. Today she earns close to $40,000 and says with undisguised triumph: "I've worked for four major companies [Lever Bros., American Home Products, and the Honig Cooper & Harrington advertising agency before Continental], and none has made less than several million dollars from my efforts. With a track record behind me, I sense that American business is so short of talent and so hard-nosed about results that being female will never again hinder my career."

Closeups of Corporate Bias

Any survey of the corporate world quickly reveals that the dice are still loaded against women executives in a multitude of cases. Herewith are some true stories about companies that, naturally, do not want to be identified:

1) A West Coast financial institution rejects a woman computer-marketing expert as head of its new department of computer-marketing services, choosing a less-qualified company man on the ground that it prefers to promote from within. Then it fills his job with an outsider, a male.

2) Confiding to a senior executive that he doesn't really hit it off with the woman who heads his department, a young manager at a service company gets informal permission to report directly to the senior executive. Comments the department head: "Can you imagine that happening if I were a man? That young twerp couldn't care less that I'm a woman, but he knows it bothers the v-p. So now he has a direct line to top management, and where am I?"

3) Feeling the effects of economic adversity, a California bank shrinks its corporate lending staff by six. It moves its six women corporate lending

officers to less prestigious positions in trust, portfolio management, and other areas. It leaves its 70-odd men corporate lending officers exactly where they were.

4) The only woman vice-president at a major consumer goods company observes that she is also the only vice-president who has no company car, whose office is off the executive floor, and whose salary (she discovers by discreet detective work) is 20% below that of her counterparts. Taxed with the discrepancies, the boss who appointed her replies indignantly that a woman should be grateful to have the post at all. "Of course I could file suit," says the woman. "And that would be the end of my career."

Profiles of Success

"I'm a builder, not a runner," says Kay Mazuy, describing her progress from marketing research studies with management consultant Arthur D. Little Inc., to marketing research manager with Polaroid Corp., to work with a new Citicorp division that developed novel marketing strategies, to her own firm, Mazuy Associates, which offered marketing advice to banks, to Shawmut, a satisfied client that now pays her $10,000 as senior vice president for corporate marketing.

But the builder's former boss at Polaroid, Stanford Calderwood, remembers her primarily as a fighter. "She was quietly aggressive," he says. "She would stick by her guns if she saw the figures differently than others. She had the courage to say 'No, you're wrong.' "

"Being a manager requires a tremendous amount of toughness," says Juliette M. Moran, 58, who received more than $130,000 last year as executive vice-president for communication services of GAF Corp., a chemicals-based conglomerate with New York headquarters. "I believe in team management. We all argue in my department. But it's my responsibility at some point to say yes or no."

Management calls for the same qualities in women as in men, Moran believes: physical stamina, dedication to the job in hand, backbone, and knowledge ("It's important to know your field, but note that I put that last"). For women of her generation, she adds, the opportunity to achieve success called for something more—luck.

Luck—in the form of World War II—took Moran and her chemistry degree out of the sales staff of Macy's New York department store, into a Signal Corps lab, and from there to a GAF lab. Her own abilities and a willingness to deal with budgets and reports, tasks generally spurned by scientific types, took her up to the chemical division's commercial development department—another break, Moran says, because a small, new department taught her a whole range of corporate activities.

None of this would have carried her further, she notes, except for still another lucky break. It is one that appears regularly in the histories of older management women and often even in the histories of younger ones. In commercial development, Moran worked for "a gentleman who had the talent to move ahead in the company and the self-confidence not to be upset by female competence," Jesse Werner, president and chairman of GAF. Even able young men often need powerful mentors in order to advance. But until yesterday, an able young woman apparently needed that rarest of birds: a powerful mentor unfazed by the fact that she was a woman.

For Kellogg, too, World War II provided the opportunity to use her graduate physics degree in GE's general engineering lab. The first vice-president promptly assigned her to arranging advanced courses for scientists and engineers and then sent her to school to learn psychological testing.

That was her particular piece of luck, Kellogg believes. With much of the important work in industrial psychology being done between 1945 and 1955, "the field was growing, and I was able to grow along with it," she says.

A former GE colleague who remembers her in her 20s—Karl McEachron, now a dean at Case Western Reserve University in Cleveland—suspects that her fierce devotion to work neutralized potential opposition during a period when GE seldom promoted women for fear that marriage and children would interrupt their careers. "Marion wasn't married, and she sure didn't sound like she was planning to be," he says. "She was planning to be a career gal."

Between 1946 and 1958, Kellogg ran placement testing and broad-based educational programs as personnel placement supervisor for the general engineering lab and organized a management and professional development section for the aircraft gas turbine division as supervisor of its supervisory and technical personnel. As manager of employee relations for the flight propulsion lab, GE's first woman section level manager, she devised and installed a performance appraisal system at GE's Cincinnati plant that became the model for the whole corporation.

By 1958, when she went to headquarters as manager of individual development methods services, Kellogg was ready to teach pioneering management-by-objective methods that integrated psychological techniques into the planning process—for instance, in a sales manager's "negotiating" sales quotas with salesmen rather than handing them down. In 1968 she began concentrating on developing GE marketing managers and in providing management consultant services internally and externally. Her travels became mildly legendary: to Germany for Kuba Co., to France for Bull Co., to Italy for Cogenel, Olivetti, and Pirelli, to South Africa for Barclays Bank, to Sweden to Volvo, to England for Massey-Ferguson, to Lesotho, to Swaziland, and on and on.

Along the way, executive advancement gave her authority over men long before such authority was remotely usual. "When I was assembling my group at Lynn," she says, "I knew the problem was the first man—and not just him but him telling his wife and his wife telling her bridge club. So I picked him carefully."

When GE named Kellogg vice-president last year, the reaction within the company overwhelmed her. "So many people wrote that it would have happened a long time ago if I had not been a woman," she says. "Personally, I think it was a great plus being a woman at this particular time. And, of course, the people who said I didn't get it just because I was a woman warmed me. Some of the women said, 'We really thank you. It gives us hope.' "

Hershner Cross, the senior vice-president who promoted Kellogg, insists that her sex played no part in the decision. "I guess Marion thinks that it did, but she's a little modest," he says. He cites a disciplined mind, a strong profit orientation, great energy, familiarity with both technical and nontechnical fields, skill at interpersonal relations, and "terrific ideas" as the factors that counted. GE executives, most of whom have worked with her for years, apparently accept her new status with ease.

Indeed, Kellogg, who recalls being smuggled through the kitchen to a business meeting on the second floor of the Downtown Mohawk Club in Schenectady because the club barred women above the first floor, finds the present era remarkably free from sex-consciousness. "Sometimes, when a meeting breaks up, we'll all go right down the hall together to the rest rooms, then suddenly realize that we are not going to the same place," she notes with pleasure.

Does Sex Matter?

Younger women executives (perhaps because they have less drastic memories of discrimination) tend to feel that the business world still contains plenty of sex-consciousness and plenty of antifemale attitudes. Many say flatly that the most competent woman in the world could be stopped dead by a male superior so threatened psychologically by her abilities that he created obstacles, and neither the EEOC nor any other earthly power could prevent it. Like Kellogg and other older women executives, however, they seldom challenge the opposition head-on.

Says Continental Air Lines' Diane Levine: "I care about how men feel about woman managers, but I'm not there to resocialize anyone. I'm paid to do a job that will affect sales and profits. If someone won't work with me for whatever reason, I will work around him, under him, over him, whatever is possible to move a project."

If Levine illustrates one similarity between older and younger women executives, she also illustrates two differences. Like her contemporaries, she speaks of seeking and grasping opportunity, not of happening upon and taking advantage of it. And her job history—five companies since leaving Columbia—separates her utterly from her predecessors, who never job-hopped, although men always did. A woman manager lucky enough to establish herself with one company would hardly risk another.

Today no one blinks when ᴊudith N. Frank, 34, follows eight years as a professional planner for three architectural and engineering firms by enrolling at UCLA B-School. Now director of studio developments at Fox Realty Corp., 20th Century-Fox's real estate unit, Frank aspires to corporate management.

Four years ago Frank filed an EEOC complaint when a Santa Monica architectural firm fired her after 30 days on the ground that male planners and designers could not work for a woman planning director. In her present job, she feels that being a woman is more of an asset than a liability because her husband's salary as assistant to the president of a major homebuilder frees her to take risks that a male breadwinner might duck.

Pushing a proposal to build 140 condominiums on 13 acres of Fox land, a $26 million project, Frank says: "I recognize the magnitude of the proposal, so I keep telling them that I am willing to put my job on the line." She believes that Fox is studying the plan seriously, with no lack of confidence based on her sex. "My approach is this," she says. " 'These are the best figures I can come up with. Take them or leave them, but I tell you, I've got the cost sheets down to the gnat's eyebrows.' With that kind of attitude, I don't detect a lack of confidence."

Why, then, in a country increasingly populated by Judith Franks, are there still so few top women executives?

For one thing, since large numbers of women have entered the corporate world so recently, they are too far down the management pipeline to be candidates for top posts yet. For another, in a still male-oriented society, the problem of juggling home, family, and job handicaps many women executives who do not choose to remain unmarried or childless. And—more fundamental than anything else—social conditioning prevents many competent women from functioning effectively as executives and prevents many competent men from accepting them fully in that role.

Where Women Start

Max Ulrich, president of Ward Howell Associates, a New York-based executive recruiter, offers two illuminating figures: It takes 15 to 25 years for a manager to become a top executive and women made up only 1% of management trainees back in 1965. "In most industries," he says, "women are just beginning to come into the pipeline." But they are coming in fast.

At the University of Pennsylvania's Wharton School in Philadelphia, where women averaged less than 4% of the students between 1968 and 1970, women constitute 25% of the present class. A Stanford University in Palo Alto, Calif., where 1969 B-School students included less than 1% women, they total 20%. At UCLA, women MBA graduates get jobs months ahead of the men and command salaries 5% higher.

Some industries remain male preserves, primarily those that require engineering and those with many small companies—the latter because the EEOC seldom squanders its limited funds on small companies. Over all, however, the woman newly equipped with management credentials faces rosy prospects.

The next step up the management ladder is harder. On one hand, women moving into middle management may meet resistance from male counterparts unenthusiastic about new competitors—and zealous competitors at that, pioneers thrilled to be breaking new ground. On the other hand, an overeager company may set them up for a fall by moving them too fast.

Jack O. Vance, managing director of the Los Angeles office of McKinsey & Co., management consultants, cites as an example the chemical company vice-president who was "clearly underqualified and named over the emotional favorite of the technical support group." Says Vance: "Management should have known that her subordinates would bag her. She never did get the support needed to market high-technology products, and she lasted less than a year."

To upgrade management women effectively, says Barbara Boyle, president of Boyle/Kirkman, a New York-based management consultant firm that specializes in women, companies must consciously track and educate high-potential women and move specialists from one area to another to broaden their experience. Many do just that, she says, describing the career path of a market researcher who was eased into preparing research materials for sales presentations, moved into selling in the field, and then promoted to sales manager. "She's headed for director of sales; everyone knows it," Boyle says.

In effect, these companies are doing for women what they formerly did for men and what a handful of exceptional women formerly did for themselves. Mary Joan Glynn (pp. 289–90), general manager and operating head of the Borghese Div. of Revlon Inc., recalls that she painstakingly taught herself a new skill at each step up because she could not have performed each new job without it. "I was vice-president for product development at Doyle Dane Bernbach [the New York advertising agency] before I learned how to prepare a budget," she says. "I sat down with the accountant and studied how."

From the company's viewpoint, middle management is the trouble spot. It is inhabited by the reluctant boss and the sensitive underling, the man who needles women and the woman who sees male chauvinism everywhere, the manager who will not dismiss an incompetent woman for fear of the EEOC and the manager convinced that any woman who holds a managerial job owes it purely to the EEOC.

Middle managers bear the brunt of change (unlike young managers with no memories of a womanless past and top managers who do not yet have women peers), and change is always unsettling. Nevertheless, a University of Southern California survey of companies that moved women into corporate positions formerly occupied by men reveals that almost all experienced fewer problems than either the men or the women had expected.

Surveying the field, experts say that women have moved furthest into middle management in consumer goods, where they already had management experience, and in areas where large pools of women professionals provided both the pressure and the talent, such as banking and data processing. And some experts regard the whole subject of middle management progress with skepticism.

"I see 10- and 15-year women veterans in good staff-line jobs still not being promoted," says management consultant Theodora Wells, who teaches female management development courses at UCLA. "I see solid female professionals—tax lawyers, cash flow specialists, market researchers—who should be prime candidates for upper middle management and would be if they were male. Companies feel free to play games with young MBAs. But they won't spend the money to give their experienced women staffers what they need—accelerated growth in a controlled situation under the guidance of a male sponsor."

Some executives conduct cosmetic searches for middle-management women, says Janet Jones, an executive director of Management Woman Inc., a New York executive recruiter specializing in women. They require such extensive credentials from the women they seek that they clearly do not want to find them, she says, merely to establish (for the benefit of the government or the company president) that they fruitlessly sought them. She cites the case of an elderly executive who demanded 35 references from an esoteric specialist and, when she produced them, chose a less-specialized company man for the $35,000 post.

But the affirmative action goals that invite gamesmanship also set limits to it, notes William E. Carmell, EEO programs manager at Union Carbide Corp. in New York. A manager's EEO record figures in his performance evaluation at most companies and, if Jones' executive cannot bear to hire this particular female middle manager, he will have to hire another one sooner or later if he wants to advance, Carmell suggests.

Since the attitude of top management is the single most important variable in determining women's corporate progress—a fact stressed by observers of both sexes and all ranks—women's continued ascent depends in great part on the rise to power of men receptive to women. Since younger men are generally more receptive than older men (another universal observation), women's prospects must necessarily improve as these younger men move up.

Right now, most experts believe that women are in sight of posts on the lower rungs of top management. Some already occupy them. A few may soon reach the very top of the heap—in traditional areas, they predict, but not at major industrial companies.

"For a woman to become chief executive officer of such a corporation, she would have to be in the pipeline now, at the right age, no more than 40 or 45, and already at the senior-vice-presidential level," says GE's Kellogg. "There's no one like that.

"It will happen," Kellogg says. "But I won't see it."

Marriage vs. Job

"The world is not set up for working mothers," says Shawmut's Kay Mazuy, who comes closer than most to harmonizing home and career. A housekeeper takes care of the Mazuy children, and her husband pitches in willingly when Kay Mazuy cannot perform such tasks as serving as nursery school "mother-helper" (a title now transformed to "parent-helper"). But she still feels a twinge when the pediatrician's receptionist, asked for an appointment late in the day, implies by her voice that Kay Mazuy is probably a neglectful mother.

Like most dual-career households, the Mazuys live organized lives. They rise at 6:15 a.m., breakfast, drive to their downtown offices together, drive home at 5:30 p.m., dine with their two children at 8:30 p.m., put them to bed an hour later, and relax briefly before bedtime. Although Kay Mazuy often brings home business reading, she keeps weekends free for gardening, cooking, skiing, and biking, all activities shared with her lawyer husband.

"I very much don't feel that your job should be all of your life, and I feel in no way compelled to think about it all weekend," she says. "There are too many interesting things to do and you can only go through life once."

Few women executives manage as deftly as Mazuy, who stresses, like others in her position, that she couldn't do it without a supportive husband and a cooperative employer. But even with both, someone has to take care of the children. As a result, married women executives typically have fewer children than other women, and they have them later in their lives, when they can afford outside child care.

Child care, indeed, determines the course of many careers. Lois Miller, vice-president for sales promotion at Halle's department store chain, recalls that she stayed in Cleveland, rather than seeking job offers elsewhere after an early divorce, because her mother was there to take care of her daughter. Julia M. Walsh, vice-president of the Washington (D.C.) brokerage house of Ferris & Co., attributes much of her success to a deal struck years ago with her mother-in-law. A young widow whose earnings had suddenly become vital rather than incidental, Walsh offered the older woman 20% of her commissions if she would take care of her home and children.

"I was the only career woman in the world with a wife," Walsh says. "She made sure that a crying child didn't disturb my sleep if I had to be sharp the next day, she packed my bag in a hurry when I phoned from the office. It was ideal."

Day-care centers, helpful to mothers with 9-to-5 jobs, work less well for the woman executive, who cannot abruptly take three days off when her child catches cold, or leave the office right on the dot if there is a business emergency, to pick up her child before the center closes. Certainly she cannot do this if she hopes to advance.

Even the childless married woman executive faces problems that her husband never faced—but is beginning to: how to run a household, what to do about a promotion that would involve geographic separation, what happens emotionally, when the wife's title or salary outranks the husband's.

In some cases, companies have taken the initiative in solving dual-career problems—for example, by seeking a new job for the husband (or wife) when they want to transfer the wife (or husband). In other cases, executives have arranged their lifestyles to fit their careers.

Continental Air Lines' Levine takes turns with her husband, a San Francisco management consultant, in commuting weekends between their two homes. Earlier in their careers, when she worked for Level Bros. in New York and he for Scott Paper Co. in Philadelphia, they made their home midway in Princeton, N.J., and waited each morning on the same railway platform, she for the train heading north, he for the train heading south.

Sandra Kresch, 30, a vice-president of Booz, Allen & Hamilton Inc., Chicago-based management consultants, typifies a more common pattern. Divorced from her first husband, she shares a Chicago apartment with the second (also a vice-president of Booz Allen), but sees him almost in passing.

Kresch works a 60-hour week and spends 80% of her time on the road. With her husband also traveling, "We have to work very much harder than most at maintaining our relationship," she says. "Certain times we allocate as our times, to let off steam and to get to know each other again."

"Sandy has totally dedicated herself to her career," says Dr. Alfred E. Goldman, Kresch's boss at Booz Allen. "That means she is totally willing to subvert her own needs, such as leisure and family, to the job. She has been able to do that very effectively, though at great cost."

Kresch apparently does not regard the cost as high. "Sometimes it's difficult to realize, 'Hey, I'm being successful and accepted in the business world,' but it's delightful. It's fun," she says. "In the consulting environment there's lots of opportunity for individual stars, and there are people looking to you for answers. It's a very gratifying environment."

Some of the older executives express faint regrets about what they may have missed. Says Betty McFadden, 53, who earns more than $50,000 as group vice-president for the direct marketing division of Jewel Cos. in Barrington, Ill. "Sometimes I think I would have liked to have developed more friendships and interests." But then she recalls that, years ago, she tried a routine job in order to spend more time with her husband, and the job nearly drove her mad with boredom. When Jewel offered her a more challenging post requiring 50 to 60 hours' work a week, she jumped at the chance.

How to Get Along

"We have met the enemy, and it is us," says Clare C. Daniels, chairwoman of the Michigan Commission on Women. In the sense that she uses the word, the woman manager's enemy is not only us (women) but them (men) and mainly the society that formed both—men in psychological patterns suitable for the corporate world and women in patterns that conflict with its aims and methods.

"Little boys learn to play on the same team with other boys they don't even like. Their relationships focus on achieving objectives," says Dr. Anne Jardim, director with Dr. Margaret Hennig of the graduate program in management at Simmons College in Boston. "Little girls are very select about their friends. They emphasize the quality of a relationship with no set goal." As a result, men and women feel differently about aggression, self-confidence, planning, risk-taking, and strategy, Jardim says, "and business organizations fit the male experience." To succeed as executives, women must resocialize themselves, she says.

"Boys make plans, girls carry them out. Boys take risks, girls think twice," sums up Evelyn Berezin, president and founder of Redactron Corp., a New York manufacturer of word-processing equipment. "That's why so many women feel more comfortable as assistants or technicians."

That is also why, in a quiz given 5,500 managers of major corporations by Jardim and Hennig, 90% of the women did not know what they wanted to be doing in five years and 90% of the men did. The men were trying to manage their careers and the women were just drifting, Hennig says.

Until recently, this conditioning worked so effectively that successful women executives often followed career paths that somehow enabled them to play by the female rules. Phyllis A. Cella, 55, vice-president for field management and marketing for Boston's John Hancock Mutual Life Insurance Co., recalls that she never once competed with anyone for a higher post. She developed new responsibilites in her old job or identified the need for a new one, which she then filled.

"I was never a threat," Cella says. "I was never after anyone's job. I didn't plan on being a vice-president. All I wanted was a better job with a little more money."

Strikingly, even the outspokenly career-minded Kellogg had never replaced a man until she succeeded Dr. L. C. Maier Jr. in her present post last year. Every previous job had been a new one.

Like others in her generation, Cella has changed with the times. "After I was made a second vice-president in 1972, I did want to be the first woman vice-president in the company," she says. "I suppose I should aspire to be the first woman senior vice-president. I do know I'm not going to sit here for 10 years until I retire."

The male form of social conditioning is even more crucial to women managers. Men may be equipped to function in the corporate world, but they unconsciously expect something quite different from the women they encounter there—at the same time that they consciously expect businesslike, "male" behavior from anyone who seeks to achieve corporate goals. And it is these ambivalent men who control the woman executive's career.

"In situations where men say, 'This is what I want and deserve' and get a yes or no, a woman's requests are treated as demands," says Booz Allen's Kresch. "People are surprised and ask, 'Why is she such a hard-driving lady?' "

"It's a damned-if-I-do and damned-if-I-don't situation," says Marion M. Wood, assistant professor of management communication at USC's B-School. If the woman executive comes on strong, she risks alienating her male superiors, and if she comes on soft, she convinces them that she lacks management qualities.

Boyle/Kirkman uses a standard ploy to sensitize male managers to their own contradictory attitudes. In the morning, the consultants ask the managers to list attributes desirable in an executive (experience, assertiveness, and all the rest). In the afternoon, they present as a job candidate a fictitious woman who possesses all these attributes. And the men turn her down.

"Men are taught to strap their six-guns on and shoot it up in the office each day, and then they'll get to be divisional manager," says a young executive of a major manufacturer. "Older managers know how they'd feel if they had to explain to their buddies that a woman beat them out for a job. So, left to themselves, they'll hire or promote a man who's B-plus over a woman who's A. And they'll certainly pick a successor who reminds them of themselves. Isn't that human nature?"

Even if the woman gets the job, male conditioning affects her every step of the way. At least one in every random sample of women middle managers tells the same story: Her male colleagues all go to lunch together and she never learns about business projects discussed at lunch till weeks later. Dianne McKaig, vice-president and director of consumer affairs for Coca-Cola USA in Atlanta, lists "funny little myths" believed by male managers—that a woman with children wouldn't want a job that involves travel (so she never gets a chance to accept or refuse it), that customers wouldn't want to deal with saleswomen, or that saleswomen wouldn't be aggressive enough (so the department sticks to salesmen, never learning whether the fact is true), that some man wouldn't work for a woman (so the woman who rates the job doesn't get it).

Despite its widespread currency among male managers, top women executives tend to dismiss the proposition that men will refuse to work for women.

Says Kellogg, with a smile: "Oh, sure, but I never made a man a job offer that was turned down."

Says Dorothy M. Simon, corporate vice-president of research for Avco Corp. in Greenwich, Conn.: "It is the power of my position, not whether I am a man or woman, that determines whether people will work with me. They know who I am and what I do."

And G. G. Michelson, vice-president for consumer and employee relations at Macy's in New York, notes coolly that few managers, male or female, have many options regarding who they work for. They work for someone who was successful enough to become a boss, and they accommodate to him—or her—as best they can, she says.

Further down the line, however, women executives cannot afford to dismiss so lightly any male belief that influences their future. Still less can they dismiss their own confused beliefs regarding their proper behavior as managers. Leslie Mowry, 27, brand manager for Downy at Procter & Gamble Co. in Cincinnati, recalls her quandaries when she first started at the company. How much credit was she supposed to take for joint projects? She did not want to be too self-effacing or too pushy. Was her boss treating her like a secretary when he asked her to photocopy papers? Maybe it was part of her job. With no female counterparts, she had no one to ask.

And that points directly to the woman executive's single greatest handicap—the lack of someone to ask, the lack of a role model.

"What does she wear at each level? When does she start to call her boss by his first name? What's the right tone of voice?" asks Pearl Meyer, executive vice-president of Handy Associates, New York-based executive recruiters. "Men can find out by looking around them. Women know it's important, know it's part of the process of moving up, but they've no one to copy."

In desperation, some women become fake men, says Meyer—"ladies in black suits with pearls, the nearest thing to that old gray flannel suit." Combined with superefficiency, this male impersonation frequently works on the lower or middle management level although it dehumanizes the woman manager, Meyer says. Above that, where executives use subtle social signals to deal with their peers (and potential peers), women managers usually hit a stone wall, she notes.

"Most women don't realize the importance of sports talk, for instance," says Meyer. "That casual talk about yesterday's football game or the chat at the 19th hole on the golf course may give an executive the feel that, yes, this man will fit into our operation or, no, he won't." Joining in the football talk or joining the golf foursome does not draw the woman into the communications skein; especially among older men, her mere presence destroys it.

Women on Trial

For sex, awareness of sex, and behavior based on sex are realities that no amount of government pressure or genuine belief in intellectual equality can erase. An AT&T manager describes walking into an airport lounge with a younger woman colleague, en route to a business conference, and suddenly realizing that everyone in the lounge is leering at him. Later he wonders whether anyone actually leered or whether it was all in his mind.

"I can remember, as a young product manager, going to the director of research and wanting to talk confidentially about a new product," says Continental Air Lines' Levine. "I went in, closed the door, and the guy couldn't even stay seated at his desk. He kept moving around the office until finally he went over and opened the door. Then he was able to sit down and talk. He was so concerned that someone might think something was going on behind closed doors!"

And sometimes something *is* going on behind closed doors—if not physically, then psychologically. Sex messages are part of even casual relationships between men and women, says Barbara K. Shore of the University of Pittsburgh's school of social work, and this complicates business relations. Younger women managers may receive special consideration from their male colleagues or superiors.

Sex consciousness also handicaps women by denying them what sociologists call a support system and women executives call the old boys' network. Says Janet Esty, 34, president and founder of Neomed, a

Boulder (Colo.) surgical-equipment company: "I can't join any of the business clubs. I can't mix socially with the businessmen. There's no one to ask hey, who's the best accountant. I know I've made some mistakes because I couldn't use the network."

In corporate centers, the network may disseminate news of a job opening, provide insider friends to push a candidate for the job and, if he succeeds, warn him of the dangers of tangling with his new executive vice-president. Later it may direct him to a supplier and banker, thus simultaneously benefiting three old boys.

To help create an old girls' network, *Executive Woman,* a New York newsletter, holds an annual dinner at which up-and-coming business-women explain in good, clear voices who they are, what they have to buy or sell, and what they seek or offer in the corporate world. Women's conferences, seminars, publications, and organizations perform the same service less directly. They form a kind of counterpart industry to the consultants, recruiters, psychological testers, training specialists, and other experts who help companies minimize the risks of upgrading women.

Both processes are freakish—the short-order creation of a long-range support system and the complex labors to absorb into the corporate world women who are the sisters, wives, and daughters of men already in it. Freakishness is inevitable because the corporate woman—although headed for normalcy by her own efforts, pushed toward normalcy by the sheer mass of young women behind her—is still abnormal. She is still, in the despairing phrase of Francine Gordon, the Stanford University professor who co-authored *Bringing Women Into Management,* "that fabulous first."

"We are still in the first woman syndrome at most companies," Gordon says. "And that puts a tremendous burden on the woman."

"If I were a male, I could probably make at least one small mistake without disrupting my career," says Jo Ann Fikes, 43, one of the first female corporate lending officers at the United California Bank. "As a woman, I know there's no room for even one. I exhaust every possibility before I make a loan because I'm putting my career on the line every time."

"All it takes to convince both men and women that females don't make good bosses is for one woman to fail," says Robert H. Marik, a planning executive at TRW Inc. in Los Angeles. USC's Wood backs him up with data from a recent management study. It found that top management generally accepted a certain male failure rate as a matter of course, but regarded female failure as an argument against further female promotions. Even the confident Diane Levine worked six days a week, eighteen hours a day, during her first months at Continental Air Lines to make double, triple, quadruple sure that she did the job right.

In brief, a so-so man is old stuff to management and probably no great burden to himself. A so-so woman is, in management's eye, proof that she holds the job simply to satisfy the unreasonable demands of an interfering government, and, in her own eyes, a disaster. Trying to make it in a man's world involves such a heavy emotional investment that even moderate failure must be avoided at all costs.

"Corporate women feel that they must perform at 300 percent efficiency all the time," says Del Goetz, 37, president and owner of Dowd's Moving & Storage Inc., in Mill Valley, Calif. "Now that business schools are turning out so many females, maybe they'll allow themselves to be just 150 percenters. Really, what women are fighting for is the right to be just as mediocre as men have been."

Barriers are Falling

Since most women managers have not yet shucked off the obligation to be symbols, let alone won the right to mediocrity (at least in positions that serve corporate rather than EEOC goals), the typical woman executive is anything but ordinary. On the contrary, she was usually marked from the first with the sign of the achiever. In an ultra-typical sequence, Patricia Cloherty, the eldest daughter of working parents who emphasized self-reliance and a scholarship girl who helped pay college bills by cooking in a California logging camp, winds up at thirty-three earning a base salary of $30,000 as vice-president of Alan Patricof Associates, a New York venture capital firm. When management troubles imperiled the Patricof interests in Childcraft last year, she took over as president of the educational toy manufacturer, whipped the company into shape in six months, handed it over to the current (male) president, and went back to deals involving everything from a secondary lead processor to an Agency for International Development grant for a group of Dominican businessmen.

Cloherty can visualize any number of future career paths: expansion of her present activities, investment in and ultimate direction of a company, a public service post, perhaps something she had not yet considered. She will avoid areas that still bar women (such as the international financial community that was her first business interest, she says) and find opportunities where barriers are falling or are ready to be knocked down by a strong hand.

The sound of barriers falling—and normalcy a-coming—rings through the corporate woman's world, although seldom as clearly as for Cloherty. Dagnija Lacis, industrial marketing manager for Detroit's Burroughs Corp., travels extensively, just like her three male counterparts, discerning no particular differences "except that I started as a programmer and they started as salesmen." Georgia-Pacific's Hodgson, who suspects that she made her first sales "because customers were worried that if they didn't buy something, I might break down and cry," ensures further sales by crawling tirelessly through customers' warehouses to spot gaps in inventories and checking old invoices to learn buying habits. And a Midwestern middle manager notes happily that "no one says I think like a man anymore. They say that I think like a manager."

Even when all the barriers are down and the corporate world demands neither more nor less of women than it does of men—on a date no one is bold enough to predict—the woman who wants executive status will still pay a stiff price for it: the price men pay.

Many women today are unwilling to pay that price, says an industrial executive. "They're not sure they want to work all those extra hours, live with the tension of make-or-break decisions, assume leadership of outside organizations, do all those extra things. A woman, or man, must want badly the risk-taking, power-controlling type of position to accept all that," he says. Once women make the commitment, he adds, "there's no holding them back."

The younger generation (and particularly its female members) appears ready for the change. "When I became a corporate vice-president," says Kellogg, "a man who reports to me told me that he had told his daughter that his new boss was a woman, and she had said, 'Oh, Daddy, how wonderful!' "

Kellogg smiles broadly. "I think that's great," she says.

Appendix: Mary Joan Glynn vs. James J. Shapiro

If some aspects of the corporate world are different for the woman executive than for the man, at least one aspect is the same: the hazards of dealing with a difficult boss.

When Mary Joan Glynn, 46, left a vice-presidency at Bloomingdale's department store in New York to become president of Simplicity Pattern Co. last January, she was heading for a job with a notorious man-eater—James J. Shapiro, chairman of the family-run company, who had just fired his brother from the presidency. Shapiro told her, Glynn insists, that he had made the change in order to strengthen Simplicity and reclaim its slipping market share before he retired.

To that end, she says, he proposed to give her full charge of merchandising and other areas of the special expertise she had acquired as merchandise editor of *Glamour*, vice-president for product development and fashion groups at the Doyle Dane Bernbach advertising agency, and a notably successful vice-president for advertising, sales promotion, and public relations at Bloomingdale's. Shapiro was to supervise finance and related areas temporarily while she honed her skills in them, Glynn says, and then cede full authority to her.

Pitfalls. Six months later the new president quit. Shapiro was running the show, including her special areas, Glynn says, and it was obvious that no one else would ever run it while he was around. "I had this sense of drowning," she says. "I was unable to preserve my business identity."

Says Shapiro: "She was a very, very nice lady, with great talents. But she wasn't for us and we weren't for her."

Now general manager and operating head of the Borghese Div. of Revlon, Glynn absolves Shapiro of sex bias ("he just needed to keep everything in his hand") and wonders in retrospect why she had not seen the pitfalls in advance. An outsider might guess why ambition blotted out caution for such an experienced executive. How often does a woman get the chance to become president of a company?

31
The Two-Professional Marriage: A New Conflict Syndrome

ELLEN BERMAN, M.D., SYLVIA SACKS, M.S.W., and HAROLD LIEF, M.D.

ABSTRACT

The two-professional marriage that begins during the period of preprofessional or professional training is apt to break down during the immediate post-training period. Reasons for this occurrence are discussed in the light of marital dynamics and adult developmental issues, with special emphasis on female professional role development.

As more and more women enter professional schools formerly largely reserved for men, marriages between students in these schools are increasing. Although the majority of these partnerships remain stable after the completion of training, an increasing number have been developing severe problems. These problem relationships often lead to divorce within the first few years after the end of school and with the assumption of professional roles by both partners.

Although the divorce rate in the general population has increased greatly recently,[1] the dynamics of divorce vary among different types of couples. The authors feel that examining the patterns of current marital problems in specific types of couples may shed some light on more

Originally published in the *Journal of Sex & Marital Therapy* 1 (3) (Spring 1975). Copyright © 1975 by the *Journal of Sex & Marital Therapy*.

Dr. Berman is Assistant Professor of Psychiatry, University of Pennsylvania School of Medicine, and Director of Training, Marriage Council of Philadelphia. Mrs. Sacks is Senior Supervisor, Marriage Council of Philadelphia. Dr. Lief is Professor of Psychiatry, University of Pennsylvania School of Medicine, and Director, Marriage Council of Philadelphia.

general present trends. In this paper the authors identify a clearly definable new syndrome common to certain types of dyads who begin their marital life as fellow students and continue it as fellow and equal professionals. As the number of these couples requesting either marital counseling or individual psychotherapy has gone up dramatically in the last 5 years (a 15-fold increase—Marriage Council unpublished statistics), we feel that this pattern is noteworthy and suggests areas for new therapeutic consideration and for further research.

This paper does not direct itself to specific methodology and techniques, which are well covered in the literature on interpersonal relationships and therapy.[2,3] The focus is rather on a new conceptual framework in which to better understand the breakdown of the two-professional marriage. This paper seeks to describe (a) a review of the literature, (b) case studies, (c) patterns of marital dynamics and marital breakdown, (d) a discussion of the syndrome, and (e) implications for therapy with conflicted couples.

Review of The Literature

The literature pertaining to the requisites for marital success is extensive but confusing. Various authors have come to the conclustion that : (a) the traditional marital pattern with fixed and defined sex roles is the more stable (see Laws[4] for review); (b) the "companionate" marriage wherein roles and power are shared fairly equally is a better system;[5] (c) most research is so full of male bias as to be useless.[4] Indeed, there is still no satisfactory, agreed-upon definition of marital success, whether it be lack of legal divorce, self-report of happiness, or other dimensions (see Laws[4] for discussion). For the purpose of this paper, we define marital success as a relationship that is legally stable and appears, both to the couple and to the therapist, to provide some continuous measure of satisfaction to each of the pair.

Certainly marital success results partly from the mutually gratifying interaction of two personalities; however, it is becoming increasingly clear that existential and cultural factors play a major part in a functioning marriage. Mudd, Mitchell, and Taubin[2] have extensively discussed criteria of successful interaction. At least one crucial component is some common goals or values. In fact, one of the common periods of marital stress is the point at which one or both partners move from an explicitly or even implicitly agreed-upon defined common ground.

Professional marriages, especially those in which the husband is a physician, have come under periodic scrutiny.[6,7] In spite of stereotypes to the contrary, the divorce rate for the one-professional marriage in which the husband is the professional is lower than that in the general population.[7] The divorce rate for physicians is lower than that of most professionals. There is no evidence that the amount of unhappiness among married male professionals is any higher than for the population at large. Women professionals, however, have a higher divorce rate than the general population.[7] Since 80% of women physicians marry physicians or other professionals, it is safe to assume that the two-professional marriage is one at risk. A recent study of physicians' attitudes toward marriages in which both partners are doctors indicates a much higher likelihood of divorce. A study of nonprofessional working wives showed no consistent connection between employment and divorce.[5]

We have been unable to find longitudinal studies or descriptions of the stages of the two-professional marriage. We therefore offer these clinical observations as the beginning of other evaluative studies.

Case 1

Two physicians who had been married for 4 years, without children, requested marriage counseling the 2nd year of residency for both.

Presenting problem

The couple bickered constantly. Mary was dissatisfied with all aspects of the marriage. She particularly complained of her husband's "intellectual dullness" and overbearing qualities. Ron voiced confusion over the arguments but had no specific complaints.

Marital history

Mary and Ron had met during their 1st year in medical school and were married during the 2nd year. Describing their early relationship, Mary stated, "He was the most interesting man around, and helped me study at a time when I was very anxious. I felt protected and feminine." The intensity of their early relationship resulted in the exclusion of all others. The husband believed that his role was to encourage Mary to study and in general to organize her life. Mary concurred, although she carried out more of the household tasks. Even at that time, however, Mary noted that her husband was argumentative with medical school faculty and distant with friends, and she was often called upon to help him out of interpersonal situations. After medical school, the decision to remain in the city for the internships was principally Ron's. Mary acquiesced without much argument or even thought. He acquired a prestigious orthopedic surgery internship while she took a less desirable psychiatric internship in the same city, a fairly common pattern in the two-professional marriage. However, she subsequently acquired a much more desirable residency, while his 2nd-year contract was not renewed. He had to accept a lesser known hospital for the completion of his training, and was acutely devalued in both their eyes. Mary's self-confidence and mastery in child psychiatry rose rapidly. She changed her style of dress and acquired many new friends. Ron became more and more involved in orthopedic surgery and less and less interested in any other aspect of their life. Already feeling uncomfortable about the relationship, he began to talk about a large country home and having children "to settle her down." As she resisted, and he found that he could no longer control her decision-making, he became angrier and angrier. While Mary was away on a 2-month clinical rotation in another city, both of them initiated a series of extramarital liaisons. When she returned, the fighting escalated and she briefly left home. At this point both of them became frightened and mutually requested marital counseling.

Significant personal history

Mary came from an emotionally cool Protestant home. Her father left home when she was 6, and she never adequately understood nor mourned the loss. She was a bright and determined girl, although she had few other significant male relationships before meeting Ron. Ron, an only child, came from a closely knit and intensely interdependent urban, Catholic household. His father was lawyer and his mother a devoted housewife. Ron always had dreamed of a large family for himself.

Course of therapy and resolution

An attempt was made to point out to the couple how much added stress had been placed on their marital system with their assumption of professional roles. This period brought Mary's markedly different needs and goals. Time was spent trying to help them understand how they could now be supportive of each other. Ron, however, was made acutely anxious by any kind of therapy. He did not wish to change his own long-range family and marital goals and dropped out of therapy after approximately 3 months. His wife continued in long-term individual psychotherapy, trying to decide what to do about their relationship, and finally decided to file for divorce.

Case 2

A lawyer, Bill, married for 4 years to a doctor, Jane, with a 2-year-old child, came for marital counseling 4 years after both had completed their professional education and were employed.

Chief complaint

Jane stated that Bill was withdrawing from the daily relationship and from sexual play, making her very unhappy. Bill felt Jane's energy and interest no longer included him. Neither wanted to break up the marriage.

Marital history

The couple had met when Bill was in law school and Jane was in medical school. Until she met her husband, Jane had been dating very little and considered herself a failure socially. They had a whirlwind courtship and were married shortly thereafter. Bill was physically handsome, and achieving and well known in the academic community. His looks and achievements gave new support to Jane's insecure social-sexual view of herself. The relationship was described as good by both of them until after the birth of their child when they were both 1 year out of school. After the birth of the child, Jane realized that she loved her baby daughter but had little interest in physically taking care of the baby. She and her husband decided that she should return to work. She rapidly rose to a position of considerable importance in the hospital as an excellent research person and chief resident. Her husband had mediocre success in his early law practice and was dissatisfied with his achievements. He became very unhappy and complained that when he came home there was no one to support him or talk to him. Jane agreed, stating that she was exhausted by the demands of her work and when she came home she felt that she first had to tend to the child, and that little emotion was left for Bill's demands. Sexually, he showed a lessening interest, which heightened Jane's anxieties. Both were frustrated and talked of divorce.

Significant personal history

Jane came from a home that included a highly achieving father and a socially prominent mother. Jane's mother had always perceived her daughter as "an old maid" and put much pressure on her to achieve socially. She always gave her daughter subliminal messages that she would, in fact, be a failure. Bill's parents had worked together in a family business. He anticipated that his marriage would also be close and with mutual sharing, but with children being secondary. A working wife seemed quite acceptable to his view of marriage.

Course of therapy and resolution

The early focus in therapy involved helping Jane to understand how much pressure she had placed on herself for success in all spheres, and to reevaluate her needs and priorities in terms of her husband. The therapeutic process enabled each of them to understand the early marital needs that brought them together and how these had changed as they became emerging professionals. Sharing and communication increased, and sexual activity was renewed. The couple are ending therapy 1 year after treatment was begun, and the marriage appears stable.

Emerging Marital Patterns

The two couples described above reveal typical marital histories that can be broken down into the student and professional periods of the relationship.

During the student period and courtship, goals are somewhat similar. The prospective husband and wife usually meet as students, as members of either the same or geographically contiguous schools. At the time of courtship the couple are drawn together by a commonality of interests and their conscious desire to find a "companion partner." The husband, especially before children become an issue, appears to be a "liberated man," who tends to see the marriage as one of genuine equals and companions and who is apparently comfortable with his own sense of masculinity. The wife, usually attractive as well as bright, tends to see herself as unfeminine, intellectual, and often as somewhat dependent and needing guidance. Academically bright, these women have often led relatively quiet social-sexual lives, even more than most of the men. The women's needs are to feel desirable and to acquire emotional security in their social and human relationships. They usually choose men who are thought to be in some way superior—older, smarter, or more popular.

Our clinical impressions lead us to believe that underlying the overt illusion of an equal relationship is a covert traditional stance, that is, a superior, strong male and a more helpless, dependent female. This early covert "contract" tends to result from the wife's early self-image, her underlying needs, and her cultural assumptions, and is supported by the underlying expectations of the man. Crucially, these are usually subliminal or unconscious, hidden from both partners.

In the first period of their relationship, early marital coping patterns tend to include sharing of household tasks, studying, and minor decision-making. However, major decision-making, such as place of residence after graduation, is often, without conscious recognition by either, left to the husband. This is especially true if he is further ahead in his education or has finished his professional training before his wife.

The second period of the marriage begins with the two in professional practices, after the wife acquires her first economically productive professional situation. Usually the husband begins to work slightly earlier. As the wife acquires professional status, her perception of herself and of her husband begins to change drastically. A greatly increased integration of her feminine self-image with her professional self takes place in the ensuing year or two. This integration involves the self-confidence of finally achieving mastery of her profession and is reinforced by a group of new admirers who have not seen her depressed, frightened, or overweary before examination—only as an exciting and professional woman. She now begins to see herself as more capable, masterful, and desirable. These feelings underlie the first crucial and significant change in her former self-perception and introduce a new influence in her marital relationship.

In the professional period, an important second and concurrent change occurs. Her opinion of her husband shifts, so that he is now no longer seen as a brilliant student but as a coworker. The husband's changes in the self-perception and in his appearance to the outside world tend to be far less dramatic than those of his wife. In general, his integration of his masculinity has always been linked to his profession, and although he may acquire somewhat more poise or authority, he remains much the same. He is now in fact often on a genuinely equal footing professionally. (Sometimes, after 2 years out of school, his wife may even be doing better than he economically or professionally.) The effect on the marriage of this sudden shift in the husband's apparent status occasioned by both the wife's rise to being a fellow-professional and the husband's apparent drop in "superior" rating is in itself confusing to both, but particularly for the wife. She is still demanding unconsciously that her husband be her superior (her old conditioning) while consciously she expects him to be an equal (her new ideals). Therefore, particularly and most noticeably in dysfunctional couples, the husband, who is now truly an equal, is seen as weak and less desirable at a time when other men around the wife appear strong and challenging. Her husband, of course, cannot move either way, because if he attempts to reestablish his superiority, she balks; yet his willingness to accept her new status tends to be perceived as weakness. The bind each feels caught in generates increasing frustration and hostility, accentuated by feelings of helplessness because of their inability to understand what is happening.

Pattern of Marital Breakdown

A rapidly increasing number of arguments over apparently innocuous subjects, such as food preparation, walking the dog, and the like, usually signal the beginning of overt conflict. These arguments have as their covert thrust the attempt of the husband and wife to each establish superiority and to feel in control of the relationship. Nursing untended emotional wounds, each withdraws.

Because of the heightened tension, a series of brief, casual affairs is often initiated by one or both. For the woman particularly, these affairs are often an early attempt to find out what she has missed. Now less invested in her husband's reassurance of her femininity, she begins to talk about her dissatisfaction, usually with other women professionals or with her lovers. From them she usually receives much support for pulling out of the marriage, usually couched in terms such as "Women shouldn't be tied down" or "Men are oppressive."

It is at this point that the woman often seeks a therapist, usually a female, to try to untangle her confused feelings. She tends to choose a woman therapist because her conscious perception of the marriage is one of oppression by the husband and a sense that "only another woman could understand my dilemma." In addition to the fact that the woman tends to be the one more overtly dissatisfied with the marriage, there is also the cultural norm that it is the woman who is the help seeker. Her husband protests more or less according to his own degree of rigidity. The more determined and inflexible both spouses are, the more the conflicted situation escalates.

The situation is often made even more difficult because it is at this point that the husband's earlier wishes for a liberated wife may also undergo some revision. Now that the wife is out of school, the issue of having children becomes more crucial. If a child is born, a new conflict is highlighted. Many husbands who were quite happy to share all household tasks with their wives now find a tighter, more demanding schedule of their own. The husband now suddenly discovers the usefulness of having a wife who will be home with the children most of the time. The husband's homemaking expectations for his wife put additional strain on the relationship at a time when the woman is discovering the joys of being an independent, professional person.

Another separating factor is that the professional interests of such couples may also unexpectedly diverge. For Couple 1, for example, there was the traditional rivalry between the surgeon and the nonsurgical specialist, and there were many disagreements on such things as the number of hours appropriate to work, what was important to read or think about in the medical world, and in forms of "patient as a person" care. Example: "He only reads about body functions; he hasn't read a novel in 4 years." This diverging emphasis is in marked contrast to their common interest in learning as students, and it puts additional strain on an already dysfunctional relationship.

One of the major issues in the development of marital breakdown is the point in time when the couple finally seek therapy for one or both partners. The longer they wait, the more likely it is that the pattern will proceed to dissolution of the relationship. If no attempts are made to reestablish a newly emerging basis to the relationship, the chances are that the couple will split within 6 months to 2 years after severe overt conflict begins.

Developmental and Existential Issues

The authors feel that this syndrome of breakdown of two professionals in their marital functioning, in the second period after education has been completed, is a developmental and existential syndrome, as well as a psychopathological one. Not enough attention has been paid in the professional literature to the developmental and existential issues involved. Recent papers by Gould[8] and Levinson[10] enlarging on the work by Erikson[9] on the developmental stages of adulthood point to the fact that there are separate developmental tasks that must be accomplished in the adult years, and that the failure to accomplish them in reasonable order, or the failure to recognize a disparate growth rate of two people living together, produces more problems.

In reviewing the developmental stages, the necessary tasks of people in their 20s can be described as intimacy versus isolation,[9] implying that the marital pair has achieved independence and self-reliance, a task Erikson had assigned to adolescence. With the delayed maturation created by professional dependence on a highly organized structure such as medical or law school, many professionals begin practice without a true sense of personal autonomy.

Levinson,[10] however, describes the period of the 20s as provisional adulthood, and does not limit the term to professionals. Simply stated, the tasks of this period involve the final breaking away from one's parents and starting a life and career of one's own. According to Levinson, although most people see themselves as reaching adulthood in the 20s, they are still doing what they were "programmed to do" to be an adult. They have not yet really chosen the path themselves.

Although such plans initially appear secure and rewarding, the period of provisional adulthood ends in a developmental crisis somewhere around the ages of 28 to 32. At this point the person for the first time looks back and reevaluates his or her life. For many, the life that appeared secure and rewarding now appears immovable and stagnant. The crisis comes over the issue "Where do we go from here?" A major reversal of goals is frequent. Age 30, rather than 45, can be seen as the first major adult crisis period. The 30s, according to Levinson, bring autonomous, self-directed adulthood.

In the cases cited, there is a sudden transition—a sharp discontinuity—when "school is over." At about age 28 the person achieves not only apparent adulthood but new, real power. (When the integration of a professional self-image occurs more gradually, with increasing responsibility and a sense of competence, this crisis is apt to be muted.) The sudden access of power that comes with the professional title is often coincidental with a fresh reevaluation of one's life. Those couples who have married as students now face several transitions at once: (a) the transition from student to powerful professional, which is most marked in the woman, and produces a major discrepancy in growth rate; (b) the transition from provisional adulthood to age-30 crisis; and (c) the first stage of dissatisfaction of the average marriage—"the 7-year itch." The authors feel that the primary source of difficulty in these dysfunctional marriages is caused by a particular combination of (a) and (b), that is, the different growth rates of the male and female professional, and the different paths they wish to take through the age-30 crisis.

The overwhelming impact of the differential growth rates needs real consideration. It is the authors' contention that for the woman, the growth spurt comes later and more precipitously than for the man. The growth spurt comes in specific ways that would be calculated to disturb even the most placid of marriages. For the man, masculinity and a career have been practically synonymous and developmental; for the woman, however, femininity and a career have been antithetical during most of her growing up years. Her personal integration of her femininity and her career comes much more forcefully with her first experience as a full-fledged professional, and is often overpowering in its effect.

As an intense female student, she felt looked upon as a "little odd," but now, as the female professional, she finds many new colleagues who tend to be male and who seem greatly interested in her, both as a professional and as a sexually aware (married) woman. As she begins to receive more external validation of her achievements as a professional and as a female, and then returns home to a boring, traditional, or already conflicted relationship, she begins to feel more and more that she can "go it alone." The effect of her late growth spurt is to weaken her investment in the marriage relationship. In addition, her dilemma is increased by the current societal encouragement for women to have professional careers and to remain single. During the age-30 crisis she is likely to change her traditional career and motherhood concept to a more solitary and autonomous path.

The impact of the differential growth rate is felt by her husband at a time when he is beginning to make the developmental transition into his 30s. For the man this period often revolves around wishes to settle down and to find contentment in the home. Two varying growth rates, two varying transitional sets of emotions, responses, and expectations—and the marital dyad begins to pull further apart.

The authors feel that this breakdown syndrome is an important new observation and in some ways a new phenomenon. This pattern is somewhat analogous to the older one of the husband being financially supported through school by his secretary-wife, whom he divorces when he realizes how far apart they have grown. We feel that the pattern being described differs from traditional breakdowns in two specific ways: (a) the marriage originally appeared to be a very good marriage of equals; and (b) it is principally the woman in the conflicted two-professional marriage whose demands are changing and whose self-perceptions have changed. The man in this dyad is often comfortable with the marriage and with his concept of their equality. It is the woman whose transition period is so marked and now unexpectedly conflicted.

The situation has grown more acute in the last decade. Previously, the married-woman professional traditionally stopped working for a few years after graduation to have children, while the man became the principal breadwinner. Her major involvement with family life held the couple in many ways to a traditional marriage pattern, and the woman's transition during her age-30 crisis was made in the home, rather than outside of it. She integrated her female self with her professional self much later, and seldom became truly the equal of her husband in terms of their professional status. The husband generally was still seen as the major decision-maker and wage earner.

Traditional views in occupational and family roles gave the earlier professionally educated woman a system of "conditional emancipation."[11] Many women chose to assume the chief responsibility of children and home care. This choice restricted their early marital freedom as an individual, and thus there emerged a concept of the "the two roles of women"; that is, domestic tasks preceded a period of economic and professional equality.

Today, the dual-salaried, young marital dyad as a life-style is increasing for all couples. Statistics indicate that 42% of the young women polled in 1970 favored the housewife's role. In 1972 a similar study found that the percentage had dropped to 35%.[12] An increasing number of women are favoring an executive or professional role. In the last 4 or 5 years, more and more women have begun delaying having children, or, if they start a family, they assume less responsibility for homemaking roles. Today, many women begin their professional careers earlier. In addition, career women have been receiving far more social acceptance if they choose to move out of the marriage and find new relationships elsewhere.

The Question of Psychopathology

Contrasting a developmental approach with a psychopathological one, the authors do not see any consistent pattern of individual pathology in members of these dyads. Although in some of the couples involved, one or both spouses could be given a psychiatric diagnosis, there is no established pattern to them and none of the members of these couples were psychotic or even seriously ill psychiatrically. All individuals were functional in society and in most of their relationships. There is some suggestion that the delayed integration of the sense of femininity and power on the part of the woman may indicate a more problematic upbringing than that of her male counterpart, pointing in particular to problems in identification with her mother. It is difficult to tell, however, how much of this is in fact an expression of family and individual pathology, and how much is confusion resulting from the conflicting values given to the adolescent girl to be a high achiever and to compete in a predominantly male and highly competitive career system.

The Focus of The Treatment

The focus of the therapeutic approach was to explore each person's developmental history and its effect on the interpersonal relationship. It is not one of individual psychopathology. It is crucial for the couple involved that they be seen together, even if the woman originally presents herself as an individual patient who is dissatisfied with her marriage and confused. Complete information from both partners as to their coping patterns, motivation, and capacity for change must be obtained for the therapist to arrive at an accurate marital diagnosis and to provide the right kind of therapy. Therapy focuses on examining the stresses that their new positions have brought to the marital system. It involves an examination of what the professional roles mean for both, and also an examination of the woman's confused demands that her husband be both an equal and a superior. Therapy also examines personal issues of power and self-esteem. Both partners must come to realize how much both of them, particularly the wife, have changed in the preceding year or two.

Treatment is also focused on examining the whole issue of commitment and choice. The issue of commitment to a marriage, even during bad times, is one that is currently becoming more and more difficult to deal with, especially at a time when all of the old rules of why one should stay in the marriage have been open for question. It is important to recognize how much conscious social conditioning of the new generation of professionals is directed toward serial monogamy, or complete lack of legal bonds. This conditioning is furthered by increasing debate on how to estimate appropriate "loving." A growing spiral of high expectations and low tolerance for frustration leads to ever-increasing difficulty in handling interpersonal problems.

Therapists need to acquire new professional awareness that they, as well, may be caught in this bind. Influenced by the same social system as their clientele, therapists may be more accepting of the patient's behavior and their new theories than is necessary. For example, the therapist, hearing of a brief series of extramarital affairs, must realize that these must be seen not necessarily as an appropriate attempt to become a liberated woman, but more as an attempt on the woman's part to cope with her developmental problems, fulfill her fantasies, and begin to pull out of a disappointing relationship. In our therapeutic experiences, therefore, we have not encouraged the two to find sexual or personal satisfaction elsewhere, but rather to attempt to use what little time they have to modify their expectations and to get closer to each other. Particularly in the two-professional marriages where the professional demands are so high, the emotional energy necessary for one good long-term relationship is immense and difficult to find; the emotional energy required to sustain several long-term intense relationships is almost always lacking.

From the female clients seeking to understand "which one of us is sick," we have been struck with the frequency with which these women have originally seen other therapists—mostly male—who have been unaware of the role changes we have discussed. The male therapist is often unable to relate sex-role stereotypes and marital history to this new syndrome, and does not carefully separate the woman's original complaints from her current confusion and strivings for independence and interdependence.

Prognosis

In most cases seen, divorce has been the result—generally because the needs of the couple, particularly of the woman, have changed drastically and because the affectional ties have been completely eroded by the time the couple seek treatment. In most cases, divorce occurs because the woman feels she has to have the freedom to experiment with the other life choices she had missed while going through her intense academic career. It is the authors' clinical experience that if the couples can be helped through the transition period in a supportive atmosphere of looking at their real and imagined needs, more of these marriages can stay together in an appropriate and mutually supportive way. However, in many of the relationships neither member can, in fact, fill the new needs that the other member has developed after completing their student years. For these couples it is hoped that relationship counseling can make the separation less destructive and more understanding for both, with the hope that they can have a more realistic assessment of their needs and a new partner to fulfill them.

Implications

The implications for the future of the marriage of two professionals, or of any of the well-educated, achievement-oriented couples, are of great significance to any society. The authors believe that marriage problems today can be integrated into what will become tomorrow's customary marriage. This paper is an effort to identify the emotional anachronisms involved and to sort them out. The long-range outlook could be a weary stalemate, or, with fresh therapeutic study and observations, we can share a more hopeful philosophic view. As Erikson[13] wrote: "To fathom the limits of human existence you must have fully experienced, at some concrete time and space, the 'rules of the game.' To live as a philosophical 'stranger' is one of the choices of mature man; to have that choice the immature person must, with our help, first find a home in the actuality of work and love."

Notes

1. Marriage and divorce: *Divorce Statist*, March–April 1974.
2. Mudd E, Mitchell H, Taubin S: *Success in Family Living*. New York, Association Press, 1965.
3. Ard B, Ard C: *Handbook of Marriage Counseling*. Palo Alto, Calif, Science and Behavior Books, 1969.
4. Laws J: A feminist review of the marital adjustment literature. *J Marr Fam*, 482–516, August 1971.
5. Bernard J: *The Future of Marriage*. New York, World, 1972.
6. Family problems are worse for women doctors: *Med Econ*, 191–202, April 30, 1973.
7. Rosow I, Rose KD: Divorce among doctors. *J Marr Fam*, 587–598, 1972.
8. Gould RL: The phases of adult life. *Amer J Psychiat* 129:521–531, 1972.
9. Erikson EH: *Identity—Youth and Crisis*. New York, WW Norton, 1968.
10. Levinson DJ, et al: The psychosocial development of men in early adulthood and the mid-life transition. In DF Ricks, A Thomas & M Roff (Eds), *Life History Research in Psychopathology*, Vol. 3. Minneapolis, University of Minnesota Press, 1975.
11. Dahlstrum E (Ed): *The Changing Roles of Men and Women* (G. Andermas & S Andermas, trans). Boston, Beacon Press, 1971.
12. Institute of Life Insurance: Community series, 1973.
13. Erikson EH; Uprootedness in our time. In *Insight and Responsibility*. New York, WW Norton, 1964.

32
The Two-Career Family

HAROLD H. FRANK

ABSTRACT

Young men aspiring to become corporate executives today are likely to be married to women who also have professional ambitions. This situation has serious implications for the traditional structure of these marriages.

Until recently, both husband and wife concentrated their combined efforts on the husband's career. The wife of a career-oriented executive usually worked as many as 70 or 80 hours a week at managing a household. She cooked and cleaned, looked after her husband, reared their children, and participated in church and community affairs. In short, she did everything necessary to make the family function as a unit.

The wife's occupation inside the home made the marriage relationship interdependent: the husband was free to work at his career more than full time only because the wife shouldered all familial responsibilities.

This *modus operandi* is impossible in a two-career marriage. When both the husband and wife are pursuing professional lives outside the home, they're not interdependent; in fact, they often end up being counterdependent—or resisting dependence on each other. They may find they cannot meet each other's needs and still maintain their independence.

Changing the Contract

What happens, unfortunately, is that a two-career marriage often evolves into something different from what both partners initially

305

intended. The emotional contract made at the time of the wedding is no longer fulfilled, a change that probably developed so gradually and imperceptibly that neither partner was aware of it until both are faced with a *fait accompli*.

A two-career marriage faces other problems a one-career marriage does not. For example, three researchers at the University of Pennsylvania's Marriage Council have found that although a couple may initially agree to a coequal marriage, expectations change as the years go by; the wife wants her independence, while the husband realizes he wants a more traditional wife.[1] Or, less often, the working wife may want to exchange her role for a more traditional one, while the husband is unprepared to be the sole breadwinner.

Partners in a professional, two-career marriage often meet at college and are close in age. When the man becomes increasingly successful in his career, he may feel that he has "outgrown" his wife. The wife, on the other hand, "knew him when" and often worked to provide the schooling that made his career possible in the first place. Neither he nor his position hold a mystique for her by the time he starts to "make it."

In some cases the man will replace his wife with a younger one, hoping to gain the recognition his older college-mate has withheld. Although there is a slight trend in the other direction—a successful wife leaving a husband she has outgrown—seeking a new partner is usually a male's solution.

Should a women out-perform her husband, serious marital crises can result. Professional success and masculinity are closely linked for many men. It is not at all uncommon for a husband to resent his wife's professional success and perceive it as a threat to his masculinity. Because of this perception, it is a threat of the gravest kind.

In most cases a woman's dilemma is different. The emotional contract at the start of a marriage is usually more traditional: a woman's career, if she has one, is likely to be subordinate to her husband's. Later on, especially when the children do not require constant attention, the wife may demand the same prerogatives, perquisites, and consideration her husband has enjoyed. He may be unwilling or unable to comply. If she insists on having a career, she often finds herself with one full-time job— her career—and another more-than-full-time job managing the household.

That more women in these circumstances have not succumbed to nervous breakdowns speaks well of the stuff they are made of. But since a woman, too, is only human, the difficulty of coping with an uncooperative husband and family may lead to divorce or, because of that notorious consistency of blood, she may regretfully and resentfully neglect or abandon her own career.

Barriers to Communication

Communication between marriage partners is an age-old problem, but it is even more troublesome in a two-career family. In the traditional family, that lack of communication is at least institutionalized. Because the husband's professional life has little to do with his home life, the family tacitly agrees that he does not have to discuss it at home.

In a two-career family, where both marriage partners may live in completely different professional worlds with completely different language systems, the problem of communication can take on added significance. What kind of common intellectual bonds are there between a college professor and a vice-president of sales, or a financial analyst and an orthopedic surgeon?

Children

Children constitute one of the greatest challenges to a two-career marriage. A couple originally may decide to remain childless so the wife can pursue her career. But as she approaches her thirtieth year—typically felt to be the age before which a female should bear her first child—the husband may realize he does want offspring and feel a deepening resentment toward his wife's profession. Thus, children are born because the wife succumbs to this external pressure, her own guilt feelings and desires, or a combination of all three factors. Even if children arrive because of an initial and mutual decision, the wife and now mother may feel increasing hostility: the children stand in the way of the career for which she was educated.

Only the bearing of children requires femaleness. The obvious solution is for husband and wife to take joint and equal responsibility for the youngsters, so that both partners can pursue their careers. Such a joint decision requires equal treatment of *both* careers, difficult to attain in these days when a man's advancement is still given more concern than a woman's.

Marriage has always been at best a mixed blessing to humankind. Sexual exclusivity, real or fancied, is not enough to hold a marriage together today, and it probably never has been. Psychological intimacy is more important.

Existential Realities

A major function of marriage in these times, when distractions from personal relationships are so much greater both in number and in kind than ever before, is providing a relationship where partners can obtain psychological refuge from superficial encounters and overstimulation by the environment.

The real challenge of modern life is an existential one. The meaning life has is the meaning we give to it. If we sit passively, reacting only to those issues which are most pressing, we will be forced into what managers call "fire fighting," or crisis management. The alternative is to be pro-active, to define goals and to manage the events and circumstances needed to accomplish them. In industry, this process is called management by objectives, or "MBO." It seeks to mate individual and corporate needs so the accomplishment of one results in accomplishing the other.

More people would benefit from the discovery that a pro-active approach applies to their marriages as well, especially to those where neither partner can give full-time attention to the marriage because both have full-time professional lives.

Notes

1. See Berman. Sacks, and Lief, "The Two-Professional Marriage: A New Conflict Syndrome," pp. 291–304.

References

1. Bralove, Mary, "Working Partners," *The Wall Street Journal*, May 13, 1975.
2. Fogerty, Michael, Rapoport, Rhona and Rapoport, Robert. *Sex, Career, and Marriage*. Beverly Hills: Sage Publications, 1971.
3. Otten, Alan L., "Two-Career Couples," *The Wall Street Journal*, July 29, 1976.
4. Rapoport, Rhona and Rapoport, Robert, *Dual Career Families*. Baltimore: Penguin Books, 1971.

APPENDIX

Matrix of Associated Readings and Cases

(This matrix is designed as a guide to the selection of background reading for individual cases. Some readings may be more relevent than others while readings which have not been recommended also may be relevant. The reader is encouraged to adapt the matrix to meet his/her specific needs.)

Readings

CASES	Barbara Parker 1	Nina Ritchie 2	Marlene Rubin 3	First Shelter Corporation 4	Donna Fogel 5	Mary and George Norton 6	Women's Medical College of Pennsylvania 7	Sue Carson 8	Susan Bronson 9	Northside Health Care Facility 10	Vanessa Green 11	Evelyn Robinson 12	Ellen Leder 13
Ch.													
14. Government in the Lead—Michael H. Moskow	X	X									X		X
15. U.S. Laws Against Discrimination on the Job—Association of American Colleges	X	X									X		X
16. Guidelines on Discrimination Because of Sex—U.S. Government	X	X									X		X
17. The Sources of Inequality—Janita Kreps					X			X					
18. The Workplace Woman—Harold H. Frank and Katherine Hooks			X					X	X				
19. Equal Opportunity for Woman is Smart Business—M. Barbara Boyle						X							
20. Statement of Purpose of the National Organization for Woman—NOW	X			X									
21. A Review of Sex Role Research—Arlie Russell Hochschild	X	X	X										
22. A Bright Woman is Caught in a Double Bind—Matina Horner	X		X	X							X	X	
23. Fear of Success: Popular, but Unproven—David Tresemer	X		X	X							X	X	
24. Woman as Nigger—Naomi Weisstein			X	X	X						X	X	
25. Assertiveness Training—Harold H. Frank				X	X	X					X	X	
26. The Solo Woman in a Professional Peer Group—Carol S. Wolman and Harold H. Frank				X	X	X					X	X	
27. Strategies of Women Academics—Karen Folger Jacobs and Carol S. Wolman					X	X	X		X		X		
28. "A House is Not a Home": Women in Publishing—Laura Furman	X	X					X		X				
29. On Being Black and Female and an Accountant—Jacqueline Thompson	X					X		X				X	
30. Up the Ladder, Finally—Business Week						X						X	
31. The Two-Professional Marriage—Ellen Berman, Sylvia Sacks, and Harold Lief	X	X		X	X							X	X
32. The Two-Career Family—Harold H. Frank	X	X		X	X							X